Multiculturalism and the Mouse

Multiculturalism and the Mouse

Race and Sex in Disney Entertainment

DOUGLAS BRODE

University of Texas Press ◄◊► Austin

Requests for permission to reproduce material from this work should be sent to:

Permissions
University of Texas Press
P.O. Box 7819
Austin, TX 78713-7819
www.utexas.edu/utpress/about/bpermission.html

⊗ The paper used in this book meets the requirements of
ANSI/NISO Z39.48-1992 (R1997) (Permanence of Paper).

LIBRARY OF CONGRESS CATALOGING-IN-PUBLICATION DATA

Brode, Douglas, 1943–
Multiculturalism and the mouse : race and sex in Disney entertainment / Douglas Brode.
p.   cm.
Includes bibliographical references and index.
ISBN 978-0-292-70960-7 (pbk. : alk. paper)
1. Walt Disney Company.   2. Minorities in motion pictures.   I. Title.
PN1999.W27B77   2005
791.43'652693—dc22
2005004589

For my son, Shea Thaxter Brode
A Disney fan from Day One

Contents

Acknowledgments

All photographs/stills included in this volume were either mailed or hand-delivered over the decades to the author, in his longtime capacity as a professional commentator on movies, television, and the entertainment media, by publicity people representing Walt Disney Productions, Buena Vista Releasing, Disneyland (the park), and/or RKO Motion Pictures. This was done with the understanding that, under the existing rules of fair usage, the author would then employ all such unsolicited visual properties in order to positively publicize the films, television shows, and other entertainment media of Walt Disney in various print forms. Current copyright law holds that such materials may be included in books of an educational nature if they are deemed necessary by the author to precisely illustrate the thematic points being made in the text itself. It is with such an understanding firmly in mind, and for that purpose alone, that these photographs/stills are included in this current academic analysis of Walt Disney and his life's work.

Multiculturalism and the Mouse

WALT DISNEY, AMERICAN. Observers can argue whether Disney was a liberal or a conservative; like the hero of Orson Welles's *Citizen Kane*, simple labels interfere with our understanding him as a highly complex American. Here, Walt delivers the dedication for the California theme park on July 17, 1955. (Copyright 1955, Walt Disney Productions.)

I Had a Dream Is a Wish Your Heart Makes
In Defense of Disney, Part 1

There is nothing good or bad, but thinking makes it so.
—WILLIAM SHAKESPEARE, 1606

Perception is reality.
—ANDY WARHOL, 1966

*B*eginning in the early spring of 1963, the New York World's Fair played host to several attractions designed by Walt Disney's initial team of "Imagineers." Corporate-sponsored pavilions, each in some distinct way, combined Disney's ongoing fascination with showcasing in the present a vision of where we as a people had realistically been and where we most likely were next headed. However popular *The Carousel of Progress* and *Hall of Presidents* were, an attraction called *It's a Small World* quickly emerged as most fairgoers' favorite.[1] Satisfying tourists from around the globe, and not a little startling owing to then-innovative ideological implications, *It's a Small World* offered a vision that would not characterize the thinking of mainstream America for another quarter century.

The term "diversity"— exclusive to the vocabulary of a radical minority only ten years ago, in the lexicon of most people today—has become such a staple of our everyday speech that we may forget such an idea did not exist, even among liberals committed to the civil rights movement, during the century's first half. At that time, "integration" remained the key byword. Those of the Old Left called for a full assimilation of ethnics and others deemed "different" into the vast national middle. They were opposed by strict segregationists, the Old Right that reeled in horror at the thought of any mingling of the races. Significantly absent from our ideology at midcentury, and the popular culture expressing that zeitgeist, was anything akin to what we now consider a preferable alternative to either extreme: Multiculturalism, based on the maintenance of any one group's beloved background while simultaneously asserting that all lingering value distinctions as to worth, based on race, gender, or other arbitrary, outmoded, intolerable standards, must be eliminated.

With one key exception. Disney—and Disney alone—offered a portrait of the future that ought to be hailed in intent and impact as a prototype, perhaps even progenitor, of the way we perceive the world today. Disney's innovative pavilion was created for UNICEF with full cooperation from Pepsi-Cola, one of many instances in which Walt served as a creative bridge between an idealistic cause in need of proper funding and the financial strength of a major corporation. Employing a highly regarded illustrator of children's books, Mary Blair (who had begun her professional career at Disney), with her talents augmented by designers Marc Davis and Claude Coats and songwriters Robert B. and Richard M. Sherman, Disney offered the public a diversion (or so it seemed) consisting of a boat ride along a picturesque canal that passed through miniature re-creations of the world's various regions. Diverse peoples were signified by children living everywhere from the frozen north to the rain forests of Africa, via a collection of 297 puppets, augmented by another 256 toys.[2] Each wore authentic clothing from his or her land, while their coloring accurately reflected specific regions. Yet these "representations offered a common face, modified a little for skin color and racial characteristics," while Blair's "compelling color schemes underlined" rather than ignored "regional differences."[3]

Each child sang the same title song, in his or her own language. At the end, all the children of the world joined together, performing the song in unison—offering a rich variety within the through-line that is the human race.

Today, some critics—those who find a reason to attack any offering that bears the Disney logo—complain that these are stereotypes, reductive instead of realistic. To a degree, they are correct. "Rather than a caricature of individuals," Walt himself stated in defense of his approach, "our work is a caricature of *life*."[4] His meaning reverberates today: No one group was ever singled out for caricature or stereotyping in Disney films; all people were equally open to the same artistic approach. As an aesthetic, caricature is benign, so long as it is not misused for negative purposes. Caricature rests at the heart of literary works by Ben Jonson and Miguel de Cervantes, the paintings of Henri de Toulouse-Lautrec and

Pablo Picasso. When democratically applied, in a work that does not reserve caricature for any one ethnic group, there is nothing invalid about it—at least not to any mind that remains open during the observation process, and free of the limitations that any strict ideology, left or right, imposes.

Such open-mindedness is precisely what's missing from much of the current devastating criticism of Disney. As to one specific ethnicity and its depiction, Marisa Penalta (of the Rafael Hernandez School), speaking on the current Disney regime's portrayal of Latinos, comments about *Oliver & Company* (1988) and its characterization of Tito, a small Chihuahua (voiced by Cheech Marin). Aghast, Penalta asks: "Why this thing with Latinos as dogs?"[5] She does not note that, in the film's animated approach to Charles Dickens's novel, every human character had been reimagined as some breed of dog. Her statement suggests that Latinos alone were singled out for caricature as animals. Had that been the case, Disney would be liable to charges of vicious bigotry. Obviously, that isn't what an objective viewer encounters. The Disney company employed a storytelling tradition that reaches back at least to Aesop, in which animals uniformly substitute for people. The French woman is (naturally) a poodle, etc.

The whole point of the film is that to succeed as a society, the onscreen dog characters must celebrate their diversity while also finding the essential connection that belies differences. All the dogs, here representing varied human ethnicities, are initially suspicious of one another. In time, though, each grows morally, accepting the others as part of a greater canine heredity they all share. They learn to tolerate, then understand and enjoy, each other's uniqueness. By the end, they become a working community, without any among them needing to assimilate so completely as to divest him- or herself of essential ethnic identity.

It's a small world, after all.

As to that pavilion: Following the closing of the World's Fair, the attraction was relocated in Disneyland, California (premiere date: May 28, 1966).[6] Each new Disney park built over the following decades also featured an identical pavilion. From the moment of its inception, *It's a Small World* managed to entertainingly educate people (adults and children) about what would, in time, gradually emerge as the predominant multicultural view. To what precise degree people's exposure to the ride created a new generation that would envision and then insist on diversity is

"IT'S A SMALL WORLD, AFTER ALL." The guest list at Disneyland lived out the lyrics to Walt's favorite song. Clockwise, from upper left: Japan's Emperor Hirohito and Empress Nagako (1975), Egypt's Anwar Sadat and his wife, Jihan (1966), India's Prime Minister Jawaharlal Nehru (1961), and Jordan's King Hussein and son Prince Hamzah (1981). (Copyright 1975, 1966, 1961, and 1981, Walt Disney Productions.)

impossible to say. What can't be denied is that exposure to mass media experiences—be they theme park diversions, the music that forms our aural environment, or the omnipresence of televised programming—subtly but significantly alters our vision of the world.

This idea is asserted also by those who disparage Disney and is fundamental to their complaints. In her documentary *Mickey Mouse Monopoly,* writer-producer Chyng Feng Sun warns that children are apt to learn from all the pop culture they are exposed to and unconsciously absorb. Such children are most strongly influenced by films that, like Disney's, are seen over and over again, and by generation after generation. That is true, and it negates a statement made by Richard Schickel in *The Disney Version* (1969), the book that initiated the ongoing attack on Disney. Schickel explained why he felt no necessity to analyze any of the comedies and dramas, lumping such beloved favorites as *20,000 Leagues under the Sea* (1954), *Old Yeller* (1958), and *The Absent-Minded Professor* (1961) together with minor fare like *The Monkey's Uncle* (1965) and *The Ugly Dachshund* (1966) as "live-action features that most people scarcely remember," adding that "there is really very little point in discussing these movies critically."[7]

As I hope to prove, Disney revealed more of his personal ideology in such fare than in elaborate animated classics. Even if most of those films (though not, certainly, *20,000 Leagues*) were hardly ambitious enough to be evaluated as art, that hardly diminishes their social, political, and cultural impact on the audience that eagerly consumed each on its original release, and has continued to do so over the years thanks to TV and home video. As Gale Dines (Women's Studies, Wheelock College), a contemporary vocal critic of Disney, says in the documentary *Mickey Mouse Monopoly:*

> Encoded in media images are ideologies about how we think about the world: Belief systems, constructions of reality. And we develop our notions of reality from the cultural mediums around us. One of the most important cultural mechanisms that we have today is indeed the media. It gives us a wide array of image stereotypes, belief systems, about race and class and gender. It's really important to analyze the institutions of media in order to understand how we, as consumers and citizens, understand the role the media plays in socializing us into certain belief systems.

Dines's assessment is apt. My sole argument is that she then condemns Disney as perhaps the worst perpetrator of outworn if notably long-standing myths.

There can be no arguing with the fact that Disney entertainment—from the most prevalent single media conglomerate in existence—exerts a greater influence on our line of vision than any of its competitors. Whether Disney provides negative conditioning is the issue. In my previous volume, *From Walt to Woodstock: How Disney Created the Counterculture* (2004), I argued that the films made by the company during Walt's working years (1921–1966), largely written off by the academic elite as grossly commercialized and superficially conventional, contained then-radical ideas. As a result, Disney films played a key role in paving the way for the youth revolution of 1967–1972. The cult of the antisocial outlaw, the back to nature movement, radical environmentalism, a glorification of then-controversial rock 'n' roll, animal rights activism, antiwar attitudes, disparagement of raw capitalism, the defense of free love and communal living, an early awareness if not acceptance of an abiding drug culture, and the glorification of long hair were all introduced in Disney movies and television shows that, amid the otherwise bland media environment of the late fifties, future hippies saw and absorbed.

The aim of this current volume is to extend that thesis to issues of race, gender, sexual preference, and various other forms of "difference." *It's a Small World,* unveiled only three years before Disney's death, offered the first significant glimpse of this new avenue of perception. As I learned, to argue that Disney set the pace for political correctness is to open oneself up, however paradoxically, to charges of political incorrectness. Disney—whether one means by that term the works of the man himself or of the company that today still displays his name—has been bandied about as the primary symbol of an American mid-cult sensibility that projects the precise opposite of our modern view. To try and alter that perception (not to argue with the essential precepts of political correctness) is to challenge a notion that for years has been set in stone to such a degree that many believe any argument ought not be raised.

I became painfully aware of this when I mentioned in an e-mail to a young Fulbright scholar, who in the past expressed great admiration for my work, that I was in the process of completing a book on Disney and diversity. My announcement was met with enthusiasm. The scholar explained that he uses clips from Disney films in his own American Studies

INITIATING A REVISIONIST VIEW OF HISTORY. Movies from Hollywood's Golden Age are notorious for caricaturing and marginalizing all ethnic groups, on those rare occasions when such people were present. Even then, Disney consistently portrayed Latinos *(Elfego Baca)* (TOP) and African Americans *(The Swamp Fox)* (BOTTOM) as three-dimensional characters who are totally integrated within their heroic communities. (Copyright 1958–1960 Walt Disney Productions; courtesy Buena Vista Releasing.)

courses abroad to illustrate how offensive the Disney vision is. When I explained that in my book Disney would be defended as an early proponent of diversity, I was greeted with the cyberspace equivalent of stony silence.

After recouping, my colleague offered an example of how abhorrent Disney is by mentioning a sequence he employs in classes to reveal Disney as both a racist and a sexist. Donald Duck, in *The Three Caballeros* (1945), literally "strafes" (in the style of a World War II dive bomber) a group of Latino women on a Rio beach, the Duck's desire for sex literally transforming into an act of implied violence. How, the scholar argued, could such a sequence be viewed other than as one of the most odious examples of insensitivity to race and gender in Hollywood's dubious history? In answer, I could only argue that to remove that sequence from the film's context, as well as Disney's oeuvre, is to utterly misrepresent it. To label Disney as politically incorrect on the basis of that sequence, then (for consistency's sake) we also ought to attack writer Larry McMurtry and director Martin Ritt for the sequence in the former's novel (*Horseman, Pass By*) and the latter's film (*Hud*) in which Hud Bannon attempts to rape (he succeeds in the book) his attractive middle-aged housekeeper, Alma (Patricia Neal).

If that sequence were presented at face value—if the reader/viewer were encouraged to "side" with Hud at this moment in the narrative— the book and film surely would rate as offensive to any woman or man possessing modern enlightened values—even more so in McMurtry's book, where she is a woman of color. That is not the case when one considers the entire drama. The point-of-view character is Lon (Brandon de Wilde), Hud's young nephew. Early on, Lon idolizes the lazy womanizer. But as Lon grows to maturity on their contemporary Texas ranch, he rejects what, to a naïve mind, seemed charmingly roguish. We are meant to share Lon's arc and—if the reader/viewer did once, like Lon, find Hud appealing—finally reject the man as fully and completely as the young protagonist does. That is how the rape scene functions in *Hud*'s context.

Likewise, in *The Three Caballeros*, Donald is an offensive character. The Duck was initially created when Walt realized he needed a foil for the gentlemanly (by the mid-forties, if not before) Mickey Mouse, Disney's alter ego and a role model for the audience.[8] In contrast, Donald emerged as Disney's designated jerk. We are induced to reject his vicious actions when he similarly "strafes" his harmless nephews Huey, Dewey, and Louie

IN THE REALM OF THE SENSES. Uptight white-bread Ugly American Donald Duck finds his long-standing sexual hang-ups tested after arriving on Acapulco Beach in *The Three Caballeros;* the Latina women of color are portrayed in a highly positive light, their naturalness and ethnicity in no way stigmatized. (Copyright 1945 Walt Disney Productions; courtesy Buena Vista Releasing.)

(a trio of "Lon" figures) in a variety of short subjects including *Donald's Snow Fight* (1942) and *Trick or Treat* (1959), then to cheer those children when they give Donald his comeuppance at each movie's end. Whether a child abuser or a sexual predator, Donald becomes the subject of ridicule, for other characters in the film as for those watching. In *The Three Caballeros*, when Donald is humiliated, we laugh at—not with—him. The film's context makes clear that the women he attacks are, like the three nephews, the positive figures. Context is everything; in context, Donald's vicious approach—like Hud's in Ritt's adult movie—is presented as the kind of male behavior to condemn.

Disney films are ripe with respect for women, an attitude that derives from the filmmaker's childhood. "My mother," Walt liked to recollect, "used to go out on a construction job and hammer and saw planks with the men."[9] Such words were spoken with glowing admiration. Just such a tone surrounds the memory of Jeremiah Kincaid in *So Dear to My Heart* (1949), Walt's most autobiographical film, when he recalls Grandma (Beulah Bondi) plowing the family farm's rock-strewn fields. Her strength and tenacity are akin to those of men who perform such hard physical labor in movies by other Hollywood legends. In George Stevens's *Shane* (1952), Joe Starrett (Van Heflin) engages in such exhausting duties, while his wife, Marion (Jean Arthur), remains in the cozy cabin, perfectly kempt, humming sweetly as she bakes a pie intended less for her hardworking husband than for the elegantly handsome stranger (Alan Ladd) who has fortuitously arrived on their Wyoming homestead.

Disney's women have no time for such romantic drivel, even when they do happen to be young and beautiful. Texas cattlewoman Katie Coates (Dorothy McGuire) in *Old Yeller* (1958), though every bit as pretty as Marion, dutifully plows the land just like old Mrs. Kincaid. Like Grandma, Katie wears an unglamorous man's slouch hat while she works. When a handsome cowboy (Chuck Connors) happens by, she does not, like the heroine of Stevens's more "adult" movie, develop a crush on him. They maintain what, in modern terminology, can only be considered a gender-free relationship. Katie speaks to Burn Sanderson on a person-to-person basis, even as her husband, Jim (Fess Parker), would if he hadn't left with a cattle drive. In the *Encyclopedia of Frontier Literature,* Mary Ellen Snodgrass cites *Old Yeller* as one of the rare Westerns to feature a strong, independent woman as the focal character.[10] Other studios showed no interest in Fred Gipson's novel, though Disney eagerly optioned and filmed it. The result was a cinematic tribute to the frontierswoman, *her*story rarely if ever brought to the screen. Even in those rare cases where other filmmakers depicted such women (Victor Seastrom's *Wind,* 1922), they likely focused on females who go mad owing to their inability to survive (as "stronger" men do) on the plains. Disney's women, like those in books by Ellen Glasgow (*Vein of Iron*), Edna Ferber (*So Big*), and Willa Cather (*O Pioneers!*), endure — often without a man around to help.

These are no mere exceptions but ongoing examples of an attitude toward women present from Disney's first female character, the diminutive heroine of the *Alice in Cartoonland* series (1924–1927), in which a real-life girl entered an animated world. "Alice," a diehard Disney critic can claim, "had no real character beyond a certain willingness to try anything and therefore get into 'situations.'"[11] One could conversely argue that such an orientation constitutes Alice's character. Further, we may read an entire attitude toward women (a positive one at that) into not only Alice's propensity for adventure, but also the end results of what occurs. Alice does, in film after film, discover that curiosity may indeed kill the cat. Often, her life is in peril as a result of a gamesome, willful, nonchalant attitude toward inherent dangers in the world. Always, though (and this is consistent in the Alice shorts), she in the end extricates *herself* from the latest difficulty. Grinning at the audience as any film fades out, Alice is no worse off for her mischievous exploit. If anything, she emerges stronger as a result of solving its problems on her own.

For purposes of contrast, we can compare Alice to Lois Lane in the Max and Dave Fleischer animated renderings of the Man of Steel and his inamorata. All but identical to Alice in outlook, Lois perversely must always go where the "wise" patriarch (newspaper editor Perry White) tells her it's too dangerous for a "mere girl" to venture. One difference is Lois always finds herself trapped by villains, unable to do anything but scream for help until Clark Kent assumes his secret identity and — the ultimate symbol of masculine prowess — hurries to rescue the damsel in distress. The Disney paradigm is precisely the opposite. In the 1955 TV serial *Corky and White Shadow,* the child-heroine (Darlene Gillespie) ignores warnings by her patriarchal father (Buddy Ebsen) against venturing into dangerous places and does so anyway. Her heedlessness proves to be a positive thing, in this hardly cautionary fable, when she captures two bank robbers that her dad, the sheriff, could not apprehend.

Moving from gender issues to those involving race, one quick example

FOLLOWING WALT'S LEAD. The contemporary Disney Company was the first Hollywood studio to release a movie in which Native Americans (Adam Beach and Eric Schweig) play the leads in *Squanto: A Warrior's Tale*. The studio takes its cue from Walt himself, who set the pace with movies like *Tonka*. (Photo credit, Attila Dory. Copyright 1994 and 1958 the Walt Disney Company; all rights reserved.)

from another Western should suffice. Were a contemporary filmmaker to produce a movie about a young Native American and cast anyone other than a Native American actor in the lead, we would rightly consider that an implicitly racist decision by contemporary standards. To so charge Disney for casting Italian American Sal Mineo as White Bull in *Tonka* (1958) would be to unfairly judge him by a standard that did not exist at that time. Major Indian roles were played by Anglo actors until Chief Dan George in *Little Big Man* (1970); he won the part only after producers first considered Laurence Olivier, Richard Boone, and Paul Scofield. Also, since Disney's project was a commercial undertaking, there was the significant need for a nominal "star" to attract youthful audiences.

The proper way to analyze *Tonka*—what made it so innovative at the time—is to point out that this was the first (and, incredibly, only) theatrical motion picture to entirely depict Custer's Last Stand from a Native American point of view. Even *Little Big Man* did not go that far. For a hero, Arthur Penn chose a white (Dustin Hoffman) sympathetic to the Indians, not an actual Indian. Lest we forget, only one live-action movie has been made in our own time that, like *Tonka*, portrays the great encounter of whites and Indians from the Native American point of view. *Squanto: A Warrior's Tale* (1994) stars Adam Beach (a Native American actor). Not surprisingly, it was produced and released by today's Disney company.

Here then is another premise: Though I will, as in my previous volume, concentrate mainly on films that Walt personally supervised, I also argue that the current Disney studio adheres, progressing along a continuum, to social and political attitudes set in motion by Walt himself. It's important to note that longtime CEO Michael Eisner's Disney company, when not fending off critical attacks by the radical left, had to deal with equally angry complaints from the reactionary right. The venom of Southern Baptist Convention president Richard Land's attacks, as well as those of other groups (the American Family Association, the Catholic League), derives from their openly expressed fear of the current Disney regime's "promotion of homosexuality." [12] In the eyes of the extreme right, Disney is indeed politically correct, explaining why its activists are so upset. To prove this, rightists point to the Disney theme parks, which allow gay organizations to openly express their lifestyles and pride while on property. "I think it would be a travesty," Eisner retorts, "for us to exclude anybody." The right rejects today's Disney films owing to a belief that what passes for "Disney" in our time breaks with what they consider the "wholesome" tradition of an earlier era in Disney entertainment.

Nothing, I hope to prove, could be further from the truth. Disney went out of his way to anger the Christian fundamentalists of his time (and was threatened by them with a boycott of *Fantasia*) when he represented Igor Stravinsky's *The Rite of Spring* with, as the film's narration puts it, "a coldly accurate realization of what scientists believe went on in the first few billion years of life on earth." This was taken as a personal insult by rightists who were "still determined to scourge Darwin as a heretic." [13] Twelve years later, when Walt re-created Main Street, USA in Disneyland, he made certain every possible type of building was included except a church. He had, since childhood, considered organized religion to be a source of dangerous divisiveness, even though he did fervently believe in God. The belief by today's Christian right that their predecessors loved, and were well served by, Disney is mythic and untrue. Ignoring such enlightened attitudes on the part of either Disney or Eisner, Chyng Feng

Sun describes how the company's output is generally accepted as "wholesome family entertainment," recommended by parents and teachers as a good influence on children. True, most parents and (elementary school) teachers do adore Disney. These people are part of families that exist somewhere in the vast American middle, squarely at the center or, in mild degrees, somewhat to the left or right politically, culturally, and socially. They despise extremism, be it from the reactionary right or the radical left, those polar opposites that at last have one thing in common: mutual hatred of Disney, past and present.

With this in mind, the academic demonization of Disney seems not only wrongheaded but takes on a strikingly antipopulist quality. This became clear to Dr. Henry Giroux (Pennsylvania State University) when, following the publication of his own anti-Disney diatribe,[14] he made numerous media appearances across the country. Giroux claims to have been stunned at the rabid hostility he encountered, "especially talk radio interviews in which the public would call in," angrily chastising him. The elitist dismissal of Disney's work typified by Giroux initially coalesced in Schickel's aforementioned book, expressed in that author's open contempt for Disney as one who both reflected and helped create "the culture of the American majority."[15]

In such a condescending context, Schickel insisted that what Disney offered was the polar opposite of true culture, in its most exalted state—work comprehensible only to highly educated persons of elevated intellectual tastes (i.e., "cultivated"). Disney was but an artist of the people, connecting with what Schickel patronizingly tags "the lumpen bourgeoisie." As José Ortega y Gasset once commented, most epochs contain "two different types of art, one for [elitist] minorities and one for [the] majority."[16] Disney self-consciously attempted to create the former only once, if at all, with *Fantasia* (1941). Even there, despite inclusion of highbrow music, the obvious intent (whether cheered or scorned) had been to bring culture to the masses—a move that endeared Disney to neither the cultivated few nor the vast public.

Another critic, Rudolf Arnheim, disparaged "the general, artistically untrained public" and its crass (in his opinion) appreciation of ultra-realistic art.[17] Arnheim preceded Schickel in damning Disney for not experimenting with more abstract visual forms. In fact, there are no more abstract images within the context of commercial cinema than *Fantasia*'s experimental segments. Nor are there more expressionistic and surreal sequences than those awaiting rediscovery in *The Three Caballeros.* Disney's critics cannot forgive his attack on "culture" as something essentially "un-American . . . sort of snobbish and affected—as if it thought it were better than the next fellow."[18] This can be taken as the words of an unregenerate urban redneck, with no appreciation for the finer things in life, or accepted as the honest assertion of a true populist of a variety known nowhere but in these United States.

That Disney's statement in no way suggested resentment toward the classical tradition is made clear in *Fantasia,* rich with symphonic music. The idea was to make such material, beloved by Walt, accessible to the public at large, which at the time failed to rise to his level of expectation, as the film's original box-office failure made clear. However disappointing the commercial and critical results when it was released, the dream for *Fantasia* was decidedly democratic: to strip away the stigma of "culture" that proved off-putting to the blue-collar audience and reveal to them, by marrying such stuff to the antics of the Mouse, that great music was nothing to be afraid of. To borrow a current term and apply it to that situation, Disney set out to demystify symphonic music for those intimidated by it. He believed that what had become the domain of a self-proclaimed elite could, when properly packaged, prove every bit as appealing to the common man. One way of interpreting *Fantasia* is to see it as a work that, however unconscious the desire may have been, set out to forever end the distinction between the two cultures José Ortega y Gasset described. No wonder that for closure to his above-quoted discussion of culture, Walt felt the need to add: "As I understand it, culture isn't that kind of snooty word at all."[19] For him, culture at its best implied a realm of imaginative experience in which Ponchielli's *Dance of the Hours* could be accompanied by balletic hippos.

Despite a desire on Walt's part to expose the public to both classical music and then-contemporary avant-garde visuals, Schickel's (quite incongruous) line of attack insists Disney held an abiding "contempt for art."[20] This notion of the man derives from a single statement he once made: "I've always had a nightmare. I dream that one of my pictures has ended up in an art theater."[21] Precisely such a statement was made by Kenneth Branagh on the eve of his four-hour-plus *Hamlet* film's release in 1996. The actor-director wanted that film to play at the multiplex, not on the arthouse circuit, hoping to bring ordinary people in to see the Bard. This explains Branagh's use of American stars in Shakespearean films. He hoped to remove *Hamlet* from the world of high culture into which it has been absorbed, returning the work to Old Will's original audience. That is, the Elizabethan era's equivalent of that vast middle class which many observers condemn Walt for playing to—the very audience that, in the first half of the twentieth century, fell in love with Disney and, in the second, with the work of Disney's key descendants, most obviously Steven Spielberg and George Lucas.

Disney never felt, much less expressed, *any* contempt for art, be it high-, middle-, or lowbrow; visual, aural, or literary. His ongoing attempts to bring the best in music to the masses—which, following the financial disaster of *Fantasia,* had to be scaled down—make this clear. Films like *Make Mine Music* (1946) and *Melody Time* (1948) attest to the truth. So does Disney's insistence that his animators regularly attend art classes at the finest Los Angeles schools. What Disney despised was not art but the self-aggrandizing attitude of those who openly identify themselves as artists. What he hated was pretentiousness, particularly that of the specialized sector of the creative community composed of self-conscious artists.

These are the people who like to announce that they are indeed artists; therefore, anything they produce automatically falls into the realm of art. For Walt—as for other similarly minded American filmmakers such as John Ford, Frank Capra, and Howard Hawks—the self-conscious artist puts the cart before the horse. Disney and his colleagues were intent on creating works that displayed the highest level of craftsmanship. If someone wanted to tag them as art, that was their business. The true artist is too busy *doing* to talk much about what he's done.

What Disney accomplished in *Fantasia,* whether he was aware of it or not, was to pioneer the breakdown between elitist and crowd-pleasing art so necessary in a rough-hewn democracy like our own. This began a reexamination of what "the finer things in life" really were. And resulted during the turbulent Woodstock era in such works as *Zen and the Art of Motorcycle Maintenance* (1968), that book's very title attesting to a sea change in values. Modern popular culture studies—serious attention paid to everything from rock 'n' roll to poster art, from Fonzie's black leather jacket placed on display at the Smithsonian to Roger Corman's once-déclassé drive-in horror flicks receiving a retrospective at the Museum of Modern Art—proceeds on some level from Disney daring to suggest that Mickey Mouse and Leopold Stokowski were not incompatible.

Schickel pejoratively dismisses Disney as an "untutored" man.[22] If a formal education were required for the highest level of competence at any artistic endeavor—if the title "artist" automatically accompanied a university degree—then every graduate of New York University, the University of Southern California, and Northwestern University who headed for Hollywood would swiftly prove more influential than Spielberg. For he spent approximately two years at Long Beach Community College, eventually leaving sans degree. Certainly, Disney did have a sense of the vast American middle, as Shakespeare did for the audience of his time, Spielberg and Lucas in our day. The total filmmaker, Charlie Chaplin, had it more than any other twentieth-century artist. It was he who inspired Walt to become a filmmaker, which helps explain why Mickey Mouse is the Little Tramp reimagined as an animated character.

Chaplin, incidentally, never made it through grade school.

Others have understood and appreciated what Disney, like Chaplin, achieved. *Time* magazine, in its review of *The Living Desert* (1954), noted that a viewer felt enraptured by "the sense that the camera can take an onlooker into the interior of a vital event, indeed into the pulse of the life process itself."[23] Mark Van Doren, a leading intellectual figure of the 1950s, insisted that Disney "lives somewhere near the human center and knows innumerable truths that cannot be taught."[24] In fact, though, those truths can be taught. Not to Disney, who sensed it in his soul without any need for advanced "tutoring," like other intuitive geniuses from Shakespeare to John Lennon. But *by* Disney, to *us,* through his work. No truths contained in Disney films are more significant than the teaching of tolerance and acceptance through a heightened understanding for the full range of diversity among members of the human race. This was particularly acute at a time when such an awareness was nowhere else suggested by mass media and popular culture.

There are, as Joseph Campbell noted, myths that are regional and/or national in origin, others that are universal, found among virtually every race inhabiting the planet.[25] These basic and essential myths, when intellectually explored from our present perspective, reveal what it means to be human, even as more limited myths expose the uniqueness of any one people or place. Disney, and Disney alone in the golden age of motion pictures, had it both ways. Chaplin's Tramp, so utterly universal in appeal, never really seemed American, despite the vivid settings. Gary Cooper in *Mr. Deeds Goes to Town* (1936) and James Stewart in *Mr. Smith Goes to Washington* (1939) may have expressed a uniquely American ideal, yet Capra's output proved something of an anomaly, an acquired taste anywhere other than at home. Disney, more than any other filmmaker, proved easily accessible to a global community. Mickey could be read either way, as an image of what it specifically meant to be American or what it universally meant to be human.

In the 1960s, *It's a Small World* likewise projected just such a personal philosophy, inherent in Walt's work from the beginning. In addition to the Mickey shorts, Disney early on set about retelling ancient fables and folk tales, which, as Campbell put it, offer "the primer picture-language of the soul"[26]—particularly so when animated by Walt. Like any true artist, Disney also has his own thematic through-lines. He did not film all the fairy tales, only stories which, when interpreted—that is, presented in the Disney Version—would allow for the expression of his worldview. This more or less held true with original material. *Nikki, Wild Dog of the North* (1961) concerns a tamed dog and a wild bear cub—natural enemies who, when thrown together by accident, set aside their instinctual enmities to survive. That theme, translated to human terms, suggested before it was popular to do so that an intermixing of the human races (like animal species) was both desirable and achievable. Diversity within society could be realized without the divesting of ethnic identity. This idea was repeated in a live-action feature, *The Incredible Journey* (1963), as well as the animated *The Fox and the Hound* (1981), released after Walt's death. It is the essence of *A Tale of Two Critters* (1977). Bear cub and baby raccoon are thrown together, cooperating to survive until they are finally safe. Afterward, they part company, but with a new respect for one another as individuals and representatives of their breed.

Dines notes that Disney's "scripts are written by real people, who themselves have been socialized by this society, and they have internalized these norms, and these values. So when they produce work, it's bound to come out in some way [expressing that society]—unless they make a *conscious decision* to operate within an alternative ideology" (emphasis added). Her statement is undeniably true. What can be argued with is the assumption that Disney filmmakers, then and now, are the least likely to have made that conscious decision. I read Disney's films as a scathing indictment of the status quo.

There will be those who insist on taking this volume as an attack on political correctness. It is intended as a defense of politically correct thinking, daring only to suggest that Disney (a targeted archenemy of PC) was the single member of Old Hollywood who set what would come to be called multiculturalism into motion. His works challenge all those societal norms and once-unquestioned values in a way that no other filmmaker of the studio era dared—if, in fact, any had even thought, or wanted, to do so.

TON-C-PUB-159

RE-PRESENTING THE NATIVE AMERICAN. Most Hollywood movies portray female Indians as unattractive squaws (Beulah Archuletta in *The Searchers,* 1956), pretty virgin princesses (Debra Paget in *Broken Arrow,* 1950), or slinky villainesses (Julie Newmar in *MacKenna's Gold,* 1969). In Disney's *Tonka,* Joy Page portrayed Prairie Flower, a full-dimensioned person: appealing, intelligent, sensitive, complex, flawed. (Copyright 1958 Walt Disney Productions, reprinted courtesy Buena Vista Releasing.)

1

Return of the Vanishing American
Disney and the Native Experience

The moment the last nuclei of Red life breaks up in America, the
present generation of surviving Red Indians are due to merge in
the great white swamp. Then . . . we shall see real changes!
— D. H. LAWRENCE, 1917

Suddenly, Lawrence's then is our now.
— LESLIE A. FIEDLER, 1968

*I*n 1968, that seminal year of social and cultural upheaval, Leslie A. Fiedler
analyzed a quartet of then-recent novels—John Barth's *The Sot-Weed Fac-
tor,* Thomas Berger's *Little Big Man,* Larry McMurtry's *The Last Picture
Show,* and Ken Kesey's *Sometimes a Great Notion*—as exemplifying what
he called "The New Western."[1] During a turbulent and transitional era
of culture shock and an all but complete reversal of conventional values,
revisionist tomes suddenly overturned long-standing genre clichés. Now,
Indians were the good guys, whites bad. This resulted in a "social trend
among the young which has led to books on Indian history filling avant-
garde bookshops from San Francisco to St. Germain-des-Pres."[2] Simultaneously, members of the Woodstock generation adorned themselves with
accoutrements of Native American culture. Wearing feathers and fringe,
bedecked with beads, they adopted Indian insignias and passed peace
pipes back and forth, smoking peyote in hope of achieving *visionquest.*

Hair!—a Broadway show exploiting the youth culture for mainstream
theatergoers—was suitably subtitled *The* Tribal *Rock Musical* (emphasis
added). Historian Dee Brown earlier noted that, as Native Americans
were banished to reservations during the waning days of the nineteenth
century, shamans (including Wovoka, of Ghost Dance notoriety) had
predicted that in a hundred years the long-dormant spirits of seemingly
vanished natives would return and seep into the bodies of white children.[3]

An entire generation would be possessed. Teenagers, as a result, would turn against their parents.

Little wonder, then, that a popular 1971 song—written by white artists, speaking from a Native American point of view—stated:

> Took the whole Cherokee Nation,
> Put us on a reservation.
> Took away our way of life,
> The Tomahawk and Bowie knife.
>
> Though I wear a shirt and tie,
> I'm still part red man, deep inside.
> But wait, and someday, they will learn!
> Cherokee Nation, will return,
> Will return, will return . . .

Fiedler, writing before the Raiders expressed this sentiment through the then newly respectable medium of rock 'n' roll, argued that like the beatnik who preceded him, "The hippie [is] one more wild man seeking the last West of Haight-Ashbury in high-heeled boots and blue jeans." But with a significant difference. Unlike the cowboyish beatnik, this

> ultimate Westerner ceases to be White at all and turns back into the Indian, his boots becoming moccasins, his hair bound in an Indian headband, a string of beads around his neck—to declare that he has fallen . . . out of the Europeanized West into an aboriginal and archaic America.[4]

This is the very America that visionary author D. H. Lawrence had, a half-century earlier, hailed as "the world once splendid in the fullness of the other way of knowledge."[5] That *other way*, derived from ideas dating back to the Romantic revolution, prefers savagery to society, simplicity to sophistication. It was, by 1967, "the way" of hippie youth, who turned their backs on traditional Hollywood movies in favor of a new American cinema: *Bonnie and Clyde, Easy Rider, Alice's Restaurant,* and *The Graduate,* the latter starring the first countercultural movie star, Dustin Hoffman.[6] Belatedly, then, Hollywood took its cue from literature and reinvented the movie Western with Arthur Penn's version of *Little Big Man,* starring Hoffman.

A number of such films—*A Man Called Horse, Soldier Blue, Flap,* etc.—appeared in rapid succession during the 1970–1971 season. In these and

A PRECURSOR TO THE PROGRESSIVE VISION. Nearly a quarter century before *Dances with Wolves, Andy Burnett* offered an Anglo (Jerome Courtland) who drops out of his own culture to join a Native American tribe. Better still, Disney provided an accurate depiction of Indian culture as compared to Kevin Costner's error-ridden and romanticized vision. (Copyright 1957 Walt Disney Productions; courtesy Buena Vista Releasing.)

similar films, contemporary attitudes were anachronistically conveyed in period-piece settings. Indians were portrayed as a pure, peaceful ethnic minority, victimized by vicious white imperialists, here symbolized by the once lionized cavalry, now dismissed as nineteenth-century equivalents of those contemporary soldiers who massacred Vietnamese civilians. When Custer attacks Black Kettle's village at Washita in *Little Big Man,* youthful audiences cried out: "My Lai!" "Each of these films," Philip French argued, "presents Indian life as a valid counter-culture, a more organic, life-enhancing existence than white society."[7] Film historians cite *Little Big Man* as the first such Western;[8] *Dances with Wolves* (1990) would win the Best Picture Oscar and become the most famous such film, leading many to wonder why it had taken so long for Hollywood to show proper respect to Native Americans. But while many golden-age Hollywood filmmakers had been negligent, Walt Disney consistently assumed a subversive approach to the conventional Western—doing so three decades before *Little Big Man.*

Animated Indians
Pioneer Days (1930)
Little Hiawatha (1937)
Melody Time/"Pecos Bill" (1948)
Peter Pan (1954)

Disney's supposed "kiddie films" were more complex, emotionally and intellectually, than ostensibly more adult movies. The first animated short to feature Indians appears unenlightened at first glance. Like such feature films as *The Covered Wagon* (1923) and *The Big Trail* (1930), *Pioneer Days* portrays the crossing of the Great Plains from an Anglo viewpoint. Mickey and peaceful friends are the heroes, a tribe of attacking Indians their antagonists. Disney, however, provided a notable innovation. Every human aspect of the pioneers' lifestyle—their singing, dancing, and other elements of camaraderie—is paralleled by crosscuts to the Indian village. Native Americans repeat those same gestures. The notion of an underlying sameness between seemingly different peoples is established, rare for Western films of that period.

Disney's first significant onscreen Indian was the title character of *Little Hiawatha,* a short subject inspired by Longfellow's once-lauded epic *Song of Hiawatha* (1855). The poem now seems at best quaint, at worst patronizing, little more than the literary equivalent of a cigar-store Indian. Disney's film, however, holds up nicely, Longfellow's stentorian verse invoked only to be undermined. This approach reverses Anglo clichés about Indians, humanizing them in the process. "Sure of foot was Hiawatha," the purposefully pretentious narrator intones, even as Hiawatha slips from his canoe and falls in the lake. "Mighty warrior, Hiawatha," we hear, as the boy finds himself unable to kill nature's small creatures, then runs in terror from more formidable beasts. This employment of an ironic sound track qualifies Disney as a proponent of what Soviet filmmaker/theorist Sergei Eisenstein regarded as the proper use of language in sound-era cinema. The meaning derives not from what we see or what we hear but the sophisticated relationship of the one to the other.[9]

Disney's critics argue that his attitude toward the Native American is most vividly (and, by today's standards, embarrassingly) expressed in the animated works "Pecos Bill" and *Peter Pan*. In the former, the legendary Texan creates a Western landmark after being attacked by "Injuns." As the Eliot Daniel and Johnny Lange song, performed in *Melody Time* by Roy Rogers and the Sons of the Pioneers, informs us:

> *He gave them redskins such a shake-up,*
> *That they jumped out of their make-up,*
> *And that's how the painted desert got its name!*

The film's onscreen Comanches are, certainly, grotesque caricatures of Native Americans. Then again, Bill is a notably over-the-top caricature of the Texas cowboy, while an outlaw gang Bill encounters is composed entirely of stereotypes of trashy rednecks. In their case,

> *When Bill caught those nasty villains,*
> *He knocked out all their fillin's,*
> *And that's why there's gold in them thar hills!*

Anglos (heroes and outlaws alike) are as stereotyped as the onscreen Indians. Their portrayal, then—while hardly an example of political correctness—cannot fairly be considered racist, for Indians are treated, in the context of the film's stereotypical approach to all its characters—good or bad, Anglo or Indian—with rough-hewn equality. Disney does not laugh (or ask the audience to laugh) at the Indian in a film that glorifies the Anglo. He kids each and every type of human that inhabited the American Southwest. "Caricature" well describes Disney's overall approach, but not his means of portraying any one group of people.

Likewise, in *Peter Pan,* the Chief emerges as a grotesque buffoon, pompously crossing his arms while caricatured braves dance around a campfire. Again, had Disney reserved such exaggerated satire for characters of color, his approach could rightly be considered offensive by today's standards. Actually, the Chief's stance is identical to that of Captain Hook, the equally pompous white leader of pirates. Hook's men are likewise caricatured as they dance in an identical circle aboard their ship. Back in London, the

THE ART OF CARICATURE. No one can deny that the Chief in *Peter Pan* (1953) is a stereotypical figure, but that ought not leave Disney open to charges of racial caricaturing. The Chief does not embody a caricature of Native Americans, but of overbearing fathers; earlier in the film, Disney had presented an almost identical caricature of the Anglo Mr. Darling. (Copyright 1953 Walt Disney Productions; courtesy RKO Radio Films.)

self-important father of the Darling family provided a target for Disney's satire. What Disney pokes fun at, then, is not an Indian per se but the patriarchal male. Women, particularly independent-minded women, receive far more respect. The Indian maiden, Princess Tiger Lily, is as brave and intelligent as the white "princess," Wendy. Even Mrs. Darling, though trapped in a suffocating late-Victorian-era marriage, represents the positive female principle as expressed in Disney films.

Injuns Got Rights Like Everybody Else
Davy Crockett, King of the Wild Frontier (1955)

Disney created a series of live-action films, fulfilling what in 1968 Fiedler would define as the genre's essence: "The heart of the western is the encounter with the Indian, that utter stranger for whom our New World is an Old Home." [10] The first Disney Western introduced attitudes that would be expanded in subsequent features. Even the animated opening credits reveal an optimistic approach toward accommodation. A long rifle of the type frontiersmen employed, comfortably crossed with a tomahawk, creates Disney's initial icon of possible reconciliation between initially hostile races.

At first, *Davy Crockett* appears to be shaping up as one more variation on the "heroic whites versus marauding redmen" theme. An immense animated war arrow decimates a painting of Fort Mims, the Tennessee outpost overrun by Choctaws in 1813, initiating "The Creek Indian War." During the first violent confrontation, Choctaw/Creeks are indeed presented in the typical movie manner as "The Threat":

> The movies are after all an expression of the dominant culture. Consequently the Indians are invariably viewed, whether sympathetically or not, from the point of view of victorious pioneers . . . a terrifying all-purpose enemy ready at the drop of a tomahawk to spring from the rocks and attack wagon trains, cavalry patrols, and isolated pioneer settlements. [11]

As Davy Crockett (Fess Parker) and friend Georgie Russel (Buddy Ebsen) [12] scout for General Andrew Jackson, a hostile band climbs a mountaintop as George Bruns's musical score telegraphs danger. Later, Chief Red Stick (Pat Hogan) [13] leads warriors in a wild dance about the campfire, as Davy and Georgie peer down. Shortly, other Creeks are glimpsed firing arrows at an army patrol under the command of (fictitious) Major Tobias Norton (William Bakewell).

Disney, unlike his Hollywood contemporaries, introduces this cliché only to dismiss it, along with corresponding audience expectations. The large-scale battle (a compilation of several historical confrontations, most notable among them Talladega) begins as Jackson (Basil Ruysdael) orders a dawn attack on a Creek village. The general employs what, by today's standards, are considered racial epithets, ordering Crockett's volunteers to "stir up them red hornets." Significantly, the film's hero/role model never speaks in such terms, and will in time come to loudly and emphatically dismiss what are portrayed as Jackson's racist attitudes toward Native Americans. During the combat sequence, Disney reverses the expected protagonist/antagonist outcome. When Davy and Red Stick face off, Red Stick wins. Red Stick also proves himself a better strategist than Jackson.

His braves escape by outmaneuvering soldiers with single-shot rifles. Ordinarily, a Western's big battle is placed at a film's end. Disney reserves that spot for the creation of peace. Crockett has tracked Red Stick's band to the Florida swamps,[14] where Indian and Anglo are reconciled after Crockett offers to face the chief on Indian terms:

RED STICK: Indian law no good for white man.
CROCKETT: Why not? White man's law'd be good for Indians, if you'd give it half a try.

The concept may be simplistic, even (as history attests) patently false. Nonetheless, Disney's drama, at the very least, ought to be tagged "unrealistic" in the best sense of the term, deriving as it does from an idealized vision of integration, presented to the child-audience as a positive thing. As Crockett and Red Stick shake hands, a chorus of Tom Blackburn's ballad (excised from the theatrical film, though present in the original TV episode) insists:

> He give his word, and he give his hand,
> That his Injun friends could keep their land.
> And the rest of his life, he took the stand,
> That justice was due every redskin band.
> Davy . . . Davy Crockett . . .
> Holding that promise dear.

Epithets like Injun and "redskin" strike modern audiences as politically incorrect. Yet they are terms that would have been employed by an early-nineteenth-century folk balladeer. The ideas and emotions, on the other hand, are enlightened, resulting in a positive fusion of historical accuracy for the tone and contemporary outlook for the theme.

The war behind him, Crockett journeys to the uncharted Obion River territory. Here, the integration theme is furthered as Davy confronts the film's second key Native American. Charlie Two Shirts (Jeff Thompson), a neighboring farmer, is, with his family, described by a likable white settler as "real nice folks." For the first glimpse of these Cherokees, Disney creates a traditional aura of threat. While Crockett and Russel work their farm, Indians scurry about in the brush. When the heroes pursue, they are surprised to meet peaceful people, beaten and thrown off their land by greedy whites. Embodying the redneck/racist element is Bigfoot Mason

(Mike Mazurki). This allows for an action sequence, as Crockett boxes with him for Indian rights.

Shortly before their fight commences, a short interchange allows full expression of Disney's values:

CROCKETT: My friend here says you threw him off his land.
BIGFOOT: Since when is Davy Crockett a friend of Indians?
CROCKETT: Always been a friend to the Cherokee. Got no bones to pick with the others, now they've signed the peace treaty.
BIGFOOT: This land's too good for Indians.
CROCKETT: Injuns got rights, just like ever'one else.

Even as *Crockett* reached theaters, school integration dominated newspaper headlines. In this context, a statement by Philip French takes on major significance: "the Indian has often been a surrogate Negro in liberal Westerns of the 1950s." [15] Hollywood's progressive element would, during the 1950s, bring contemporary issues to the screen, if—to maintain commercial viability—in thinly disguised form.

A powerful moment in the original TV version occurs after Charlie kills a redneck before the man can shoot Davy in the back. Disney does not attempt to conceal from his impressionable young audience the reality that people of color were treated unequally under the law. Instead, he champions the need for progressive Anglos to justifiably lie in order to further the civil rights cause. "Anyone asks who fired that shot," Georgie whispers to Charlie, "just remember, it was *me!*"

Shortly, Crockett runs for his first elected office (state legislature in Nashville) solely to defeat Amos Thorpe. Bedecked in suit and tie, this fictional opponent victimizes Indians with his brain as ruthlessly as Bigfoot did through brawn. Crockett angrily insists that Thorpe's campaign coffers were filled with "money he made on them Indian land grabs!" The greatest such villain—amazingly so, in a "kiddie film" made during the McCarthy era, when any social commentary and pointed criticism of American icons could be taken as proof of communist subversion—will prove to be Jackson, now the president. Expansionist-minded, he introduces his Indian Bill to Congress in hopes of moving peaceful Cherokee off their land and far to the west, where hostile tribes will prey on them. [16] "You put a strain on a fella, Mr. President," now-Congressman Crockett complains. Shortly, Davy's speech before Congress introduced the child-audience to civil rights activism of a type never before encountered in American movies, much less family-oriented Westerns:

> CROCKETT: Sure, we got to grow. But not at the expense of things this country was founded to protect. Expansion ain't no excuse for persecutin' a whole part of our people 'cause their skin is red!

Crockett storms out of Congress, quitting the political arena,[17] with its potential to corrupt even him, and heads for Texas—the final frontier, a place where natural man—Rousseau's best man—can still live close to the earth.

Or, in Davy's case, die there. As the film's final act commences, a Native American is at last totally integrated with Bustedluck (Nick Cravat), a Comanche encountered on the way to San Antonio. Crockett "speaks" with Bustedluck via sign language, incorporating the ongoing Disney theme of full (and nonverbal) communication as a means of bridging cultural gaps. A gambler companion, the fancy-suited Thimblerig (Hans Conried), is unhappy about the latest addition to "Crockett's Company":

> THIMBLERIG: I for one do not trust that perfidious savage.
> CROCKETT: We better trust him. He's the only one knows the way to the next waterhole!

In the subsequent shot, all four fall to the ground, drinking from a spring; Crockett was right, the gambler wrong, about Bustedluck.

Even Thimblerig will, in the film's final moments, arc enough to accept Bustedluck as an equal, as the two die side by side on the Alamo walls during the final battle.[18] Earlier, upon their arrival, Colonel James Bowie (Kenneth Tobey) asks how many reinforcements Crockett has brought. Davy—without hesitation—answers, "Four."[19] Bustedluck is a full equal among them. Davy regularly translates orders from Colonel William Travis (Don Megowan) to Bustedluck; the multilingual man is, in Disney, to be admired for his ability to communicate universal truths across ethnic lines. In return, the Comanche aids Davy, insisting Crockett use his favorite rifle, Old Betsy, to fire at a Mexican cannon crew slipping close to the fort. Bustedluck—and Bustedluck alone—comprehends the weapon's mythical power.

As the film moves toward its conclusion, Bustedluck becomes central to every sequence. Though Thimblerig still refers to him as an "aborigine," the Comanche bests the gambler in a game of chance after several Texicans have lost. Bustedluck stands beside Crockett when Travis draws the legendary line in the sand. Only after Bustedluck steps across does Thimblerig sum up the courage to join the others. When Crockett and Russel exchange final words of friendship on the Alamo's wall, Bustedluck sits between them, central to the shot. Finally, Bustedluck dies on the walls during the assault, courageously giving his life to keep Thimblerig (they are now close friends) alive. The gambler, then, in a symbolic moment, seizes his fallen companion's tomahawk, fighting with it. He has learned from the "savage" rather than, as was the case in more conventional films of the era, teaching him.

Blamin' the Indians Was A-Proven Untrue
Davy Crockett and the River Pirates (1956)

The second series of Crockett TV shows, and the subsequent truncated film version, were drawn from the *Almanacks*—predecessors of pulp fiction and comic books—published during the final decade of Crockett's life (1826–1836) and for a considerable time thereafter. The resultant work retells an apocryphal 1810 contest between Crockett, King of the Wild Frontier, and Mike Fink (Jeff York), King of the River. The sequel is fashioned in broadly comic strokes, approximating a nineteenth-century tall tale rather than the more historical approach of the first film. Still, Disney endowed this yarn with a serious subtext that challenged all the clichéd images of Indians then prevalent in American thought and Hollywood films.

Captain Cobb (Clem Bevins) and other Ohio keelboatmen are unable to round up proper crews. Cobb informs Davy that everyone's "heard about the Indians" upriver, ambushing boats and killing the rivermen. Only Mike Fink's braggarts dare travel the route, until Crockett rounds up some friends and agrees to race Fink to New Orleans. Shortly, "Indians" attack Mike's boat, in the lead. Davy and company arrive to reinforce their friendly rivals against what appear to be members of the Kaskasia tribe. We, however, know better. Disney's camera pulls back to reveal white river pirates, ashore near Cave-In Rock, disguising themselves as Native Americans.

After the keelboat race ends in tenuous victory for Crockett, Mike transports Davy and Georgie downriver. The frontiersmen ask to be dropped off in the land of friendly Chickasaws. They are captured by braves and brought before the chief, who informs Davy his people are planning war "to avenge the murder of our brothers," Kas-kasias whose village (including women and children) was devastated by whites, out for vengeance. The film's previous lighthearted tone dissipates, as the chief— wise, decent, and played by an actual Native American actor, a rarity at the time—speaks in simple yet eloquent English:

> Know this, Davy Crockett. We have always wanted peace with the white man. But he does not want peace with us. He makes treaties and calls us brother, but he believes any evil he hears of us.

Anyone expecting Crockett to defend the whites, or their government, was shocked to hear the film's hero fully agree. Nonetheless, Davy asks for (and receives) a few days to avoid further bloodshed by enlisting Mike's help in rounding up the pirates. When our heroes again engage the gang, in a large-scale battle, faux Indians are stripped of their costumes. Heroic river-men lift Indian "scalps" (wigs), revealing dastardly whites lurking beneath. As the child-audience watched in amazement, Indians are fully exonerated of the crimes that most matinee movies of that time held them responsible for. This chore completed, America's "kings" go their separate ways.

> Kept his word to Mike and his crew,
> Kept his word to the Indian chief, too!
> For the river was clear and *all* men knew
> That blamin' the Indians was a-proven *untrue.*

Two Medicines Are Better'n One
Westward Ho the Wagons (1956)

Initially, *Westward Ho* seems a giant step backward. In the opening, Hank Breckinridge (Jeff York), grizzled scout for a mid-1840s Oregon-bound wagon train, entertains exhausted pioneers before a roaring campfire with harrowing tall tales of battling the Blackfoot (Breckinridge refers to them as "savages") during his mountain man days. As all are held spellbound, an arrow appears as if magically summoned by his story. Shortly, Breck-inridge, wagonmaster James Stephen (George Reeves), and John "Doc" Grayson (Fess Parker) discover an unknown man's body. Through this ruse, Pawnees steal horses.

Indians are, at this point, once again the traditional movie-threat to "heroic" whites. Three action sequences, following one another in rapid succession, further this image. When teenager Dan Thompson (David Stollery) rescues his beloved horse Chieftain from Pawnees, Doc shoots down pursuing Indians. After capture, Dan flees (in the manner of real-life frontiersman John Colter) on foot. Climbing a foothill, he kicks down rocks, killing a brave who earlier taunted the bound boy. Finally, the train—pursued by hundreds of war-painted Pawnees—makes a wild rush for South Pass, firing at Indians who fall from horses in the conventional movie manner. Ironically, the sequence was directed by a part-Native-American stunt coordinator, Yakima Canutt, who had earlier mounted the famed chase for John Ford's *Stagecoach* (1939).

Even in such a traditional action sequence, however, Disney manages to overturn the cliché that attacking Indians are out for blood. "A Pawnee would rather have a horse than take a scalp, any day," Doc explains. When they release extra horses, the Indians disperse; Disney's Indians only wanted fair payment for passage. Disney also breaks new ground by placing the battle at his film's midpoint, violating genre expectations and causing one critic to dismiss *Westward Ho* as "one of Disney's more forgettable live-action films."[20] In fact, Walt dared to innovate. As Robin Wood wrote of Alfred Hitchcock's groundbreaking decision to kill off his heroine halfway through *Psycho* (1960), this

> completely undermines our . . . sense of security . . . It also constitutes an alienation effect so shattering [at a first viewing] we scarcely recover from it. Never . . . has identification been broken off so brutally . . . we are left shocked, with nothing to cling to, the apparent centre of the film entirely dissolved.[21]

Likewise, as smoke clears in *Westward Ho*, we're left wondering what the remainder of this Disney film can possibly be about. Shortly, we learn: A vision of Native Americans as equally human if notably different, along with a practical blueprint for multicultural communication between races. The film's early episodes occur almost entirely at night; Disney's depiction of Western clichés conveys the darkness of a preexisting racist view. The latter part, however, unfolds largely in daylight. Overcoming cultural bias is (as the film's night/day dichotomy implies) an enlightening experience for the mainstream Americans in the film and those who received it.

At daybreak, the train arrives at Fort Laramie, where the pilgrims are greeted by Bissonette (Sebastian Cabot). A French-Canadian trader, his doors are open to white and red man alike. Bissonette makes no racial distinctions. All are his "customers," he tells people in the manner of an ardent but unprejudiced capitalist. A notable contrast can be made between Disney's view of a character who espouses such values and John Ford's.

Though Bissonette will emerge here as a complex yet essentially positive person, the Indian agent Meeker (Grant Withers)—who expresses those sentiments in precisely the same words in *Fort Apache* (1948)—is a hypocritical villain out to exploit Indians and whites alike. For Disney, a man who speaks about his own blindness to racial issues eventually lives up, in a positive way, to his words, rather than revealing that they were merely a mask to make more money.

Camped nearby are Lakota. "Sure good to see friendly Indians again," Doc sighs. Though we learn these people are in an ugly mood, Bissonette explains why: "Last train through here killed a couple of their braves"—an unprovoked action. In history, as in this economically modest yet morally ambitious film's vision, transformation of the Sioux from a friendly nation to a hostile force was caused by whites. Disney, always at heart an artist in the Romantic tradition, simultaneously dramatizes Wordsworth's edict that "the Child is Father to the Man." When the children of the covered wagon (the title of the book this film was based on) visit the trading post, they're treated with respect by medicine man Many Stars (Iron Eyes Cody) and Chief Wolf's Brother (John War Eagle).

Indian roles in the second half are entirely played by Native Americans. Intriguingly, villainous Indians in the first part were rendered by swarthy white actors. Disney implies through casting that the Indians we now meet—proud, decent, peaceful—are the "real" Indians, while those encountered earlier—hostile, threatening, inhuman—represented only a figment of white Hollywood's collective imagination, which Disney initially invokes only to eventually dispel. From this point, the drama is intellectual rather than visceral. Many Stars and Wolf's Brother are entranced with the golden hair of a little girl, Myra Thompson (Karen Pendleton). "Daughter of the Rising Sun," they adoringly call her.

When they touch Myra's curly locks, the child—Wordsworth's naturally wise child-as-swain—senses the essential goodness of the alternative culture and smiles without fear. Friction occurs only when an unpleasant pioneer, Spencer Armitage (Leslie Bradley), misinterprets the innocent gesture as molestation. Armitage is, like the corrupt, overly civilized adult of nineteenth-century Romantic poetry, a man who has entirely lost touch with his primal sympathy. He would do well to appreciate the simple, near-silent wisdom of Myra (her name an anagram for the biblical Mary) as the Indians instinctively do. Shortly, Disney makes clear that youth may well set aside the racial antagonism of their parents. Two groups of young people—from the covered wagon and Sioux village—accidentally encounter one another. At first, each appears fearful, grimacing at possible danger. Then, an Indian child, Little Thunder (Anthony Numkena), produces a handmade top-on-a-string toy and spins it. Dan returns the gesture, drawing an identical item from his pocket. Even beatific children, though, can miscommunicate. When Dan attempts to shake hands, Little Thunder wrongly interprets this as an invitation to wrestle. Still, the children accept it as an agreeable game. Problems occur only when several braves happen by, precisely as Dan bests Little Wolf. That a Sioux child could be defeated insults the self-image of adult Indians, causing Wolf's Brother to angrily break up the fun.

Disney does not sentimentalize his Native Americans. Adult Indians are as prone to ego as their white counterparts. But if either culture proves more appealing in the film's context, it is the Lakota, who arrive at the pioneer camp carrying peace pipes. After learning that Myra is an orphan, they hope to adopt her into the tribe, offering rich gifts, including religious white buffalo robes and a tribal flute guaranteeing the caravan's unmolested passage. Now—and this is exceedingly rare for a Hollywood film, particularly one marketed mainly to children and adolescents— there is no human villain. The antagonist is, as in the best adult drama, a situation—the lack of understanding between different if equally worthy people. The agreeable wagonmaster overreacts with a loud "No!" The Sioux are insulted by rejection of what they consider a generous offer. Only Doc—the consummate Disney hero—attempts conciliation through communication. "We know the honor [the Chief] pays us," he makes clear via the multilingual Bissonette, "but we cannot part with the child." While such words soothe the immediate conflict, they can't end the problem. The Sioux won't allow the train to leave until the child is turned over, which the pioneers won't consider.

Then, a seemingly unhappy accident provides the solution, when Little Thunder falls from his horse during a game and breaks his clavicle. Many Stars performs religious rituals, but they cannot keep the child from growing comatose, his silent suffering rendered in heartbreaking close-ups. At this point, Doc offers to bring his limited knowledge of medicine into play, not by replacing Many Stars but by collaborating with him. "Two medicines are better than one," Breckinridge informs the Sioux. In less certain hands, the story's thrust could have degenerated into incipient if unintentional racism, white man's medicine proving "superior" to Indian "superstition." Not in Disney. Breckinridge suggests that the medicine man's invocations to Lakota gods have indeed worked. Having heard them, the

AN UNFINISHED JOURNEY. In *Westward Ho the Wagons!*, Anglos meet and befriend Native Americans, as (in the tradition of the nineteenth-century Romantic poets and philosophers) the child proves to be father to the man: adults learning the ways of peaceful coexistence from their offspring. (Copyright 1958 Walt Disney Productions; courtesy Buena Vista Releasing.)

higher powers sent Doc to augment, not supplant, the native approach. Phrased this way, Doc's offer cannot be refused; perception is reality.

Still, Disney refuses to choose between the two forms of "medicine" or the two equal nations—Anglo and Indian—from which they are derived. Doc employs his surgery, which should succeed but apparently doesn't—until the "magic" flute is placed in the child's hand. Then, the boy stirs, his eyes open, and everyone breathes a sigh of relief. There's no way we can know which approach worked, or whether it was indeed the happy combination of the two. The power of the resolution derives from Disney's intended ambiguity. Clearly, positive results are achieved by mixing—and believing in—alternative approaches. The Sioux, accepting that they cannot adopt Myra, drape her in sacred robes and hang a flute around her neck. Total integration between two American "tribes" does not occur. They have different points of view, different goals. Yet multicultural respect has been achieved. Pioneers now reverently carry Sioux objects, while they have given the Indians the greatest gift: the returned life of a beloved child.

The final image rejects the mythic vision of every other wagon-train Western, in which caravans, having defeated Indian enemies, reach their destinations. Disney's caravan pushes on, with the Sioux riding on either side. The two groups do not intermingle, though they travel in parallel directions, maintaining respectful distance. Yet this does not imply separate but equal, in the reactionary sense, so much as the tolerant respect of difference inherent in diversity, a radical notion at the time. "Instead of a denouement," Leonard Maltin complained, "the film merely stops." [22] While there may be no *conventional* ending, what we experience is more, not less, rewarding than what we expect from a traditional Western. If we do not see the wagon train reach its destination, this is because the train serves as Disney's objective correlative for America. Until full tolerance has been achieved, our journey, like the journey of these people (or, more correctly, peoples), is far from over.

Good and Bad on Both Sides
The Light in the Forest (1958)

The Light in the Forest forsakes the cinematically well-traveled route of the mid–Oregon Trail for the rarely explored, onscreen at least, first frontier. In 1764, still-untamed territories in upstate New York and portions of Pennsylvania remained the Wild West, geographically and metaphorically. The film begins with a treaty negotiation between British soldiers, led by scout Del Hardy (Fess Parker), and Delawares under Chief Cuyloga (Joseph Calleia). A key clause insists that all prisoners held by the tribe be returned. This affects True Son (James MacArthur), Cuyloga's adopted child.

However historically documented and dramatically rich, the concept of reassimilation into white society has a deep symbolic significance in our national consciousness. In 1862, Fenimore Cooper's *The Last of the Mohicans*—arguably the first "Western"—concerned the kidnapping and rescue of two Anglo women from Hurons during the French and Indian War. Lieutenant Colonel George Custer may have become a legend for all time on June 25, 1876, at Little Big Horn; he emerged as a legend in his *own* time eight years earlier, by daring to ride into an Indian village, demanding the release of two captured white women. Nationwide newspaper coverage of this event exalted Custer in the popular imagination over all other frontier cavalry commanders.[23] Similar stories—fact or fiction, part of an emerging Manifest Destiny folklore—portrayed White Knights (cavalry in the West, the Klan in the South) riding to the rescue of virginal damsels-in-distress held, against their will, by members of some dark race.

As Richard Slotkin, director of the American Studies program at Wesleyan University in Connecticut, explains:

> I call it the captivity myth. It dates back to the colonial Indian wars of 1622–1763, our oldest social conflict, but it's still a central theme in popular culture today. The myth centered originally on the figure of a white woman captured by Indians, an event that had great symbolic value: It represented the colonists' fear that their fundamental values were endangered by this "savage" race.[24]

In 1956, Ford confronted that myth with *The Searchers*. His protagonist, Ethan Edwards (John Wayne), reveals himself more sociopath than idealist, planning to not only recapture but also execute abducted women owing to his profound fear of miscegenation. Though *The Searchers* ends happily ("Let's go home, Debbie," Edwards whispers to his niece, played by Natalie Wood), Ford's follow-up, *Two Rode Together* (1962), insisted that such well-intended efforts are doomed to failure. Despite two stalwart heroes, a cavalryman (Richard Widmark) and a lawman (James Stewart), Ford's teenage abductee dies brutally in a tragic attempt at reassimilation. Ford's sad but unavoidable conclusion is that such an encounter cannot prove happy.[25]

Disney views the matter differently. *Light in the Forest*, filmed midway between the two Ford films, contains no shred of such fatalism. In its place, Disney offers the guarded optimism of a populist-progressive: A positive outcome will be achieved by educating both communities as to the values of the other's alternate ethnicity. To accomplish this, cooperation of "good" people on both sides (Del for the Anglos, Chief Cuyloga representing the Indians) is necessary. Del's insistence on multicultural communication (he's first glimpsed translating between British and Delawares) overrides negative influences on both sides. These include Niskitoon (Norman Fredric), always somewhat sympathetic since he advocates open warfare only after whites murder his brother, and the villain, Wilse Owens (Wendell Corey),[26] whose hatred of Indians is entirely without provocation.

Here, Disney adds a personal touch to Conrad Richter's story line. Wilse, compared to the otherwise good-natured whites, is *not* Scotch-Irish. How he could then be their blood relative is never explained, yet Disney will not slur his own ethnicity. Compounding Wilse's unpleasantness is his sexual harassment of his indentured servant, Shenendoe (Carol Lynley)—villainy extending beyond racism into sexism. Other, less enlightened movies of the period (e.g., *Rachel and the Stranger*, 1948) portrayed such male authority lightly, more or less a side benefit of that time. Disney, and Disney alone, makes clear sexism is as objectionable as racism.[27]

Still, Shenendoe's problems, however sensitively presented, take a backseat to racial prejudice. The film educates us as to the wholesale massacre of Christianized Indians by redneck whites, here called "The Paxton Boys." Adult Westerns of the mid-1950s conveniently overlooked this reality, attested to in the historical record,[28] such behavior reaching its odious nadir in 1893 at Wounded Knee. Yet Disney pushed deeper still into what were then still dangerous waters. Fiedler notes that, once captive, some male prisoners embraced the Indian experience, owing to "an uneasy longing to cast off the burden of being white, and make of slavery among the Indians a kind of freedom [and even] an almost voluptuous acceptance by certain whites of their subjugation to an alien race."[29] That aptly describes True Son, who attempts suicide by eating poisoned plants rather than return to civilization.

Fiedler mentions something even more disturbing to Anglo (particularly patriarchal Anglo) tradition. Leading mythmakers from Cooper to Ford, subscribing to Victorian notions of women as more civilized vessels than their male counterparts, tacitly avoided the historical fact that "not all of the women captured by Indians . . . actually found their captors disagreeable . . . some of them, in fact, preferred to remain with those who snatched them away by force."[30] Disney, and Disney alone, dared address this issue during the Eisenhower era. The white wife of Little Crane, forced to part from her beloved Indian husband, provides the film's most tender but also daring (for its time) moment. Later, a crisis occurs when Little Crane, learning his wife (pregnant when she left) has given birth, slips into the white community to catch a glimpse of his son. Wilse casually shoots Little Crane on sight. "Clean out the vermin," Wilse insists. In 1953, Charles Marquis Warren's adult Western *Arrowhead* offered Charlton Heston as a hero who utters those very words. In Disney, it is the villain. Wilse's murderous act precipitates a war that the positive figures on each side labor to stop. Yet for all his empathy toward Indians, Disney never allows his film to degenerate into simplistic white-bashing of the *Dances with Wolves* order. We are expected to discriminate in Disney between good and bad individuals, rather than make easy assumptions based on race.

Disney, too much of a moralist to remain nonjudgmental, insists that we judge (but never prejudge) and that we do so based on a person's behavior rather than bigotry. Here, then, is the key distinction between Disney's film and Costner's *Dances with Wolves,* the latter merely reversing long-held prejudices, arriving at a pro-Indian, anti-Anglo bias. Disney's dispels all prejudicial thinking, coming out against the very idea of bias, be it reactionary or radical in nature. So Wilse is the only cardboard character, without a shred of humanity. This remains true even at the end, when—after Johnny bests Wilse in a fair fistfight—Wilse offers to shake hands. Maltin described the scene thusly: "The only glaring weakness . . . is the finale, with Wilse . . . suddenly mending his ways."[31] In fact, Disney offers a dramatically perfect closure, at least when one fully understands the fable's moral implications.

For Wilse does *not* mend his ways. While shaking hands, he grunts what he considers to be a compliment to the man who beat him: "He's *white!*" Wilse cannot accept the notion that any red man might win, though he does (magnanimously, in his own mind) admit that other Anglos can. Wilse accepts Johnny back into society only after the youth has proven himself (in Wilse's objectionable scheme of things) able to compete with the worst of whites. Though Wilse remains incapable of change, Shenendoe arcs. This proto-hippie-princess—pure, innocent, decent, almost mute—initially expresses racist attitudes as offensive as Wilse's. The first time Shenendoe sees Johnny, head shaven Mohawk fashion, she becomes hysterical and runs away. Yet Wilse's wife, who does not share her husband's attitudes and provides another example of the female as morally superior to the male in Disney films, notes: "Yes, she hates Indians, but with good reason." Shenendoe witnessed her sister killed and scalped. Disney chronicles Shenendoe's growing realization that, the horrible incident notwithstanding, it's wrong to prejudge an entire people for isolated acts committed by specific individuals. Only when she has reached this point of enlightenment can Shenendoe accept Johnny.

He, initially as narrow in his defense of Native Americans as Wilse is in his attacks (verbal and physical), cannot at first accept what Shenendoe has seen, accusing her of lying: "Indians don't make war against white squaws and papooses," he insists. Johnny believes that only whites—whom he considers evil—are capable of such things. Painfully, Shenendoe describes what she saw Wyandottes do. Johnny, unable to refute her story, sighs: "Wyandottes? Maybe. But not Delawares!" By the end, Johnny will acknowledge he was wrong even about this. To achieve vengeance for his slain brother, Niskitoon scalps not only white warriors but women and children. "We're not *all* bad," Shenendoe earlier told him. Indians, on the other hand, are not all *good,* as he learns for himself. "There's good and bad on *both* sides," Del, Disney's mouthpiece, explains. Significantly, the film maintains this balance.

If there is any bias, though, the film favors Native Americans. "White man makes slaves of everything," Half Arrow (Rafael Campos) mutters in amazement after first hearing the concept of indentured servants, inconceivable to the Native sensibility, "while the Indian is always free!" Only heightened communication, achieved through education, will save the day for this community, Disney's microcosm of America itself. So Johnny's biological mother, Myra (Jessica Tandy, as another of Walt's incarnations of the biblical Mary), insists he learn to read and write English. Johnny fears this may diminish his Indian heritage. "You should know both," Myra—who never speaks against Indians or asks Johnny to abandon his Delaware ways—informs him. "I have no people," Johnny cries out during his darkest hour. These are precisely the words we hear from the doomed boy in Ford's *Two Rode Together*. The difference exists in context.

What Johnny perceives as his plight transforms, by movie's end, into his saving grace. Johnny realizes, under Del's guidance, his self-pitying conclusion was wrong. He is blessed with two people, Del insisting: "You have good Indian parents and good white parents." Accepting this, Johnny emerges as the cinema's first multicultural hero. Still, there are other, happier forms of education than books. Here, Disney again celebrates the sensuous side of life that, were he the strict Victorian many believe, he would necessarily have to criticize. Shenendoe—overcoming her early racism—prepares for Johnny to kiss her. Instead, Native American–style, he brushes his cheek against hers. Disappointed, Shenendoe reveals herself as one of Disney's gentle dominating teachers, seizing Johnny by the shoulders, delivering a full kiss on the mouth—a repeat of Sluefoot Sue, taking charge of naïve Pecos Bill in *Melody Time*.

When the two are to be married, each reveals respect for the other's ways of knowledge. Embracing, Shenendoe kisses Johnny in Native American manner, he returning the gesture Anglo-style. Here is the Disney statement on race relations in a nutshell. Like medicine, two ways of kissing are best; the couple that combines the beauty of both worlds is truly blessed.

INTEGRATION WITHOUT ASSIMILATION. The Disney films provide balanced images of Anglo and Native Americans learning to accept and adjust to each other's lifestyles. In *The Light in the Forest* (TOP), a settler (James MacArthur) becomes an adopted Indian. Conversely, in *Tonka* (BOTTOM), a Lakota youth (Sal Mineo) joins the United States Cavalry. (Copyright 1958 and 1959 Walt Disney Productions; courtesy Buena Vista Releasing.)

A Good Day to Die
Tonka, aka *Comanche* (1958)

There remained only one way for Disney to extend his sympathetic treatment of Native Americans: Tell a story from *their* point of view. This was
the approach in his version of the Battle of the Little Big Horn, as the film's
title suggests. Tonka is what the film's Lakota hero calls the title character, a horse, whereas David Appel's novel had been named after the white
hero's moniker for him, Comanche. The cavalry steed belonged to Captain
Myles Keogh, one of Custer's officers; the only living survivor of the fight,[32]
Comanche inspired the tradition of the riderless mount, a significant part
of military protocol to this day.[33] To achieve his aim here, Disney had to
jettison the narrative device of his source: perceiving the events through
the animal's eyes, precisely what attracted Disney in the first place.

He had, in 1954, filmed *Ben and Me,* an animated featurette retelling
Ben Franklin's Colonial-era experiences from the perspective of a fictional
mouse ("Amos"). *Comanche* provided perfect material for a live-action
film that could accomplish much the same thing. But with the decision to
make a title change,[34] a different approach was called for, obvious from
the opening credits in which the titles appear over Lakota pictographs,
with no representation of the Seventh Cavalry. "The movies," as film history tells us, "are after all an expression of the dominant culture. Con-
sequently, the Indians are viewed, whether sympathetically or not, from
the point of view of the victorious pioneers and their White Anglo-Saxon
society."[35] True, perhaps, for most movies, from *Broken Arrow* (1950) to
Dances with Wolves. But not Disney's, which breaks sharply from that tradition as well as the film's literary antecedent.

Appel's animal is first portrayed as a wild horse, captured and trained
by a Lakota youth, White Bull.[36] The novel's Indian never names his horse.
This is merely a brief prelude to a pro-Custer, pro-army tale, focusing on
the love between Keogh and his mount. Though kinder to the horse than
the other Indians are, the book's White Bull never equals Keogh in the
horse's heart as he does in the movie. The central idea of the film—the
horse forced to choose between two masters, and the races they represent,
ultimately unable to do so as he loves both—does not exist in the source.
That shouldn't surprise us, since it is a modern idea—the way we might
expect the story to be told today, in the age of diversity. Disney's version is
virulently anti-Custer, a dozen years before *Little Big Man* transformed a
onetime American hero into a villain for a new, then-emerging generation

with radically different values. Disney plays down the Keogh-Comanche element while expanding on the White Bull–Tonka Wakon ("The Great One," in Lakota) relationship.

The film's first image depicts mounted braves pursuing wild horses, Tonka among them. Relegated to the sidelines, White Bull (Sal Mineo) and friend Strong Bear (Rafael Campos) guard meat. Spotting the beautiful horse, White Bull vows to own him someday. Everything we see from that point and throughout the film's first act is what White Bull experiences. This entails a reversal of one key genre cliché: Indians as threatening rather than threatened. In *Tonka,* on the other hand, we first glimpse members of the U.S. Cavalry when White Bull returns to his village from a mountain sojourn, discovering deserted lodgepoles. Moments later, Keogh (Philip Carey) and Lieutenant Henry Nowlan (Jerome Courtland) lead cavalrymen from Fort Hays in a surprise attack. Though both officers are among the film's "positive" Anglo characters, they're initially experienced as frightening. The child-audience has assumed the attitudes of White Bull and his people.

Still, the film does not, like *Dances with Wolves,* provide a well-intentioned but false corrective to earlier clichés by offering an idealized portrait of a peaceful Lakota. Such a vision contradicts fact, for the Sioux and their cousin-tribe the Cheyenne were always, at heart, a war-loving people. Combat was an accepted, even cherished, part of their existence.[37] Unlike Costner, Disney doesn't leave himself open to the "accusation of manipulating Indians according to the political ideas and unconscious cultural predilections of [the film's] makers."[38] While such an approach may initially seem enlightening, when that happens, "the Indian remain[s] one of the pawns of the western game."[39] For the typical nouveau Western sacrifices historical accuracy to make a politically correct statement. Disney pulled off something far more significant, complex, and stimulating—intellectually and aesthetically—as he blends an accurate portrait with an overriding respect for the greatness and *uniqueness* of this alternative culture without resorting to sentimentalizing or simplifying. "Stealing horses and taking scalps," the young hero cries out, describing his two ambitions in life. We see him do both, stealing a horse from a cavalry camp, even killing the guard, then proceeding to take a scalp with the dead man's own sword. The stealing of horses from enemies, according to Lakota values, isn't stealing at all, rather a way of life, as is scalp-taking.

A difficult demand is made on the child-audience that few adult-oriented filmmakers, then or now, would dare try: discriminating between people on the basis of their words and actions as individuals. To achieve this, Disney sets up parallels that structure his film along moral lines. There are equally appealing heroes, White Bull and Keogh. Each has a close friend (Strong Bear, Hank Nowlan) in whom he confides. The film's heroes are linked by their equal love for the horse. The early sequence, in which White Bull trains Tonka to be a warrior's stallion, is balanced when, in Act Two, Keogh puts Comanche through similar training. The third and final act commences with the chance meeting (invented for the film) of White Bull and Keogh, as they cut across cultural lines (mutual love for the horse leading to mutual respect for one another). The film concludes with the two meeting again as combatants at Little Big Horn.

Also, we encounter a pair of equally offensive villains. In the Lakota camp, Yellow Bull (H. M. Wynant) is a war chief initially admired by White Bull. "Yellow Bull is a cruel man, but a great warrior," Prairie Flower (Joy Page) reminds her son. Her words also describe Yellow Hair of the Seventh Cavalry; the film's Custer is courageous yet cruel.[40] The Last Stand, portrayed more often onscreen than any other incident in American history other than the Alamo and the Gunfight at the O.K. Corral,[41] is here presented more accurately, in terms of terrain (what we see actually looks like Montana for once) and tactics (Custer and his men do not fight with sabres) than in any previous filmed version. More significant is Disney's eliciting a complex reaction to the battle. Earlier versions, notably *They Died with Their Boots On* (1941), had audiences cheering for Errol Flynn as Custer. Later, *Little Big Man* elicited boos and hisses for Richard Mulligan's Custer. While watching *Tonka,* child-viewers cheered when cruel people (Yellow Bull, Yellow Hair) died, groaned when good guys (Strong Bear, Myles Keogh) fell. Though Disney is as manipulative as previous filmmakers, he insists on provoking nonracial/antiracist reactions.

As the battle ends, our final image is of an American flag falling to the ground. Children wildly whooped with glee in 1958, much to the consternation of exasperated parents.[42] Never before had a supposedly mainstream American movie elicited, purposefully or accidentally, such a response. Many children in attendance between the ages of seven and eleven would, in the late sixties, burn American flags to protest a controversial war— one as clearly offensive to them as our government's 1876 Indian policy.

The movie's most controversial moment proved to be the ending, in which White Bull, seriously wounded while fighting Custer, stands at attention at Fort Abraham Lincoln, in blue uniform, in 1878. Now an Indian scout, White Bull is again near his beloved horse. To a degree, this is a contrivance, fiction providing a happy reunion between boy and pet. Critical reaction was incredulous: "the Indian brave, who has repeatedly shown his allegiance to his tribe and his hatred for the white man, is now an honorary member of the 7th Cavalry! Horse or no horse, it doesn't ring entirely true."[43] Such a reaction fails to take into account the fact that changing loyalties were by no means rare. The historical Little Big Man (an Indian, *not* a white convert), a former ally of Crazy Horse, joined the army, then held his onetime blood brother while a soldier bayoneted the great chief at Fort Robinson, Nebraska.[44]

The significance of the ending resides in its implication that any minority can be accommodated in the American mainstream, even those who have violently opposed our country's imperialist tendencies. White Bull and Hank Nowlan have become friends, making up for the former companion each lost at Little Big Horn. Best of all—and most enlightened on the filmmaker's part—White Bull can integrate *without* giving up his ethnicity and way of life. In the closing shot, White Bull and his horse ride the plains once more. While away from the fort, White Bull forsakes army blue for his old Lakota clothing. If this constitutes less the reality of the situation than an idealized vision of minorities achieving full equality while maintaining the essence of their own cultures, it is a dream that, nearly half a century after the film was made, has become the great hope of most modern Americans.

The Art of Omission
Ten Who Dared (1960)

Native Americans have a relatively small role in Disney's retelling of John Wesley Powell's 1869 geological and mapping expedition along the Colorado River. Still, Walt should be commended for *not* adding a fictional fight between Anglos and Indians to beef up the action, as most Hollywood filmmakers would have done. Such commercial concerns did not matter much to Disney, who here refused to compromise with historical reality.

Midway through the film, when a thinly disguised version of mountain man Jim Bridger (Roy Barcroft) meets the explorers, he's accompanied by his Native American wife. Disney portrays intermarriage in a positive light. The woman is played by Dawn Little Sky, an authentic Native American actress. Hardly surprising by today's standards, it's worth recalling that, throughout the fifties, Anglo women invariably portrayed Indians, Debra

Paget all but cornering the market (*Broken Arrow, White Feather,* etc.). Ten years after the release of this Disney film, most Hollywood filmmakers were still casting non-Indians in such roles. *A Man Called Horse* (1970) featured Corinna Tsopei, a Greek Miss Universe winner, as a Lakota.

Disney portrayed Mrs. Bridger as a highly positive person. Offering far better advice to the frontiersmen than her legendary husband, she's treated with great dignity by Powell, Disney's hero and spokesman. *Ten Who Dared* proved enlightened as to Native Americans in other ways as well. The group's mountain man turned scout, Bill Dunn (Brian Keith), and two other members of the party eventually head off on their own, attempting to reach civilization overland. Shortly, they find themselves face-to-face with a war party, led by a chief (Pat Hogan) understandably angry over the killing of some of his people by whites. Ordinarily, Dunn and his group would be attacked by the Indians, who do not discriminate among Anglos. But this is a Disney film, where the ordinary never occurs—if occasionally such stereotypical situations may be invoked only to be rejected—dramatically and, by implication, morally. Dunn explains how and why it could not possibly have been them. The chief accepts their account, letting them go.

Blood Brothers
Those Calloways (1965)

Having briefly raised the issue of intermarriage in *Ten Who Dared,* Disney fully explored this in *Those Calloways.* The film, a family drama set in New England during the twentieth century's early years, is most notable as one of the first to bring ecology to the public's attention. The eccentric, hermit-like hero, Cam (Brian Keith), respects the wilds in a way his town-oriented neighbors do not. This, we learn in time, derives from the fact that Cam is part Indian himself. Earlier movies by other Hollywood filmmakers tended to cast the "half-breed" in derogatory villainous roles; Disney made Cam a larger than life figure. We sense that Cam's Indian heritage is what makes him sensitive to the environment in a way other locals—nice enough folks, mostly—are not, at least until Cam teaches them to respect the earth. When Cam is accidentally wounded, near death in the family cabin, a decent-minded doctor (Frank Ferguson) reminds Cam's wife: "Don't forget, he's part Indian. That oughta pull him through!" A deep personal strength is implied about people lucky enough to have Native American blood running through their veins.

YOU GO, GIRL! Disney's original concept for the pagan orgy in *Fantasia* (as this rare, previously unpublished photograph of tabletop models makes clear) was to cast female centaurs as African American women. Sadly, Walt's concept didn't make it past Hollywood's nervous censors. (Copyright 1940 Walt Disney Productions; courtesy Buena Vista Releasing.)

2

Together in Perfect Harmony
Disney and the Civil Rights Movement

If the film became the main manipulator of the American
Dream, for Negroes that dream contained a strong dose of such
stuff that nightmares are made of.
—RALPH ELLISON, 1949

Literature conditions the mind and the battle, for the mind is
half the struggle.
—RON KARENGA, 1967

*D*uring the late 1960s, the Woodstock nation's interest in minority
cultures most obviously manifested itself in Native American customs
and costumes. Still, the roots stretched considerably broader and deeper.
Many young people identified as "longhairs" during the brief but intense
hippie era had, while still crew-cut during the early sixties, aligned themselves with the civil rights movement. No wonder, then, that the Afro,
newly popular among blacks who now rejected their previous emulation
of Anglo styles, was also embraced by many whites. Such cultural give-
and-take reached beyond cosmetic levels, extending to a sincere interest
in values, social and spiritual, in many cases as expressed in art and music.
The new—and decidedly tricky—question now facing minorities was
whether they still hoped to assimilate into the American mainstream, as
had been the case throughout the 1950s, or rather forge separate if equal
identities within an emerging multicultural country.

But be it integration or black nationalism, the sixties was the decade
during which the civil rights movement, which had begun taking shape
even as World War II ended, came of age. Little wonder, then, that for
the first time an African American emerged as superstar. Sidney Poitier's
roles in *A Raisin in the Sun* (1961), *Guess Who's Coming to Dinner* (1967),

and *In the Heat of the Night* (1967) instilled a heightened sense of pride within black moviegoers, while communicating a newly respectful image of blacks to white audience members. Significantly, Poitier's racial identity was never mentioned in several key movies, including *Lilies of the Field* (1963), for which he was the first African American to win the Best Actor Oscar. Clearly, this was a man, who happened to be black, demanding respect both for his ethnicity (in some roles) and for his basic humanity (in all roles), an enlightened approach that hadn't been in evidence in typical previous film or TV productions. The only exception to that earlier norm, once again, was in Disney's work. His black characters are often not identified by race, though when ethnicity does emerge as an issue, it is always handled with pride.

As would be the case with Poitier's roles, African Americans are presented in Disney films as at the very least equals and, in more cases than not, superior to the Anglos on view. This approach was to be expected in the sixties, when films reflected a transitional period during which Dr. Martin Luther King, Stokely Carmichael, and Malcolm X all became household names in white as well as black homes. Such a situation, however, appears remarkable when encountered a quarter century earlier, at a time when roles for blacks consisted mainly of self-mocking characters more often than not played by Stepin Fetchit. Disney's films, conversely, proceed from the hope that movies—a cinematic "literature" for the twentieth century and beyond—could, as Ron Karenga put it, positively condition viewers.

Early Visions
Steamboat Willie (1928)
The Opry House (1928)
The Jazz Fool (1929)
Cookie Carnival (1935)
Three Orphan Kittens (1935)

Though no one has chosen to acknowledge the fact, Mickey Mouse was the screen's first positively portrayed black character. His body is completely black, as is most of his face. The white area running from just above his eyes to slightly below his mouth appears masklike, as if the character has adopted this guise in order to "pass" and survive in the Anglo world of his time. Disney's alter ego (apparently, Walt perceived himself emotionally and spiritually as an African American) was introduced to the public in

Steamboat Willie, piloting a craft through the deep South, singing and humming nineteenth-century gospel songs. They transform, during the short subject, into an early incarnation of twentieth-century jazz. In *The Opry House,* Mickey performs ragtime for a white audience that seemingly hasn't been exposed to such music before. They take to it in a big way. In *The Jazz Fool,* the Mouse dares enter a suburban neighborhood, bringing soulful music with him, improving the lifestyle immensely. An essentially decent, good-natured character, Mickey would shortly have a perfect foil in the unpleasant (and notably white) Donald Duck.

In *Cookie Carnival,* assorted white-bread cakes and cookies dance about in a peaceable kingdom, one of Disney's utopian visions of what life ought to be like. That not-so-impossible dream is totally integrated. Gingerbread cookies and chocolate cakes dance alongside cream-colored companions, without distinction. In *Three Orphan Kittens,* when un-feeling white characters dump three helpless tabbies on a snowy night, they are rescued and warmed by the black maid at a rich white person's home. She, in her goodness, convinces her uncertain Anglo employers to accept them.

Five Black Crows
Dumbo (1941)

The first major depiction of blacks in a feature-length animated film occurs in *Dumbo.* After suffering ridicule for being different, the baby elephant silences his critics by using his large ears to fly. Dumbo, how-ever, couldn't have achieved his hard-won success without strong support from a little brown mouse and five black crows—characters of color who save the day after all the Anglos disparage Dumbo. The claim has been leveled that this was "distasteful," the crows "too obviously Negro carica-tures." [1] Leonard Maltin better appreciates Disney's motives:

> The crows are undeniably black, but they are black *characters, not* black *stereotypes.* There is no denigrating dialogue, or Uncle Tomism in the scene, and if offense is to be taken in hearing blacks call each other "brother," then the viewer is merely being sensitive to accuracy. [2]

Each crow is individualized as a distinct character, resembling the uniquely realized jive-talking denizens of a Brooklyn street corner in Spike Lee's *Do the Right Thing* (1989). While there *is* an edge of caricature, that

AMERICANIZING THE ANCIENT GREEK CHORUS. The crows have often been cited as obvious and offensive stereotyping of African Americans. What they most resemble are the lovably quirky characters in Spike Lee's *Do the Right Thing* (1989). Every character in *Dumbo* is caricatured; what distinguishes the crows is that they are positive, decent, and wise in a way the film's Anglos are not. (Copyright 1941 Walt Disney Productions; courtesy RKO Radio Films.)

ought to be set against Disney's overall approach: *Every* group, from pretentious pachyderms to crazy clowns, is here caricatured. Disney doesn't pick out blacks alone for burlesque, and in comparison to his vicious ridicule of other constituencies within the film, his treatment of the crows plays as *loving* satire. The crows do initially laugh at Dumbo, like everyone else. They are, after all, only human, or, more correctly, Disney's anthropomorphic equivalent of humans. Laughing, though, is *all* that the others do. Only characters of color reveal true humanity in the film. And when (brown) Timothy Mouse informs them of Dumbo's travails, the (black) crows are deeply touched, weeping outright. Refusing to allow Dumbo to wander away, they halt, befriend, and mentor the outcast.

As film historian Steven Watts noted: "Since the film could be viewed as an attack on unthinking prejudice, what was more appropriate than to have the most persecuted group in America, African Americans, teach the young elephant how to survive and soar?"[3] The only way in which the issue of ethnic caricaturing could have been averted would have been for Disney to *not* include blacks. That would have opened the film—and Walt—to the criticism of ignoring the African American subculture. A nonblack artist finds himself in a no-win situation, damned if he does and damned if he doesn't. Disney *did;* his decision would reach a climax less than five years later in what may be the most misunderstood movie in Hollywood history.

Nirvana in the New South
Song of the South (1946)

Song is the only Disney classic never released on videocassette or DVD in the United States,[4] for fear of reigniting a controversy that has always surrounded it. Importantly, *Song* has as many defenders as detractors in the black community. In 1946 objections were raised by several African American institutions, the editors of *Ebony* calling for an outright boycott by blacks.[5] Yet preeminent African American film historian Thomas Cripps, reconsidering the film from a cooler climate, argued that timing worked against an otherwise admirable effort, causing a movie that "might have been lauded for [its] efforts in social progress in the 1930s" to bring "down the wrath of organized Negroes" owing to the "whimsically old-fashioned roles" played by James Baskett and Hattie McDaniel.[6]

It ought to be noted that heated criticism during the initial release was largely leveled by *white* reviewers, overeager to display their newly acquired heightened awareness. This was not confined to *Song.* In 1949, African American reviewer Ralph Ellison *defended* the depiction of blacks offered by *Intruder in the Dust* in *The Reporter* (December 6, 1949), while an Anglo critic denounced that same portrait of blacks in the *Daily Worker* (November 23, 1949). Typical of the Anglo response to *Song, Time*'s anonymous reviewer insisted Uncle Remus was "bound to enrage all educated Negroes, and a number of damnyankees."[7] The final phrase reveals, ironically, a deep-seated prejudice. The reviewer's questionable assumption is that all Northern whites are nonracist liberals, whereas all white Southerners could be written off as conservative bigots. The history of race relations in America during the twentieth century and the early years of the twenty-first reveals otherwise. Even assuming that "all educated Negroes" would find the film offensive bristles with classism as well as racism, implying that blacks who haven't attended a (white) college are incapable of clear thinking. On the other hand, Herman Hill, a highly educated Negro author, defended *Song* in the *Pittsburgh Courier,* a paper published by and for that city's black community: "The truly sympathetic handling of the entire production from a racial standpoint is calculated . . . to prove of *inestimable good* in the furthering of interracial relations" (emphasis added).[8] That had always been Walt's hope; his depiction of Remus was intended to "help mould" white minds.[9]

At least one black critic of the time, Wendell Green, saw it that way, lauding *Song* as "the greatest thing Disney has ever done."[10] Over the next half century, African American film historians would insist on the need for "black roles that *challenged* the stereotypes that had been the icons of earlier times."[11] Achieving this necessitates purposefully evoking, then reevaluating, the cliché. Disney's approach ought to be analyzed and understood in terms of the time in which his movie was made. The film-maker sensed that to utterly abandon the Tom and Mammy icons would disorient a mainstream audience in 1946. Instead, he retained the myths' surfaces to subtly subvert them. As *Sepia Hollywood,* a black publication, noted: "They haven't distorted Uncle Tom at Walt Disney's studio, they have glorified him."[12]

The employment of Uncle Remus (James Baskett) as the narrative voice in itself represented a significant breakthrough. No major Hollywood film, aimed squarely at a mixed (if largely white) audience, had been narrated (the voice-over always creates an intense bond between character and audience) by an African American. Remus signifies the film's moral center, positively influencing the Anglo child-hero, Johnny (Bobby Driscoll). Remus resembles Mary Poppins (who also could be dismissed as a cliché, the prim and proper Brit) in coating the pill of moral education in an entertaining manner. He, according to the dictates of Romantic philosophy, has learned what is truly important by living close to the earth. Distraught Johnny, running away from home after his father leaves, is drawn to the warmth and beauty of the black community, enjoying gospel songs in the woods. Whenever Johnny peers back over his shoulder at the plantation house, it appears cold, aloof, off-putting. Remus's cabin is where Johnny feels completely at home—loved, wanted, respected.

"Mr. Bluebird's on my shoulder," Remus at one point sings, as an animated bluebird descends. He, like Davy Crockett, Snow White, and other Disney heroes, is Rousseau's natural man, that philosopher's *best* man. The essential irony of *Song* is, in the Romantic-philosophic vein, how oblivious adult whites (particularly Ruth Warrick as Miss Sally, the most civilized and corrupt among them) are to the true meaning of life, as compared to how open and aware the earthy and unpretentious blacks are. Only when Miss Sally realizes she must learn from Remus (something the film's sharper-minded whites picked up on earlier) does the moviegoing audience come to tolerate, if not like, her.

Remus is not only the author's mouthpiece, but Disney's most autobiographical figure. As *Song* begins, an image of a glowing hearth is accompanied by a crawl:

> *Out of the humble cabin*
> *Out of the singing heart . . .*
> *Have come the tales of Uncle Remus,*
> *Rich in simple truths,*
> *Forever fresh and new.*

If not actually born in a "humble cabin," Disney perceived himself as hailing from just such a rural boyhood.[13] In time, he matured into a "singing heart," equal in that regard to Remus or, earlier still, Aesop. Like them, Disney related tales about "critters" whose misadventures served as moral cautionary fables for humans. Like his predecessors, Walt was dismissed as a naïve primitive. The seven-year rerelease cycle of Disney features until the advent of home video and their continued popularity ever since in that medium attest to Disney's fables, like those of Remus, remaining "forever fresh and new."

Like Disney himself, Remus is at one point silenced by a "tasteful" upper-middle-class mother who dismisses his stories as "inappropriate" for impressionable young minds. Like those British censors who forbade minors from seeing *Snow White*,[14] so, too, does Miss Sally inform Remus that there are to be "no more stories—they only confuse [Johnny]." Yet when Johnny and a poor neighbor girl, Ginny (Luana Patten), are at their most distraught, Remus restores their guarded optimism with the tale of "Br'er Rabbit and the Laughing Place," revealing the need for each and every person to discover a secret spot for achieving happiness. In time, Johnny discovers his laughing place is Uncle Remus's "humble" cabin. Here, and here alone, Johnny feels, in Remus's word, "satisfactual." The eventual building of the Disneyland theme park represented Walt's attempt to create a laughing place for all of humankind. Once, Remus tells Johnny in a story/song, "folks was closer to the critters, and critters to the folks," and "it was better all around." Here, Disney speaks directly to us through Remus. That occurs again during Remus's moment of crisis, when—forbidden to relate any more tales to the children owing to

THE MASTER STORYTELLER. Preexisting barriers of class and race are brushed aside when the greatest of all storytellers brings diverse children together; what Uncle Remus (James Baskett) happily achieves within *Song of the South*, Disney himself likewise accomplished in this and other films. (Copyright 1946 Walt Disney Productions; courtesy Buena Vista Releasing.)

Miss Sally's fear he may "corrupt" them—Remus experiences an epiphany, alone in his cabin:

> I'm an old man that never did nothin' but tell stories, but they never done no harm. And if they ain't done no good, how come they done lasted so long?

Disney, at the height of censorial attack on *Snow White*, underwent a similar crisis of conscience, wondering if he ought to continue, deciding he must. *Song*, so understood, serves as a parable on the significance of storytelling. Johnny eventually begins telling Br'er Rabbit stories to Ginny and others. He can be seen as a semifictionalized stand-in for Joel Chandler Harris, learning tales from his "Uncle," or a prefiguration of Steven Spielberg, in childhood gleaning from Disney films how to eventually make his own Disney-like movies (e.g., *E.T.*) for the next generation in need of cinematic stories that confront the complexities of life. In the latter case,

Uncle Remus is Disney. And, lest we forget, the filmmaker's nickname was "*Uncle* Walt." [15]

Following *Song*'s release, the NAACP issued a statement praising *Song* for its "remarkable artistic merit" but decrying "the impression it gives of an idyllic master-slave relationship which is a distortion of the facts." [16] This evaluation derives from the mistaken (if universal) notion that *Song* is set during the pre–Civil War era. In fact, the film takes place in 1867. The film's blacks are freedmen who chose to work for wages on that plantation where they once served as slaves. The National Urban League complained that *Song* perpetuated a perception of the Negro as "indolent" and as a less advanced race that "handles the truth lightly." [17] While there is no more false or abhorrent racial myth than that of the field hand who avoids work, there are no such black characters on view in *Song*. In nearly every instance portraying blacks as a mass, they enthusiastically walk to work, work hard, or are glimpsed returning home, exhausted. Obviously, Disney set out to crush the rightly despised myth of indolence, by portraying blacks as hardworking citizens who, like other blue-collar types he admires, whistle while they work. Owing to the period, they here whistle gospel songs.

Song's black leads also are always seen working. One charming moment occurs when Aunt Tempy (Hattie McDaniel) is wooed by Uncle Remus. Tempy is discovered cooking for everyone, black and white, when Remus stops by. He carries a heavy pile of logs. Though old and clearly suffering from rheumatism, Remus performs strenuous physical work with gusto. Ultimately, Uncle Remus's greatest "work" is as a storyteller, providing entertainment to the black community as a reward for their backbreaking labor. In this context, it's worth noting that Uncle Walt—like the character who stands in for him in this film—himself preferred the task of creative storytelling to mundane manual labor. In the Remus stories, far from (as one critic put it) depicting "the Negro [as] one who handles the truth lightly," Remus (like all other black characters on view) takes the notion of 'truth' far more seriously than whites. The movie did, after all, begin with Johnny's parents refusing to tell him the truth about their upcoming separation. If Uncle Remus bends orders on occasion, this hardly implies Disney's condemnation of the character. Rather, it establishes Remus (his color notwithstanding) as a typical Disney hero (e.g., Davy Crockett, Robin Hood, Cinderella, Pollyanna, Mary Poppins, etc.) who understands authority must, when proven wrong, be challenged.

As to other supposed stereotypes: McDaniel may look, in her Mammy garb, similar to her role in *Gone with the Wind* (1939). This turns out to be another case of, in Cripps's words, evoking the stereotype only to undermine it. Having initially set the audience at ease with a nonthreatening image, Disney alters their value system by what he unexpectedly offers onscreen. Basic to the Mammy cliché is that such characters are essentially sexless.[18] Tempy, though, is attracted to Remus, while not about to let him get the best of her, adding a prefeminist element. Additionally, Disney gets in his licks against ageism. The two sing a tender love ballad ("Sooner or Later"), the first time in Hollywood history that elderly people (black or white) entered into romance without becoming comic objects of caricature and/or contempt.

The film's opening makes clear that, in Disney's view, African Americans are more in tune with the natural beauty that, as a modern artist working in the nineteenth century Romantic tradition, he perceives as superior to anything jaded civilization has to offer. Johnny (still unaware that his parents are separating) travels by coach with his mother, Miss Sally (Ruth Warrick), father (Erik Rolf), and Tempy toward the plantation owned by Sally's mother. The parents sit together, coldly ignoring one another. Johnny sits beside Tempy, warmly exchanging smiles. Nearby, a frog makes its bullhorn noise; hearing it, Tempy responds in kind, to Johnny's delight. Johnny's father—having lived in the city of Atlanta—has unfortunately "unlearned" much of what he knew while living close to nature. Yet he retains enough "primal sympathy" to respond. Miss Sally remains oblivious as the other three slip into a natural (and racially integrated) cacophony.

Shortly, we meet another African American who, though young, proves himself as wise as Remus. Johnny becomes friends with Toby (Glenn Leedy), a black child with whom he shares adventures. Toby often instructs Johnny as to proper (i.e., natural) morality. After the boys catch a frog and amuse themselves for several hours, Toby convinces a skeptical Johnny that they ought to turn the critter free so it may hurry home. Toby, though uneducated, relies on spiritual sensitivity and natural-born wisdom (as well as mentoring from Uncle Remus) to make his point by noting the frog may have children of its own. Toby allows Johnny to see the parallel (which he previously missed) between the frog and himself (his parents now live apart). This was refreshingly innovative for 1946: then, films depicting a friendship between white and black children (including Hal Roach's *Our Gang* comedies) consistently portrayed a wiser white child (Spanky) instructing a dim-witted black (Buckwheat). *Song* happily turns that situation inside out.

Objection has been raised to a line in which Toby refers to "the whole United States o' Georgia." Though far from the film's finest moment, such words should be put in proper perspective. Novelist James Baldwin argued: "A movie is, literally, a series of images, and what one *sees* in a movie can really be taken beyond its stammering or misleading dialogue, as the key to what the movie is actually involved in saying." [19] What *Song* is "saying," overall: However limited his education, Toby is a finer person than Johnny; their friendship is one of equals.

For drama, though, there must be villains. Here, we discover them in the guise of white-redneck children, the Favers boys (George Nokes and Gene Holland), who taunt the film's pint-sized protagonists. "My Mama don't 'low me to play with them," Toby confides to Johnny, adding: "Your Mom won't, either." Mothers with solid values—Toby's black mother, Johnny's white one—*do* discriminate against possible playmates, based solely on attitudes and actions. Racial prejudice is not present here, nor, for that matter, is bigotry based on class: Ginny Faver (Luana Patten) is allowed to play with the boys, though she's from the same Faver family. A natural-born lady, Ginny is acceptable as a *person*. Her qualities as an individual, Disney implies, are what matter, not her lower-class origins.

Never during the film does Toby's blackness become an issue, and at no point is the issue of race raised among adults. Johnny's grandmother (Lucille Watson), living closer to nature than her Atlanta-bound daughter, treats Remus as an old friend rather than a former slave. This might, in the NAACP's words, seem "a distortion of fact." An alternative view: As with any artist, what we here encounter is the world according to Walt, offered in hope that we might emulate what we see—an America in which race no longer figures as an issue. Pointing out that the film does not offer an objective view of history is as naïve as it is superficially correct. That could be said about Homer, Shakespeare, and Tolstoy in literature; John Ford, Sergei Eisenstein, and Oliver Stone in film. Disney's vision offers the dream of a world where ebony and ivory can live together "in perfect harmony," as one late-1960s song put it.

At the time of *Song*'s release, *Variety*'s critic complained about "the confused and insufficiently explained estrangement of the parents." [20] Properly understood, that ambiguity is basic to the film's power. The post–Civil War setting is employed as objective correlative to the 1940s, when the divorce rate in America skyrocketed owing to a postwar disorientation. Had we been made aware of the precise nature of this family's problem, the couple would have been rendered too specific. By leaving the reasons vague, the parents emerge as universal symbols for every couple whose marriage comes under pressure when the world shifts to a new order of things—a theme Disney would explore more fully in *The Parent Trap* (1961). Here, though, the focus remains on African American equality, Disney's primary ambition clearly being to parallel the story's period of postwar upheaval with the then-current one. During the waning years of World War II, President Harry Truman had ordered a belated integration of the armed forces, providing one million drafted Negroes a new motivation to serve. Meanwhile, Walter White led the NAACP to Los Angeles, where he petitioned studios, requesting a new screen image; earlier still, George Norford of the Urban League's *Opportunity* printed similar requests. Movie moguls responded with a "conscience-liberalism"[21] that vividly defined postwar cinema, resulting in such works as *Lost Boundaries* (1949) and *Pinky* (1949). As always, Disney beat them all to the punch. *Song* reached theater screens on November 1, 1946.

Baskett received a "special" Oscar. Today, that seems an act of symbolic segregation, denying him a right to freely compete for Best Actor. At the time, this move constituted a civil rights initiative. Members of the Academy, convinced Baskett couldn't win in competition, wanted to ensure that an Oscar did go to a black performer for the first time since Hattie McDaniel won Best Supporting Actress for *Gone with the Wind* (1939). The Academy's approach, however confining in retrospect, was most progressive for its time. Before the war, James Farmer and CORE could not have created the Freedom Riders, nor could Dr. King have led the SCLC in the Montgomery bus boycott. Similar conditions hold true, in Disney's dramatic context, for Remus. Though he (as an elderly slave) remained quiet for years, in the postwar *New* South, Remus grows self-confident enough to talk back, his obvious wisdom putting all whites around him to shame.

Significantly, Cripps has noted that Poitier's dignified portraits appealed to mixed audiences of the sixties even as Stepin Fetchit's eager-to-please blacks had during a less enlightened era. Cripps admitted that he was less interested in contrasting the two seemingly polar African American screen icons than in comparing them. He insisted that Poitier did not, as has generally been believed, signify a polar rejection of everything Fetchit stood for, rather offering an update for a different decade: "Like Fetchit's, [Poitier's] characters were giving and open, even in the face of white hostility. Unlike Fetchit, he stood apart—cool, reserved, and possessed of superior skills which the whites in the plot would soon need in order to avoid an awful fate."[22] Likewise, the degree to which Remus remains genial, even when condescended to by whites, was necessary at the advent of postwar cinema if whites were to be lured into theaters.

Yet the degree to which Remus possesses greater gifts than whites, who in time recognize this, derives from Disney's desire to incite social change. No wonder that, in 1946, black critic George S. Schuyler insisted that the film's friendship between a white and black child would set the pace for an equality in our real world among "the [racially diverse] children of today who are the grownups of tomorrow."[23] At film's end, Johnny lies near death, having been gored by a bull. Outside, African American characters sing gospel music and hymns. This has been dismissed as "a scene sickening both in its patronizing racial sentiment and its sentimentality."[24] Alternatively, it may be interpreted as Disney's portrayal of African Americans as more deeply spiritual—closer to God and Nature, one and the same in the Disney Vision—than whites.

Unaware that Remus has brought his father back, the boy cries out only for Remus, even when John Sr. speaks. Then, in close-up, Johnny reaches out and takes Remus's hand, black and white lovingly united. When, twelve years later, such a scene concluded Stanley Kramer's adult drama *The Defiant Ones,* the image was hailed as a major breakthrough in socially conscious cinema. Disney, as always, dared go there first, if without proper recognition. Remus reunites father and son, then slips away, precisely as the equally wise and gracious Jiminy Cricket did after bringing Pinocchio and Gepetto together, and Mary Poppins will do after achieving the same thing.

In *Song's* final shot, total integration is achieved. A recovered Johnny (privileged white) takes the hands of Ginny (poor white) and Toby (poor black) to dance together, drifting away from civilization (the plantation) into the natural world (beyond Remus's cabin). When Br'er Rabbit appears, talking to all three children, even Remus is amazed. "It's actual," he exclaims. Finally, it is the new multicultural youth who teach their parents well—onetime guru Remus included. His stories can be literally, as well as symbolically, true, if one believes in them fully. At the top of a hill, the children wait for Remus to catch up. Though they have gone without their teacher—their black Maharishi, so to speak—they could never have reached such Enlightenment—nirvana in the New South—without his influence. All four take hands, age reconciled with youth, black with white, rich with poor. If less than realistic, this ought to be acknowledged as idealism of a liberal bent, highly progressive in attitude for its time.

Still, *Song* continues to be at best controversial, more often widely damned, setting one African American film historian against another. To Donald Bogle, Uncle Remus offends by signifying "the paragon of contentment";[25] Cripps argues the opposite: "in his staunch rural balkiness he prevails over white wishes."[26] Anglo critic Frederic Mullally could, in his *Tribune* critique, sniff that *Song* was merely "a not very subtle attempt to confirm the white American's argument that the Negro was a much more likeable fellow when, like Uncle Remus, he 'knew his place' and had no impertinent" attitudes.[27] Such words hardly describe what occurs onscreen. For Disney's reimagined Remus ultimately rejects his once-accepted "place" through a display of extremely "impertinent" attitudes. Viewed objectively, the film serves as the cinema's first concerted effort at propaganda *against* the Old South, depicted as a decadent and dying way of life. No wonder, then, Cripps offered at least a mild defense—emphasizing that, however much Remus may initially seem yet another variation of the now-offensive "Uncle" stereotype, he nonetheless "shares the center"[28] of the film's stage. In fact, a study of the film's iconography reveals Remus as gradually assuming center stage, visually speaking. In so doing, he paved the way for future African American characters—and the actors playing them—to in time become the focus of Hollywood movies.

An Anthropomorphic Allegory
So Dear to My Heart (1948)

A Midwestern companion piece to *Song of the South, So Dear to My Heart* can be read as an indirect allegory for the civil rights movement. Early in the story, the train carrying racehorse Dan Patch through early-twentieth-century middle America stops in Fulton Corners. The village's white-bread population gathers around for a good look at the legendary piece of horseflesh. The way for the champion's descent is prepared by blacks, more likely than not the first that these heartland citizens have ever seen. They (and we) notice the African Americans are extremely hard workers, also extraordinarily competent at the labor they perform. However brief their appearance, the image of these dedicated black professionals offers one more welcome—and early—slap in the face to the false "indolent" myth. Disney also makes the point (embarrassing to realize today, though this was something few Hollywood filmmakers of that era dared suggest)

BLACK IS BEAUTIFUL. Disney provided civil rights allegories by attacking the age-old dichotomization of white as "good" and superior to anything black; in *So Dear to My Heart,* Harry Carey (right) forces a skeptical middle-American audience to accept a broader, more enlightened poststructuralist definition of "beauty." (Copyright 1949 Walt Disney Productions; courtesy RKO Radio Films.)

that African Americans are capable of the most complicated work. A black groom oversees the care of Dan Patch; when the animal's owner gives orders, the groom softly but firmly contradicts the white man. Realizing that the groom is far more knowledgeable than he, thus right, the owner backs down.

Dan Patch is himself black. Disney—operating in the tradition of Aesop and Remus—employs the primitive (in the best sense of that term) anthropomorphic approach to seriously if indirectly address issues of importance in the human sphere. The very idea of a *black* champion—after competition with and victory against racehorses of all colors—in 1948 allowed Walt to imply that, given equal opportunity, individual black Americans could, and would, win out over whites in pretty much any area of expertise. Little Jerry Kincaid (Bobby Driscoll) becomes spellbound by the champion and, in the Disney Version, the horse's beautiful color is essential to his appeal. "I can still feel the touch of his *black* nose," the narrator (Jerry as an adult, voice provided by John Beal) recalls years later.

Likewise, when the baby lambs are born, Granny (Beulah Bondi) comments on the color of one: "*Black* as a lump of coal!" The lamb's mother, Jezebel, pushes this twin away: "Sometimes they're like that," Granny tells Jerry, "especially when one of them's black." Prejudice, apparently, can be found even in the animal kingdom. Jerry, however, loves the lamb in large part *because* of the blackness. As the lamb reminds Jerry of Dan Patch, the boy names his pet "Danny." However fine and decent Granny may be, she represents the old heartland America—locked into a way of seeing that perceives anything black as inferior. Jerry provides an early incarnation of the new American youth that would gradually emerge during the postwar era, free of such stifling prejudices. When Jerry suggests they might make some money by shearing Danny, Granny replies: "They don't fancy *black* wool. Never did." This attitude is what Jerry sets out to change, effectively symbolizing (however unconscious this may have been on the filmmaker's part) the young civil rights activists to come.

Granny does not relent easily, continually revealing her prejudices: "He'll be underfoot; I know the nature of them *black* sheep." But Jerry persists. Scaling down his original dream to someday own a racehorse, Jerry displays Danny at the county fair. The result is a breakthrough, for the lamb becomes a local champion—the first *black* to win a prize—even as Dan Patch had been on a national level. The American Dream—the success ethic that Disney subscribes to—is, Disney insists, for blacks as well as whites. A huge billboard advertising the fair features a portrait of a white sheep. As he observes this, Jerry's concerned eyes make clear that he must overcome an abiding bigotry.

In this context, the movie addresses issues of class as well as race, notably in a key conversation between Jerry and the amiable old judge (Harry Carey):

JUDGE: What's his breeding?

JERRY: Danny isn't one of them fancy lambs. Mom's name was Jezebel. I don't know who his daddy was.

Jezebel was, of course, one of the great whores of the Bible; in that book, her progeny proved evil. Not, however, in Disney, who (virtually alone among Hollywood's Golden Age moviemakers) does not condemn a woman of loose sexuality, here or in any of his films. Everyone attending the competition laughs loudly, but Jerry won't back down. Color and class are issues which he, and Disney, trust will be set aside in a better future. Society isn't ready, in the film's turn-of-the-century setting, to go that far.

Nor was it in 1948, when Disney released this film, though that situation would shortly change—perhaps, at least in a small way, as a result of this and *Song of the South,* and the friendly persuasion they offered to a vast American audience in need of a liberal education on civil rights.

Understandably, then, Disney opted for a bittersweet ending. Danny doesn't win, though he does (and none too believably) in the source, Sterling North's *Midnight and Jeremiah* (1940). Still, the judge played by Carey (John Ford's original silent screen star and symbol for heartland America, employed in just such a capacity here) isn't about to let the issue die. When Carey speaks, his attitude can be read as traditional America admitting its attitudes have become outdated, also that it's willing to open the way for more progressive thinking. First, he informs Jerry that his lamb is indeed something special, then adds that Danny doesn't fit into the current thinking about winners:

> Only trouble is, it's *black.* Not much market for black wool. Puts your lamb in a class by himself. [The gathered white farmers laugh.] I'm not joking, folks. This lamb *is* in a class by itself. Though he's got no pedigree, this lamb *is* a champion, in *every* sense.

Jerry is awarded a special prize. One wonders if perhaps Disney thought back to James Baskett receiving a "special" Oscar, thereby paving the way for a future in which Sidney Poitier could, and would, win the Best Actor award. Gradual change, according to Disney's vision of life, is something the American public can and will accept, in every aspect of life. This includes the breaking down of color and class barriers (as Nemo puts it at the end of *20,000 Leagues under the Sea,* 1954) in "God's good time," achieving full enlightenment. And, with it, full incarnation of everything that was always best in the American Dream.

The First Foray into Television
Davy Crockett, King of the Wild Frontier (1954–1955)

When Disney first entered the world of weekly television, a Vast Wasteland mentality remained firmly in place. If most Hollywood films remained five years behind the times, television stood, at the least, five years behind motion pictures in its depiction of African Americans. Rarely seen, those blacks on view tended to be cast either as male indolents *(Amos 'n' Andy)* or none-too-bright maids *(Beulah).* There were none in continuing dramas at all; *Rawhide* (1959–1966), one of the top-rated Westerns, did not add a black cowboy (played by Raymond St. Jacques) until its final months on the air, despite the fact that most all post–Civil War cattle drives were integrated.[29] The notable exception was Disney. Even in programs that, for historical authenticity's sake, did depict blacks as slaves, Walt treats such characters—however minor the parts may be—with notable sensitivity. One sequence in "Davy Crockett Goes to Congress" (January 26, 1955) proves most telling: Crockett (Fess Parker) rides up to the Tennessee home of soon-to-be president Andrew Jackson, where he's greeted by a black child who steps forward to take the horse.

Most shows wouldn't have acknowledged the little boy as anything other than a convenience. Disney's Crockett, however, pauses to exchange friendly and open smiles. Shortly, when Crockett and Jackson (Basil Ruysdael) are reunited for the first time since the Creek Indian War, Old Hickory is attended by a black butler. Disney establishes through gesture and body language that this man is anything but conventionally servile. He is in charge, determining what the aging warhorse will or will not drink for health's sake. Better still, he speaks abruptly and honestly to Jackson. Happily, we witness none of the groveling, so embarrassing today, found in other Hollywood films of the era. He has the final say, leaving no question that this competent, intelligent man is the general's general.

"Beulah, Peel Me a Grape!"
Legends of the Swamp Fox (1959–1961)

Disney based *Legends of the Swamp Fox* on the Revolutionary War experiences of General Francis Marion (Leslie Nielsen), commander of a makeshift South Carolina volunteer outfit. The first episode, "Birth of the Swamp Fox" (October 23, 1959), includes a scene that recalls the *Crockett* show. Once again, a black child projects dignity and intelligence rare for television—or popular culture generally—at that time. The youth, stuck in a servile position as the hero enters a mansion to attend a formal party, suggests some commonsense advice to Marion, which the hero unwisely ignores. Before leaving the event in a huff, owing to the presence of Tories, Marion pauses to admit his error, speaking to the youth as an equal as well as a friend. The episode also introduces Oscar (Jordan Whitfield), a slave owned by Marion's brother Gabe. The imagery implies a total equality among the film's good people, black or white. When Marion approaches the plantation, Oscar and young Gabe (Tim Considine) are seen working together. Everything, from camera angles to body language, suggests an abiding equality. Hard physical work is always presented as a highly positive undertaking in Disney. To confront and defeat the "indolent" stereotype, Disney's blacks and whites share the labor. Marion then treats the two as equals, via verbal greetings while warmly embracing each. The two men help the wounded Marion to the house, where Oscar and Delia (Louise Beavers) are treated more as extended-family members than servants.

Taking considerable liberties with historical probability, Disney balances that imperative with personal expression. It isn't difficult to grasp why Ms. Beavers, who quit *Beulah* at the height of its ratings success,[30] would have relished this role. The problem was never simply the fact that she had been cast as a maid—there were, and still are, black maids—but the manner in which any one maid-character is portrayed in the specific context of any one show. On *Beulah,* characters, dialogue, and situations were all demeaning. Beulah forever flurried about, flustered, trying to solve problems created by her friend Oriole (Butterfly McQueen). Though Beavers rightly earns a piece of media history as the first black woman to star in her own show, the talented actress had been allowed nothing more than to perpetuate the Mammy myth as a sexless servant. She understood that and resented it. Even her character's name recalled an earlier Beavers role as Mae West's legendary lackey in Lowell Sherman's *She Done Him Wrong* (1933), as well as the immortal (if, by today's standards, offensive) throwaway line "Beulah, peel me a grape!" Though the fame and money *Beulah* provided were welcome, Beavers felt that her self-respect and artistic fulfillment were more important. She left a show created specifically for her, the role then assumed by another actress. In the Disney series, by contrast, Delia is treated by Marion's sister-in-law as a trusted friend. Ostensibly a slave, Delia is never once seen in a servile, much less silly, situation. She displays a cutting humor, revealing independence and intelligence in every onscreen situation.

Suggesting a stereotype only to undermine it is, as mentioned earlier, an approach championed by African American film historian Bogle, at least for such a transitional period in media history. The thesis of his "interpretive history" of Hollywood is that *"all* black actors—from Stepin Fetchit to Rex Ingram to Lena Horne to Sidney Poitier and Jim Brown—have played stereotype roles."[31] Fair analysis must proceed from a realization that "the essence of black history is not found in the stereotyped role but in what certain talented [black] actors," working with enlightened (white)

THE UNTOLD STORY OF '76. During the cultural revolution of the late 1960s, African American scholars rightly complained that the popular cinema and television had largely overlooked the contribution of people of color to epic historical events; Disney alone had focused on black women (TOP) and men (BOTTOM) as nonstereotypical heroes in *Swamp Fox.* (Copyright 1959 Walt Disney Productions; courtesy Buena Vista Releasing.)

writers, directors, and producers, "have done with the stereotype."[32] That is, in seducing the audience into believing it will experience the old clichés only to be reeducated in the form of entertainment.

Which precisely describes what Beavers and Disney accomplished. In *Swamp Fox*, black characters are positively portrayed in such a way that they transcend their historically accurate slave situations and emerge as contemporary role models of a highly positive nature. When British cavalry chase Marion, Oscar rides side by side with him, in the process transformed from family servant to a variation on the best-friend character from the *Crockett* shows. Oscar—Georgie Russel–like—even writes and sings the inevitable ballad immortalizing his friend. Once Marion's men decide to hide from General Tarlton's redcoats on Snow Island, Oscar is assigned meaningful, not menial, tasks. Oscar does not serve as a guard, instead commanding others as captain *in charge of* guards—all white Southerners. They all quickly realize (and here, Disney's approach may well be wishful thinking rather than historical reality) that Oscar is in a position of power and prestige because, as an individual, he *deserves* to be. Like Remus, Oscar is the most spiritual person on view, the highest compliment Disney can pay a character, black or white. Oscar serves as the company's doctor, a man of sophisticated skill to whom the others turn in times of need.

"We would like to see the Negro presented to the world and to America as a normal American. If this were done, the films could make a real contribution to inter-racial understanding and to a better world," W. G. Still wrote.[33] Disney, more than any other television producer of the late 1950s and early '60s, responded to that valid plea. Oscar, "ordinary" in his attitudes, proves himself extraordinary via his wide range of talents. In the second episode, "Brother against Brother" (October 30, 1959), Delia likewise is presented as a person who can be trusted with significant jobs, including mothering the youngest of the Marion children. As *Bambi, Dumbo*, and numerous other films illustrate, nothing is more profound in Disney than the mother-child bond. The image in this show of white child and black mother, nestled close, was groundbreaking for 1950s television.

Throughout the series, whites are designated as positive only if enlightened as to the equality of blacks. They achieve this state by undermining the abiding master/slave relationship. Marion's beloved, Mary (Joy Page), entrusts a young Toby to run messages between herself (supposedly a

Tory, secretly an American spy) and Marion. Toby's characterization is impressive, particularly considering beloved wag Robert Benchley's comments on that era's screen depictions of Negroes, which "usually consist of the mispronunciation of big words" or "the inevitable fright which a Negro is supposed to fall into when confronted by ghosts, loud noises," and other potential dangers.[34] Disney was the first to counter such clichés. Captured the by British, Toby eats the paper containing a key message, then allows the Tory Briggs to beat him to death, refusing to reveal what he knows. The lad's father (Clarence Muse) accidentally learns of the tragedy in "Tory Vengeance" (January 1, 1960). While driving a carriage in which Mary and General Tarlton (not yet aware that her loyalty is with the rebels) ride, Joseph overhears their conversation. Reining in the horses, he shivers with anguish, questioning Tarlton, who is shocked by such behavior:

TARLTON: Speak when you're spoken to!
JOSEPH: Toby was my son! Haven't I a right to speak, Miss Mary?
MARY: Yes, Joseph. But not here. Go on!

Disney's choice of names for this platonic couple—Joseph and Mary—hardly seems coincidental. In their special way, they give blessed birth to an integrated America, offered by Disney as an ideal that can, and should, be pursued by his audience. Once again, Disney has rethought, as well as retold, a story from the past less for its own intrinsic interest (though that is certainly considerable) than owing to its potential for positively changing our contemporary world. This is made clear when Mary arrives at the Marion home, expressing her anguish at having inadvertently caused Toby's death. Though the family cannot find words, Delia speaks loud and clear:

MARY: Poor Joseph! It's all my fault. It wasn't Toby's war.
DELIA: You're wrong, Miss Mary! It was Toby's war. Just like it's my war, just like it's all decent people's war.

The African American characters are clearly willing to share the horrors of this war for the sake of freedom. Disney's implication is that they had every right to share the benefits of an eventual victory. If that has, sadly, not been the case since the formation of the United States, then—as the show vividly illustrates—the time (of viewing the series) is right to finally correct such wrongs.

Later in that episode, young Gabe is killed by the same Tory who murdered Toby. The grief of Marion and Joseph is shared. Each weeps for the loss of the other's beloved as much as his own, mutual tragedy cementing their growing sense of equality. In "Day of Reckoning" (January 8, 1960), they set out to catch their shared enemy. Joseph identifies the culprit, Briggs, by posing as a servile black, shining shoes for white Massahs. As actor/director Ossie Davis would note, "Most of the stereotypes we know about Negroes were invented by Negroes for the purpose of survival." In precisely this mode, Disney delineates Joseph's assumed role from the dignified person we know Joseph to be. We are in on Joseph's ruse, complicit with him—Anglo TV viewers relishing as much as blacks the trick that a black (by playing, rather than being, the stereotype) pulls off on unsuspecting whites.

Clarence Muse, the actor cast as Joseph, had decades earlier been considered, along with Stepin Fetchit and Mantan Moreland, the most embarrassing of early performers who became successful "by caricaturing a certain attitude about Negro people which," in Davis's words, "we know not to be true but which certain people wanted to believe, and this idea was that all Negroes were lazy and stupid and they drawled." [35] In the twilight of his career, Muse was finally allowed an opportunity to put distance between himself and just such stereotypes. After learning Briggs's identity, Joseph pulls a gun, planning to assassinate the man, apparently with Disney's blessing. In doing this, Joseph provides a prototype of the Black Panther, the primary African American activist of the late 1960s. Explaining why that animal was chosen as their symbol, organizer Huey Newton explained: "The nature of the panther is that he never attacks. But if anyone attacks him . . . the panther comes up to wipe that aggressor out." [36] He might well have been describing Joseph as presented here.

For a black/feminist element, Delia forcibly asserts herself in "Redcoat Strategy" (January 15, 1960), wielding a stick to chase British soldiers away when Marion's sister-in-law proves unable to do so. "No fine gentleman is going to tell *me* what to do in *my* house," she tells one officer, backing the man down. That is precisely how she, Disney, and we view her relationship to the plantation in this film's fanciful (though politically correct, a quarter century before that phrase came into being) reconstruction of its historical period. When the British take the family (Delia included) prisoners, Marion's relatives can't think of a way to escape and warn him. Delia and Oscar, however, do just that—by (like Joseph) slipping into servile roles, playing dumb for their captors. In James Baldwin's words, they must "undergo a tiny, strangling death before resolutely substituting 'de' for 'the' on endless occasions."[37] The gullible redcoats believe the act; as a result, Oscar and Delia turn seeming defeat into victory.

Following World War II, the demands of African Americans were expressed in "works of protest by Blacks decrying, as [in] Ralph Ellison's 'invisible man,' the refusal of White America to see them as human beings."[38] Disney's highly visible blacks are the precise media incarnations that Ellison so rightly demanded. When Marion's men sneak into Charleston in "A Case of Treason" (January 22, 1960), planning to rescue Mary after her cover is blown, Oscar is entrusted with the most demanding jobs. He drives a hay wagon with patriots hidden under straw into the city, again playing to the redcoats' immediate if false assumptions concerning his presumed shiftlessness and ignorance. Oscar turns the Brits' unwarranted prejudices against them. We watch as he, a bright man, feigns idiocy; they—Anglo idiots—are the butt of Oscar's (and Walt's) humor. By manipulating his audience to laugh at the stupidity of all such prejudice, Disney provided a paradigm capable of altering the Anglo viewer's mind-set.

During this episode, Oscar has more screen time than Marion, arcing from supporting character to second lead to, finally, the hero. At this point, Marion chooses to remain on Snow Island, certain the cause has been lost. Even his most loyal men, worn to the bone, go home. All except one: Oscar, now Marion's conscience. It is Oscar who, like Jiminy Cricket in *Pinocchio,* persuades his friend to continue. "You're a good man to have around, Oscar!" Marion says with a smile, once his tested faith has been restored by an African American whose dedication to the cause exceeds that of even Marion himself. Once more, Marion embraces Oscar as a true brother. By this point, the audience (like Marion, like all enlightened whites) is barely (if, indeed, at all) aware of Oscar's color.

If one believes that exposure to art and/or entertainment can alter the public consciousness, then Disney set the pace for such enlightening work at a time when blacks were otherwise either invisible in television's warped window on the world, or presented in the most demeaning roles. In early *Swamp Fox* episodes, Marion was photographed alone. After isolating him from the group, the camera would slowly circle the others, Oscar (importantly) visualized as equal among them. In the final episode, "Horses for Green" (January 15, 1961), Marion sits by the campfire with the men, more their equal than leader. It is, in the show's closing moment, Oscar who now stands alone, center stage—the leader and true hero, something Marion and all his men at last understand and fully accept.

Like all Disney's positive characters, Oscar sings. His specific words are significant:

> *Let the rich man see*
> *His brother's needs.*
> *Let the lamb abide,*
> *Like the Good Book says,*
> *By the lion's side,*
> *Till the end of days.*
> *Let peace come over the land.*

Edward Hicks's painting *Peaceable Kingdom* —a Romantic's idealized but appealing image of nature as a gentle garden rather than the naturalist's vision of it as a deadly jungle—is here expressed in verse, coupled with quasi-socialist thinking (presented positively by Disney, in itself daring during the McCarthy era), with an African American character serving (as in *Song of the South*) as Walt's mouthpiece and alter ego.

How the West Was Won
Tales of Texas John Slaughter (1958–1961)

Several African Americans worked on the Arizona ranch, located not far from Tombstone in Cochise County, that was established by former Texan John Slaughter during the early 1880s. To convey that truth while simplifying the situation for dramatic purposes, Disney created a composite figure, taking his name from one real-life employee, John Raymond Swayne, nicknamed "Bat." For this role, Disney chose James Edwards, who had played a black member of the newly integrated army in *Home of the Brave* (1949). Many observers had believed that in those pre-Poitier years, Edwards—owing to his potent combination of talent and sex appeal— would quickly emerge as the first mainstream black superstar. Then came red-baiting and political blacklisting, Edwards among the many victims. Few producers would hire him even for supporting roles; Walt Disney proved the key exception.

Bat made his first appearance in "Apache Friendship" (February 19, 1960). Initially glimpsed as an uninvited stranger, entertaining the Slaughter children, Bat waits for John to appear so as to ask for a job. Self-consciously assuming (at this point) the cliché of the "Tom," Bat establishes that he's nonthreatening, clearly a survival tactic he has learned by dealing with racist whites. No sooner has Slaughter established himself as a righteous white than Bat drops the façade, revealing himself to be intelligent and highly educated.

The immediate bonding with children connects Bat to Disney's adult heroes who communicate with kids (innocent, natural) owing to their innate possession of—in Wordsworth's Romantic notion—"a knowing heart, an understanding mind." When Slaughter first appears, Bat carves a whistle for the Slaughter boy. This image conveys two of Disney's most positive signifying elements, music and work. Bat is introduced working at creating an instrument to make music. Shortly, Bat proves himself able, eager, and anxious to perform *any* sort of work, ranging from simple farm and ranch duties to (like Oscar) doctoring sick men, allowing Disney to again dispel the odious "indolent" myth. While he gladly works at any job, in time outdoing all white cowhands at every conceivable task, Bat requests that Slaughter list him in the log book as a tracker, "that being my *profession*." However positive hard work may be, dedication to a single craft—true professionalism—takes a person's esteem a giant step further. Bogle would rightly complain about old movies that employed "character types used for the same effect: to entertain by stressing Negro inferiority."[39] Bat conversely emerges as a fully realized individual, while Disney insists not only on, at minimum, Negro equality but in most cases superiority to the surrounding whites. This process begins with Bat's language. His impressive vocabulary and exquisite diction put Slaughter's Southern drawl and limited vocabulary to shame.

"He's my best friend," Slaughter's son happily shouts. Neither John nor the second Mrs. Slaughter (Betty Lynn) objects. Bat then replaces Ashley (Darryl Hickman), a Southern gentleman, as the hero's closest companion. But Disney doesn't allow Bat to play second fiddle. A key to Walt's conception is revealed through costuming. Bat is established as John's absolute equal by having him costumed identically to the title character. Bat wears the high white Stetson, soft suede vest, blue jeans, and black boots that compose Slaughter's signature costume. Even Bat's given name, though mentioned only once, suggests he is the title character's black alter ego: John Swayne, John Slaughter. When John must go on the trail after rustlers, it is Bat—not one of the white cowboys—he invites to come along. He does this not to prove that he's free of any prejudice, but as the only logical decision for a color-blind person: Bat is clearly the best man around. Once on the prairie, Bat quickly proves himself invaluable:

JOHN: No one can track at night.
BAT: Except *me!*

Slaughter is stunned to realize Bat is not bragging, merely stating the fact of his superiority in terms that are neither arrogant nor humble, only openly honest. "For the present," the National Urban League asked of Hollywood, "we would like to see ridiculous, criminal, superstitious and immoral characterizations eliminated."[40] Disney, never having included such clichés in his films, now forged ahead, presaging a future in which media depictions of African Americans moved beyond anything else present in Hollywood's motion pictures to that point.

As John and Bat rest by a campfire, Slaughter passes his canteen to Bat, who drinks from it. He then passes it back, and, without hesitation or thought, John takes another sip. The notion of a white man touching his lips to an object a black has made contact with, however difficult this may be for most people to believe today, was nothing short of revolutionary in 1959. "For racism to die," Stokely Carmichael wrote, "a totally different America must be born."[41] Working in the relative safety of a period setting, as well as in the genre/guise of a Western action show, Disney offered the mass audience a dramatized vision of Carmichael's new America.

Up to this point, the only hint of racial issues is Bat's Tom-like tendency to refer to Slaughter as "sir," while John hails Bat as "boy." The terms, however offensive to modern ears, are included for historical accuracy. Now, though, the filmmaker again employs history to express in the present his highly personal vision of a more enlightened future. When the two run into Natchez (Jay Silverheels), a cordial Apache, John makes his true feelings for Bat clear:

NATCHEZ: Him?
JOHN: My *friend!* Hope he never works for anyone else.

John will never again hail Bat as "boy," nor will Bat call John "sir." Like Crockett and Russel, Marion and Oscar, they are nonbiological brothers. The issue of race has been dealt with and disposed of—the victory presented in drama as it ought to be in real life, literature (in this case cinematic) as what Kenneth Burke once referred to as "equipment for living"—or, at least, living correctly.

Natchez is also John's friend; Natchez and Bat become friends as well. Anglo, Indian, and African American—all represented by nonstereotypical

TALL, DARK, AND HANDSOME. Dozens of Westerns were popular on TV during the 1950s; only one featured an African American in a significant and positive role. Disney's *Tales of Texas John Slaughter* (1958–1961) featured James Edwards as Bat, a black cowboy who equals and often exceeds the Anglo hero. (Copyright 1960 Walt Disney Productions; courtesy Buena Vista Releasing.)

men of dignity—swiftly prove to be natural allies. Skin color matters so little that Disney refuses to allow it to be passingly considered in conversation by his few good men. That holds true for his role-model women as well. The following episode, "Kentucky Gunslick" (February 26, 1960), features a conversation between Bat and Mrs. Slaughter. Ashley has returned, now combining the earlier hubris of a Southern gentleman with a newfound Western gunfighter's cockiness. Little Willie Slaughter is at first highly impressed, though Disney ridicules Ashley's posing as a pistolero. With Bat, even-tempered and right-minded, as his mouthpiece, the auteur expresses his own liberal-progressive attitude about America's gun culture:

> BAT: Willie, a man who has to use a gun to prove he's right is probably wrong.

Mrs. Slaughter speaks to Bat, even as she would to her husband, were John present:

MRS. SLAUGHTER: Before Ashley came, *you* were his hero.

BAT: Guess that is right.

MRS. SLAUGHTER: *You* were teaching him what I *wanted* him to learn!

The lady knows a fine person when she meets one. And a superior one, all around, when Bat—extremely masculine, yet not fearful of acknowledging his feminine side—offers to help with tailoring work.

MRS. SLAUGHTER: Bat! Isn't there *anything* you can't do?

In fact, there isn't. The only skill Bat admits to being "middling" with is using a handgun, much to Mrs. Slaughter's relief. Before the episode is over, little Willie comes to see who the real hero is. In the following episodes, Bat and John bring closure to white-Indian hostilities in "The End of the Trail" (January 29, 1961) and round up outlaws in "A Holster Full of Law" (December 5, 1961). Bat is a black Slaughter, an African American Crockett, a Western John Henry.

"Cinema audiences," film historian Peter Noble complained in 1970, "regard the coloured man as a clown . . . and their contempt for him is a result of the manner in which he is invariably portrayed on the screen."[42] That has, thankfully, changed, mainstream Hollywood belatedly offering more enlightened images beginning shortly after Disney's groundbreaking work. Bogle, writing about *The Birth of a Nation*—the first major film, and the first American movie, to deal significantly (if offensively) with black characters—noted that *Birth*

> not only vividly re-created history, but revealed its director's philosophical concept of the universe and his personal racial bigotry. For D. W. Griffith there was a moral order at work in the universe. If that order were ever thrown out of whack, he believed chaos would ensue. Griffith's thesis was sound . . . even classic in a purely Shakespearean sense. But in articulating his thesis, Griffith seemed to be saying that things were in order only when whites were in control and when the American Negro was kept in his place.[43]

Bogle's assessment is right on target. Like Griffith, Disney is no mere journeyman filmmaker but a visionary, a true artist who projects his singular world-vision in every work he produces. There, the similarity ends. For in all his projects, Disney reveals himself to be in total opposition to Griffith. In Walt's vision of the world, only when blacks and whites exist in a state of total equality do we discover a proper sense of order in the universe.

A BREEZE FROM THE EAST. One key aspect of the 1960s cultural revolution was an embracing of Indian wisdom; pop icon Mia Farrow, among others, journeyed far to study with a guru. Ever ahead of his time, Walt had already presented such a paradigm, as British flower child Pamela Franklin consults Sabu in *A Tiger Walks.* (Copyright 1963 Walt Disney Productions; courtesy Buena Vista Releasing.)

3

Beat of a Different Drum

Ethnicity and Individualization in Disney

If a man does not keep pace with his companions, perhaps it is because he hears a different drummer.
—HENRY DAVID THOREAU (1848)

You and I,
March to the beat of
A different drum.
—THE STONE PONIES (1968)

*D*uring the late 1950s and early 1960s, the civil rights movement intensely focused on African Americans. In time, though, the growing consciousness of tolerance spread to other minorities, including various nonracial special-interest groups. A ripple effect had been set in place, the country continually redefining itself thereafter. An emerging mindset insisted on an ever-greater sensitivity toward anyone belonging to the diverse groups deemed "different" from the supposed (now questioned) "norm." When compared to the embarrassing exaggerations of more adult-oriented Golden Age Hollywood filmmakers, Disney's lapses are precious few. Even when they do on occasion occur, the impact is notably muted. Jock, the terrier in *Lady and the Tramp,* is defined by his thrifty temperament—a cliché long associated with Scotsmen. Being a dog, he hoards bones, not money. Significant, though, is the aura of sweet-spiritedness with which Jock is portrayed. Hardly a negative stereotype, this is one of many aspects to his well-rounded personality, all positive. Moreover, the ethnicities most often lovingly satirized in Walt's films are the Irish and Scots. Irish on his father Elias's side, Walt was Scottish on that of his mother, Flora Call Disney. There is, then, no sense of chauvinism to

THE DARK SIDE OF DIVERSITY. Walt was criticized for supposedly making the entire pirate band in *Swiss Family Robinson* Asian in ethnicity, thereby purportedly fueling anti-Oriental prejudices. Like all groups—good or bad—in Disney films, the pirates are, when closely considered, multicultural in composition. Moreover, an Asian is the leader, not (as in other pirate movies) a follower of some Anglo captain. (Copyright 1960 Walt Disney Productions; courtesy Buena Vista Releasing.)

what we encounter, as his own background is as subject to satire as those of anyone else.

It has been pointed out that the villains who attack Disney's family (ostensibly nineteenth-century Swiss, clearly signifying twentieth-century Americans) in *Swiss Family Robinson* may embody a racist slur: "The pirate rabble, as Asians, were a rather transparent rendering of the 'yellow peril' which bedeviled the American imagination in the 1950s."[1] Closer examination reveals that, though their boat is constructed in an Asian style, the pirates themselves do not neatly fit into any single nationality. There are Moors, as well as others who appear Gallic, both in physique and in costuming. Several obvious Anglos fill out the ranks. This is not simplistic anti-Asian propaganda, but a vision of evil that—parallel to the good forces in Disney—rates as multicultural. No one group is ever held responsible in this filmmaker's work for the best *or* worst of what occurs. As to the pirate captain, played by Sessue Hayakawa, Disney was the first Hollywood filmmaker to portray an Asian as the leader of a pirate band, rather than a follower, the case in most previous adventure movies. However despicable the marauders may be, we are informed through casting that Asians are fully capable of taking charge of situations, rather than remaining subservient to the Anglos in their company.

Nature's Slip-ups
Dumbo (1941)
Follow Me, Boys! (1966)

The narrative device that sets Disney's fourth animated film into motion—Dumbo's extraordinarily big ears—allows Disney to create a parable about the difficulties and rewards of being born different. Scorned as a freak by his own race, the pachyderms, Dumbo gradually (and painfully) realizes he can, through altered perception, transform difference into a gift. Once dismissed by the conformist crowd as a clown, Dumbo—having learned self-esteem thanks to true friends of dark coloring—accepts his singularity as a positive force, then "flies"—literally and symbolically.

Subsequent films concern themselves with "marginalized figures" who "come together" and, through mutual acceptance of differences, "overcome their oppressors."[2] Identification with the marginalized often entails Disney's opposition to capitalism at its worst—i.e., rawest. When circus bosses transform Dumbo into a clown, his fellow clowns greedily decide to "hit the big boss for a raise." The diminutive hero's "humiliation, it seems, will financially benefit the very people who exploit him."[3] Those characters are all savagely satirized, whereas Walt "preaches sympathy, not derision, for Nature's slip-ups."[4] A quarter century later, that held true in Disney's salute to the Boy Scouts. When an outsider, Whitey (Kurt Russell), makes a tenuous attempt to join other children, he mistakenly refers to a kid with glasses as "four-eyes." One of the scouts retorts: "No one's called 'four-eyes' around here!" Walt ranks as an early proponent of what would eventually be tagged "politically correct speech." Prejudice, even when expressed by (ironically) one "different" person to another, will not be tolerated. Scoutmaster Lem

(Fred MacMurray) refuses to allow Whitey's lower-class upbringing to be held against him, teaching the middle-class boys to judge Whitey on his merits as a person rather than share their parents' prejudice. As the rare enlightened adult, Lem realizes he has the potential to shape a new generation that will live free of bigotry. Lem makes certain the small town's only ethnic child, Quong Lee (Warren Hsieh), is treated as an equal by all the others.

The Physically Disabled
"Pegleg Pete" (character: 1925–1936)
Treasure Island (1950)
Snow White and the Seven Dwarfs (1937)
Ten Who Dared (1960)

In the waning decades of the twentieth century, the negatively loaded term "cripple" would be replaced by the more enlightened and positive concept, "physically challenged." Disney's guarded optimism set the pace for such thinking. The first such character to appear in the animated work was "Pete." A villain originally depicted as having a peg leg, Pete regularly proved himself anything but disabled. First appearing in the *Alice* comedies (circa 1925), later the antagonist of Mickey and/or Donald in thirty-one cartoons,[5] Pete—despite his deformity—proved adept at his nefarious schemes. In time, the peg leg was eliminated, perhaps suggesting Disney's growing sensitivity and so disassociating the villain with a disability.

Also sporting a peg leg was Long John Silver (Robert Newton), Walt's first live-action villain. He serves as the leader of a crew that mutinies against the proper captain of the *Hispanolia* during a perilous journey from England to the Caribbean. Despite his physical disability, Long John—though a killer—is intelligent in a way the other pirates are not, qualifying him as a natural-born leader. He also displays a sensitivity to young Jim Hawkins (Bobby Driscoll) that at least partially redeems him in the audience's eyes. Simply, Long John is anything but "a cripple." However evil he may be, everything about this man appears remarkably functional.

Had Disney only presented villainous portraits of the physically challenged, he would be wide open for criticism. Instead, he achieved some-

CRIPPLED IS AS CRIPPLED DOES. No Golden Age filmmaker did more than Disney to convince American audiences that there is no such thing as a "cripple," or that a disability is merely a challenge to be overcome; this is as true for villains like Long John Silver (Robert Newton) as for many of Walt's admirable heroes. (Copyright 1952 Walt Disney Productions; courtesy RKO Radio Films.)

thing never before even attempted by portraying the disabled as heroes. One oft-quoted anecdote has Walt telling Lillian that, for his costly first feature film, he had decided on *Snow White and the Seven Dwarfs*. His wife purportedly recoiled, her more conventional nature causing Lillian to complain that "There's something so *nasty* about them."[6] Instead of dissuading Walt from moving forward with the project, Lillian's attitude appears to have inspired him to design the dwarfs so that they would *not* appear nasty on film, to either his wife or the mainstream Americans she represented in terms of widespread prejudice. The film appears, in the contexts of this anecdote and previous screen portrayals of dwarfs, to be a politically correct propaganda piece.

Though Disney does rely on the "humour" approach that has existed in Western culture since playwrights like Ben Jonson initiated it during the Elizabethan age—each "little man" incarnates a single human trait—those personalities are, at the very least, just that—undeniably *human*. They represent a wide (indeed, the full) spectrum of human emotion(s), and none of them is in any way nasty, not even Grumpy, whose incorrigibility is charming. The film forces the public to reconsider that learned (false and unfair) "nasty" prejudice that so many people feel, or at least felt before the release of this motion picture. After all, Snow White—the delightful and utterly natural heroine with whom the audience is encouraged to identify—finds the dwarfs to be absolutely charming from the moment that she meets them. If the viewing public is not, in the film's early sequences, entirely convinced, they certainly are when Snow White sends the dwarfs off to work. She kisses each good-bye, and the viewer—who has, if he or she did indeed arrive with attitudes similar to Lillian's, arced while watching—does not find this repulsive. We perceive them not as dwarfs, with the old stigma still attached, but (as Snow White herself calls them) "little men."

In this, Disney set into motion the politically correct term, "little people," by which those heretofore known as dwarfs and midgets prefer to be referred to today. No child who has ever seen the movie needs to be told that the little men "stood tall" when, at the end, they rush to the rescue. This helps to explain the emotionally as well as aesthetically satisfying sensation of that early sequence in which the dwarfs, singing as they march home from work in their mine, cast huge shadows on the rock formations around them. The image, as the ending makes clear, was no mere technical show-offishness on the part of Disney and his animators.

Rather, it provides a foreshadowing of the manner in which we would be induced to think of these fine and decent human beings, too often in the conventional imagination (or lack thereof) reduced to freaks, and nasty ones at that. A die-hard Disney despiser can complain that Walt offered a version of the old tale that is "fundamentally different in mood from the tale the Grimms told,"[7] intending that statement as a put-down of the filmmaker's oft-criticized "sentimental" tone. Then again, we can look once more at the distinction between the Disney Version and the rough-hewn original, finding an enlightenment that was notably missing in a primitive rendering that presented the dwarfs as identical to one another, therefore advancing the vicious notion that "nature's mistakes" are not capable of having fully formed personalities, even caricatured ones.

Walt's approach was more recently assumed by the current Disney regime when, in 1996, the decision was made to produce an animated live-action feature, *The Hunchback of Notre Dame*. From a filmmaking company that had recently offered such attractive central characters as the Little Mermaid and her handsome hero, the choice might have seemed an unlikely one; in the context of Disney entertainment over the years, it makes perfect sense. The modern Disney film, like Victor Hugo's novel and all the varied cinematic renderings of the coarse Quasimodo, re-veals—despite the jeers of supposedly civilized members of society—his potent ability to feel, even think.

In his own time, Disney dared to mount an epic Western, based on a historical incident, in which the heroic lead is disabled yet overcomes any and all problems, proving himself anything but "crippled" by his physical loss. *Ten Who Dared* concerns an 1869 trek along the Colorado River headed by Major John Wesley Powell (John Beal), noted explorer and geologist. However significant that expedition may have been, no filmmaker had chosen to bring it to the screen, owing to Powell's being a one-armed man, incapable of the action expected from a typical Western hero. This only made Powell all the more appealing to Walt Disney.

A man of quiet intelligence, Powell gradually wins over most of his companions, even if they do early on deride him by using the "c" word indiscriminately. Those capable of an ethical education cease laughing and fall in behind Powell as they come to appreciate his greatness. When the endangered party eventually splits in two, several men follow a far more likely savior: Big Bill Dunn (Brian Keith), a rough and rowdy mountain man with two good arms and a weapon in each hand. Based on his previous

DIFFERENT KIND OF HERO. Disney alone chose to tell stories about significant but overlooked frontier figures, as in *Ten Who Dared,* a vivid portrayal of John Wesley Powell (John Beal, right), the one-armed army officer who overcame his physical liability and mapped the Colorado River in 1869. (Copyright 1960 Walt Disney Productions; courtesy Buena Vista Releasing.)

experience in the wilds, Dunn would certainly appear the more likely candidate to get the men out alive. Yet those who follow Dunn overland die, whereas others who listen to the logical reasons given by Powell for proceeding by boat survive. To this day, Disney's *Ten Who Dared* remains the only Western feature film in which a disabled man was cast as the hero.

Deaf but Not Dumb
Zorro (TV; 1957–1959)
The Magnificent Rebel (1962)

A key character in the *Zorro* series, Bernardo (Gene Sheldon), serves the aristocrat Don Diego (Guy Williams). Without him, early California's fictional caped crusader could not function. A mute, Bernardo feigns deafness so residents of Los Angeles, including high-placed enemies of the people, will speak freely in front of him, unwittingly revealing their plans. All such types consider Bernardo to be a fool—a common assumption about deaf-mutes on the part of the unenlightened. Actually, he is a brilliant man, able to devise plots and help the common folk in trouble, which even the lofty Zorro could not manage. On more than one occasion, Bernardo disguised himself as Zorro and made the midnight ride to save someone when Diego found himself incapacitated. At such moments, Bernardo usurped the role of hero, no longer subbing for Don Diego but literally *becoming* Zorro. Always, the audience was encouraged to root for Bernardo and laugh at those supposed sophisticates who reveal their ignorance by making untenable assumptions and poking fun at a far better person than themselves.

Disney chose to tell the stories of great composers only twice, and the initial example appears something of a purely practical decision. *The Peter Tchaikovsky Story* (January 30, 1959), based on voluminous background material gathered during the research process for the *Sleeping Beauty* film,[8] likely would not have been filmed other than as a televised promotional piece to promote that theatrical release. More characteristically, the only composer whose life Disney dramatized solely out of interest for the person's unique story was Ludwig van Beethoven (Carl Boehm), told in a two-part TV show. Before the first episode aired (November 18, 1962), Walt appeared to explain that Beethoven's entire life would not be presented. Instead, he would devote one hour each to two periods in Beethoven's career that had captured Disney's imagination. The opening hour dealt with Beethoven's extreme rebelliousness during his youth, establishing him as one more of Disney's numerous rebel heroes. The second (November 25, 1962) was devoted entirely to the developing deafness that plagued Beethoven's later years. Such a situation, difficult for any man, would appear horrific to a composer. The show detailed Beethoven's initial depression, a state of mind bordering on nihilism. What had he done to be so punished by God? Disney chose this story because, like every work in the oeuvre, it allowed for his guardedly optimistic expression of great positive achievement as a result of seemingly destructive adversity. This "magnificent rebel" in time rejects negativity, realizing that he can continue to compose, even conduct. As Walt announced, Beethoven overcame, going on to create his most impressive work *after* the infliction. A disability, Disney insists, is not really a disability if only one refuses to perceive it as such.

Eye of the Beholder
The Ugly Duckling (1931)
So Dear to My Heart (1949)
The Ugly Dachshund (1967)

All stereotypes, according to one expert, "are socially supported, continually revived and hammered by our media of mass communication—by novels, short stories, newspaper items, movies, stage, radio and television."[9] That rare filmmaker who employs mass communication for the opposite purpose—to consistently undermine all such stereotypes— qualifies as exceptional and enlightened. As always, those particular tales from Aesop that Disney decided to adapt reveal much about his viewpoint. One early entry in the *Silly Symphonies* series, *The Ugly Duckling,* qualifies (along with the birth of Danny the lamb in *So Dear to My Heart*) as atypical in one key respect. Most often a staunch defender of mothers (in contrast to, say, Alfred Hitchcock, whose portraits are grotesque), Disney deals honestly with the rejection by some mothers of offspring they believe unfit to survive to focus attention on other (more "fit") babies. Such inborn instincts are accepted as an unfortunate result of the evolutionary process, only to be challenged in our modern sphere. First, Disney condemns the situation: Nonbiological mentors (in *So Dear*) take on a maternal role, leading, in time, to great success for the once-rejected creature.

The animated films provide anthropomorphic fables to the human world. Such behavior, according to Disney, is itself one of nature's defects, which we, as humans, must—as we continue to evolve—be sure to correct. We can achieve this by totally rejecting Herbert Spencer's transference of Darwin's survival of the fittest theory to human society via the false concept of Social Darwinism. In *The Ugly Duckling,* the title character's "mother" forces him away because he's different. In the realm of uniformity and retro-mainstream thinking, "different" means "ugly," even "evil." An identity crisis follows, as the rejected creature studies his image in the lake, trying to decide what's wrong. Disney's answer, like Aesop's: Nothing at all, nor is he truly "different," other than in a narrow context. Meeting a group of swans, the creature realizes that he is identical to any of them—is beautiful when judged by the proper aesthetic.

The very title of *The Ugly Dachshund* makes clear this movie will play as a variation on the "Duckling" theme. Mark (Dean Jones) visits the veterinarian to pick up his dachshund's four female pups. While there, he discovers a Great Dane has rejected one of her litter. As the vet (Charlie Ruggles) explains,

> Duchess picked him out and pushed him away. Funny, the tricks nature sometimes plays.

As in *Duckling* and *So Dear,* the mother did this not out of cruelty but owing to instinct. There was only enough milk to go around, so one of the pups—the one she deemed least likely to survive—had to be sacrificed to save the many. That was in the animal kingdom, where Darwinism reigns. We live in an enlightened human society, we can hope, where such instincts must be rejected. Mark's decision to adopt the pup—to become his "mother"—marks him not as a foolish sentimentalist (the way a reactionary would perceive him), but one of Disney's good progressives.

Humankind reveals its worst side when imposing itself on nature in deadly ways, e.g., the mindless hunters who shoot Bambi's mother or the careless campers who, later in that film, accidentally start a forest fire. On the other hand, humans are to be admired when they interfere with nature to oppose natural selection. So Mark brings five puppies home to his wife Fran (Suzanne Pleshette), twisting the truth to make her think they are all of a litter, since she doesn't care for large dogs. We hear dialogue that expresses Disney's disdain for a mind-set that equates "being different" with "being ugly":

> FRAN: This one is funny looking.
> MARK: Why "funny looking"?
> FRAN: Because he's . . . *different!*
> MARK: *How* "different"?
> FRAN: All out of proportion. Positively *ugly!*
> MARK: He's *not* ugly.

The film focuses on Mark's desire to convince Fran that "Brutus" is attractive. He succeeds, after admitting that Brutus is indeed of a different breed. Mark does this only out of necessity, when the dog grows by leaps and bounds.

Still, as a dedicated dachshund lover (that is, a chauvinist), Fran initially cannot step beyond her prejudice until a series of circumstances conspires to radically alter her for the better. Fran realizes damage done to the house, and blamed by her on the big dog, was actually perpetrated by her beloved pups. One is mistakenly carried away by the garbage man (the pup was raiding a trash can) until Brutus intercedes, saving his "sister." Finally, Brutus effortlessly wins first prize in the Great Dane category at a local pet show, whereas Fran's prized dachshund only places second in her category.

Fran's perceptions are altered for the better. She is taught by experience to see clearly—i.e., without prejudice against anything deemed different—for the first time. More often, women in Disney see life more clearly than men. Here, it is Mark, a true artist by profession—therefore, someone predisposed to possess a singular vision. Fran is too much the conventional suburbanite, worried about peer opinion while trying to win respect and friendship with elaborate catered parties the couple can't afford. We are left, at the end, with the feeling that her long-dormant best instincts have been reawakened. In learning to see just one living thing less conventionally, Fran becomes the natural woman she always had the potential to be.

Disney and Latin American Culture
The Gallopin' Gaucho (1928)
Don Donald (1937)
Saludos Amigos (1943)
The Three Caballeros (1944)
The Nine Lives of Elfego Baca (1958–1960)
Zorro (1957–1959)
The Sign of Zorro (1960)
The Littlest Outlaw (1955)

No sooner had the United States militarily seized the Southwest from Spanish inhabitants in the mid-nineteenth century than our popular culture added insult to injury by transforming Latinos in general, Mexicans in particular, into a brutal, mindless people. Latinos were characterized, in cheap fiction and popular plays, by passionate natures: more often than not, loose morals for the women, violent tempers for the men.[10] The birth of motion pictures only enhanced, via the exaggerated acting approach of silent cinema, such negative stereotyping. Seeing, for the public at large, is (rightly or wrongly) believing. Audiences "saw" the negative myth actualized in flickers such as *Bronco Billy and the Greaser* (1914), in which the screen's original Anglo Western hero (William Anderson) put a swarthy, unpleasant Latino in his place. Such portrayals, typical to the point of being exclusive, became so abundant that in 1919 the government of Mexico contacted Hollywood producers, threatening to boycott their films if something were not done. This appeal was roundly ignored. When a particularly mean-spirited incarnation of Latinos as shiftless and slow-minded appeared in *Argentine Nights* (1940), moviegoers in that country burned down the theaters where it was showing. The threatened boycott was enacted, beginning in 1922—Mexico soon joined by Panama, then Nicaragua, setting off a domino effect. American producers, their exploitation of a considerable market threatened, finally responded, if in a half-hearted way, continuing yet softening the stereotypes.

Only Disney avoided them entirely. His hero and alter ego, Mickey, was cast as a Latin American in the second cartoon to feature the Mouse. Originally shot as a silent cartoon, though released only after sound had been added, *The Gallopin' Gaucho* features the ever-heroic Mickey rescuing his beloved Minnie from bad guy Pete—notably cast as a gringo. This constituted a reversal of the cliché, in which a righteous Anglo, in other Hollywood films of the time, would invariably save the lady from a lecherous Latino. The second Donald cartoon featured the Duck in a virtual remake. Donald was cast as a Spanish caballero, Daisy his charming Latina inamorata. By employing familiar "actors" (in this case animated ones) for such roles, Disney presented an accessible and positive vision of a culture still perceived as distant and negative by most Anglo audiences.

The first great challenge to the stereotype occurred when, in the 1940s, President Franklin Roosevelt revived our country's already existing if tacitly ignored Good Neighbor Policy. He did so for a pragmatic reason, hoping to strengthen the Americas as a bulwark against potential European enemies. Roosevelt's program entailed the creation of the Office of the Coordinator of Inter-American Affairs, headed by Nelson Rockefeller. He in turn appointed John Hay Whitney, then vice president of the Museum of Modern Art, to employ the powerful medium of motion pictures as a means of quickly correcting age-old biases. To promote what Will Hays, head of the industry's self-regulated censorship board, referred to as "hemispheric solidarity,"[11] those involved approached Disney, the only commercial filmmaker whose movies had never maligned Mexicans or any other minority, as the most logical Hollywood filmmaker to spearhead the effort.

This resulted in a pair of films, *Saludos Amigos* and *The Three Caballeros*. In mid-August 1941, Walt, his wife Lillian, and fifteen filmmakers flew to Rio de Janeiro, where they prepared initial sketches and soaked up as much local culture and street life as possible. They studied the gauchos of Argentina, the city people of Santiago, Chile, and the natural wonders of Lake Titicaca. Always, Disney perceived the trip as a means of eventually using "properly, in the medium of animation, some of the vast wealth of South American literature, music, and customs" in the context of American films.[12] Arriving back in California in late October, Disney planned a series of shorts, each illuminating viewers on one Latin American area via an entertaining tale. Movie historians have noted that, beginning in the 1940s, "films began to portray each nation differently, each possessing an individual culture and history."[13] Disney was the first to do so. For commercial reasons, the initial four shorts were packaged into an anthology. The framing device would be the trip itself, immortalized in 16 mm home movies. The result, however unconscious, offers another instance of Disney expanding the feature film by foreshadowing what would years later be considered a revolutionary approach to moviemaking, as the subject of the movie is the making of that movie.

The Lake Titicaca episode presents Donald, whiter than white, as the original Ugly American. A vulgar tourist, Donald affects native costume, urging one of the wary locals to snap his picture in front of famous locations. Disney satirizes *us,* even as he treats the area's residents with abiding respect. In Chile, the little airplane Pedro gets the mail through a terrible storm and over high mountains when his father cannot make the trek. A narrative combination of *The Little Engine That Could* and *Little Toot,* the tale by implication decimates the odious cliché of the lazy Latino, alternately projecting a people (here represented by cartoon aircraft) as dedicated to Walt's beloved work ethic. For the Pampas, Disney employed Goofy as the typical American cowboy. He encounters his doppelganger, a gaucho—educating the audience that our most beloved American institution is derived from Spanish customs. Rio allowed Disney to show the development of a sophisticated nightlife, where Donald and parrot Joe Carioca dance the night away. Throughout the film, Disney's "magic paintbrush" creates for the audience a series of maps, making the South American continent's geography comprehensible to casual viewers. The film was happily received in the countries that inspired it, both by journalists and the public at large—a key reversal of the response to previous Hollywood films about Latin America.

The combination of creative experimentation and positive propaganda would be furthered in *The Three Caballeros.* In its opening, Donald Duck receives a large gift-wrapped package, the accompanying note explaining this is a gift from his friends (fellow humanized birds) in South America. Included is a movie projector, allowing Donald to screen numerous films from varied lands. This time, Disney begins at the bottom (the South Pole) and works his way up (to Mexico). The approach allowed his audience to grasp the geographical layout through interludes between episodes that, via animation and on-location photography, illustrate the changing terrains of each country before we slip in for a visit. Continuing the concept of education through entertainment, Disney includes language lessons as well. Words and phrases are regularly translated, beginning with *Aves Rares* (unique birds), the focus on wildlife allowing Walt to illustrate his ongoing and innovative ecological themes.

Each individual sequence—from the Brazilian outback through the Uruguayan pampas to elegant Acapulco Beach, identified as the Monaco of Mexico—informs the mass audience, which remained so engulfed in splashy entertainment that they accepted as so much mere escapist fun this crash course on the joys of cultural diversity half a century before that phrase was coined. Disney's artists adopted a different color scheme, and unique style of animation, for each individual country or, in the case of Mexico (allowed more time than the others), specific regions within the country. These choices were based on close observation of the terrain experienced during the Disney crew's visit. There is surrealism for the train ride through a jungle, rich reds and oranges for a lyrical portrait of Brazil's quiet cities, and a subdued color scheme for daylight on the open plains. In the lush, lyrical animated depiction of Bahia, the camera's movements imitate the music of the samba, which—as we notice thanks to a crosscut—is itself an imitation of trees and other vegetation, swaying in the gentle winds.

Nowhere is Disney's enlightenment more clear than in his portrayal of Latin women. Grossly caricatured in other Hollywood films, they were reduced to emotionally superficial, intellectually vapid, sexually promiscuous vamps. Lupe Valez, perhaps most vividly remembered in *Hot Pepper* (1933), *Strictly Dynamite* (1934), and *Mexican Spitfire* (1940), appeared consistently intent on seducing wholesome Anglo boys away from decent white-bread fiancées. Her characters were always "unpredictable, passionate, and uncontrollable."[14] In the forties, when Hollywood attempted to modify that vision, the best it could come up with was Carmen Miranda—not a true alternative to the stereotype, only a camp queen caricature of the traditional Latin vamp, now an over-the-top joke. Conversely, in *The Three Caballeros,* Walt employed three of Latin America's most talented and beautiful stars, none ever before featured in a Hollywood movie: Aurora Miranda as a Brazilian street merchant, Dora Luz as an Acapulco sophisticate, and Carmen Molina as a female gaucho. Exquisite actresses, dancers, and singers all, they vividly bring to life three actual types of ethnic women, refreshingly opposed to the existing sex-kitten cliché. Nor does Disney go the other extreme, desexing them to diminish the stereotypical image. Each woman is, in her own way, healthily sexual—interested in the men who surround her, though never "uncontrollable." Like all Disney's liberated women, they are capable of emotional and sensual warmth, yet able to manage any and all such feelings. They are, simply, in control of their destinies. It is Donald—symbol of the white American male—who goes giddily out of control. With each woman in turn, he makes a fool of himself, turning red with sexual heat, wildly pursuing the ladies with no motivation other than unleashed libido. When Donald finally does get to kiss one, it is she—not he—who decides the time is right, always the case in Disney.

Anything but an artistic imperialist, Walt enlisted composers Ary Barroso, Agustín Lara, and Manuel Esperon, all acknowledged in their homelands, as full collaborators. The film emerged as a true pan-American effort, the most forward-thinking Hollywood filmmakers teaming with native talent to create a portrait of each Latin American country that would at once be acceptable to the people living there and comprehensible to a mass audience in the United States and, for that matter, the world. Briefly, other studios followed Disney's lead. Then, "[a]s soon as the war ended, Hollywood lost interest in its good neighbor policy and abandoned the Latin American."[15] Not Walt. In *Davy Crockett,* respect for minorities was always in evidence. The third episode, "Davy Crockett at the Alamo" (February 23, 1955), closed with Crockett's death on the walls of that fort on March 6, 1836.

Significantly, Disney refused to paint the attacking Mexican army, in broad strokes, as representing some evil empire. At no point in the film is the army ever verbally identified as being Mexican. General Santa Anna's name is mentioned; the uniforms and flags are accurate for that time, though the soldiers' ethnicity is verbally avoided. Previous Alamo movies had all been implicitly racist. And sometimes, explicitly, as with D. W. Griffith's *Martyrs of the Alamo* (1916), in which the color of the attacking force is emphasized, though we see no Spanish defenders of the fort. That remained the case in the many Alamo movies to follow over the decades. Until Disney broke the mold. As the hero enters Texas, a friendly Spanish family warns Davy of the dangers in San Antonio, then blesses him and his men when Crockett's company proceeds anyway. More sombreros are seen on the Alamo walls than either Stetsons or coonskin caps. This is in recognition of Captain Juan Seguin's "Los Tejanos," Hispanics living in Texas who chose to join the fight on the Texican side.[16] When sickly Jim Bowie (Kenneth Tobey) must be moved to the chapel, Crockett calls for help to two men: "Hornbuckle! Contreras!" As equals, Anglo and Latino carry the colonel to safer quarters.

The next logical step was to offer such an enlightened view of the Hispanic in a leading role. Disney did that twice, first as a fantasy, then in a more realistic vein. *Zorro* (based on popular pulp fiction novels by Johnston McCulley) had been filmed many times, including famous silent (1920, with Douglas Fairbanks Sr.) and sound (1940, starring Tyrone Power) adaptations by major studios. There were numerous American and international B pictures as well. Disney departed from the previous approaches, transforming the tales of derring-do into pro-Latin propaganda. His TV shows and film marked the first time a Latin actor played the part in a major American production. Likewise, the women who portrayed Diego's various love interests (Jolene Brand, Lisa Montell, etc.) were mostly Spanish, if on occasion Italian American Annette Funicello also appeared as a pretty señorita.

Spanish names and settings were employed in previous Zorro films, yet they seemed little more than window dressing, in light of the obvious Americanization of the characters. Once an audience adjusted to such elements as costume design, the story had been accepted as an Anglo

REIMAGINING THE LATINO. Disney was the first Hollywood filmmaker to discard the offensive stereotype of Latinos as sexual predators. In *The Nine Lives of Elfego Baca*, the shy title character loses the love of his life to an equally nice Anglo (TOP), while Hispanic women (BOTTOM) are portrayed as serious-minded persons of political substance. (Copyright 1959 Walt Disney Productions; courtesy Buena Vista Releasing.)

romance. In Disney's version, the opposite held true. Stories centered not so much on Zorro (often reduced to an obligatory appearance) as Los Angeles itself, particularly the teeming street life of its diverse Spanish and native populations. These ranged from elegant aristocrats to hardworking peasants, the full spectrum of Latin American humanity. Most were played by Spanish actors, and often, the Spanish language was fully incorporated into individual episodes.

Many stories were merely routine in terms of drama. Yet the whole series constituted something more than the sum of its parts. Before *Zorro*, the only Hispanic hero for children had been the Cisco Kid in the early fifties, with Duncan Renaldo cast as the traditional happy-go-lucky hero, Leo Carrillo as his dim-witted comic sidekick. In its limited way, that show did provide a breakthrough, though it never approached Disney's in ambition, as the two leading characters were often the only Latinos on view, and the tone was clearly simple heroics. However fantastical the concept of Zorro, a masked avenger, may be, Disney made it appear as real as possible. Diego emerged as a three-dimensional character, capable of pathos, particularly in those episodes involving him with his father, played as a distinguished left-leaning political activist by George J. Lewis. As for the women, they always fully joined in the physical fight against tyranny as equal partners.

The next step was to offer a real-life Spanish hero of the Southwest. Disney found such a man in the person of Elfego Baca (Robert Loggia), whose most famous adventure occurred when he found himself surrounded in a small shanty by angry Anglos. The Texans fired hundreds of rounds into the crumbling shelter over a period of forty hours. When help finally arrived, Baca emerged, in what many in the Hispanic community perceived as a miracle, unscathed. In the opening episode (October 3, 1958), Disney (in his introduction) made clear that the man's heritage would be essential to the shows. Thereafter, it was presented in a manner designed to counteract all stereotypes. Numerous studio Westerns had begun with an image of wild, disorderly Mexicans shooting up a town, only to be put in their place by a crusading Anglo lawman. Here, the opposite occurs. Cowboys are presented as a drunken, unruly lot, endangering women and children. Elfego, on the other hand, harbors only peaceful intentions, arriving in town on a business matter. He uses guns to subdue the mob only when he realizes innocent people may be hurt.

As the cowboys make clear, they are less upset about having one of their number arrested than the fact that the deputy is of the despised Spanish descent. When Elfego is forced into the hovel where he makes his gallant stand, the viewing audience was, for the first time in television history, asked to cheer for a member of an ethnic minority who stands against the ordinarily lionized Anglo cowboy. At episode's end, Elfego's good work results (as in all Disney films) in his achieving higher status within the American Dream. He's named sheriff of Socorro, the first Latin American to achieve such status in an Anglo-dominated cowtown. Disney then decimates the cinematic cliché that Latin men are addicted to gambling. Elfego closes down the worst joints, owned and run by suited members of the Anglo establishment. In the second episode (October 17, 1958), Elfego—having achieved a lofty position—uses it to ensure that innocent and productive members of his race, previously treated as second-class citizens, receive full equality.

Significantly, though, he flatly refuses to use his office chauvinistically, protecting Hispanic outlaws who blame their problems on racial prejudice, then beg Elfego for special treatment. When one particularly cruel killer, who happens to be Spanish, calls Elfego a traitor to his people for arresting him, Baca literally laughs out loud. He himself insisted on equality, and won it. Every other Latino should do the same, rather than hide behind the protective shield of victimization. Disney, alone among TV producers of that time, employed the action-Western genre to insist that minorities are capable of upward mobility within America's capitalist system. It makes sense, then, that at the end of episode two, Elfego realizes he's had enough of enforcing law with a gun and turns in his badge. He leaves to study law—the facts in this case supporting Disney's ongoing belief in education as an effective means of overcoming social barriers for minorities. Elfego returns with a degree in hand, emerging as a role model for the Latin minority watching TV's Disney hour, as well as a case study for Anglos—helping the latter pass beyond the limiting stereotype other Hollywood producers had set in place.

Before that second episode closes, Disney effectively dismisses yet another cliché. From Rudolf Valentino to Ricardo Montalban, any conventionally handsome Spanish male was typecast as the Latin Lover, more often than not targeting Anglo women. Such a male predator was, in the popular imagination, "incapable of having a normal adult relationship with a woman" that transcended sex.[17] Disney offered a reversal, at once wise and witty, of that situation. Elfego falls deeply in love with a woman of his own race (Lisa Montell), the same young lady who allowed him to hide in her sad little home while escaping the wrathful Texans. She clearly cares for Elfego, so he plans to ask for her hand in marriage. Before he can propose, she blurts out that she's in love with another man—an Anglo rancher—hoping her beloved "brother" Elfego will be best man at the wedding. Sheepishly, he agrees. The simplistic approach would have been for Disney to then characterize the Anglo cowboy as an unpleasant person, the young woman blindly choosing the wrong man. That is not the case. He's a delightful fellow, completely antiracist, sincerely thrilled to meet his fiancée's "best friend." This allows Disney to argue, as no other TV producer of the period dared do, in favor of interracial marriage. They will clearly be a happy couple, and Disney holds them up as a positive role model for young people watching.

In the following episodes, gunplay was gradually eliminated (itself a shocker for fans of violent TV Westerns) in favor of court cases. Elfego continued his upward mobility, first working as a clerk in the office of an enlightened liberal lawyer (James Dunn), becoming his assistant, then a trusted courtroom attorney, finally a full partner in the firm. Always, Elfego balances his deep, ongoing loyalty to the Hispanic community with a sense of color-blind fair play, judging any case—and any man—on an individual basis. Disney's Elfego also goes out of his way to promote what we now call diversity by defending even those minority subcultures more despised at the time than his own. In the seventh episode (November 13, 1959), "Move Along, Mustangers," he takes the case of a group of despised Anglos who, owing to their unique religious beliefs, are persecuted by both the Anglo *and* Hispanic communities. Each wants these "different" people to leave, the now belatedly accepted Hispanics no more notably enlightened than the Anglos who once excluded *them*. In the eighth episode (November 20, 1959), "Mustang Man, Mustang Maid," Elfego breaks a boycott created to destroy the Mustangers' economic base, put in place to drive them from the area. In time, the Mustangers are, their "difference" aside, gradually accepted as a part of the community at large. Yet they remain by choice a subculture that refuses to surrender its cherished uniqueness for total assimilation, insisting instead on becoming integrated with other elements of an America that is gradually learning to tolerate and accept diversity.

HE WAS NICE TO MICE. Adolf Hitler, who associated Germany's Jews with rodents, considered Walt Disney the "most dangerous" of all Hollywood filmmakers. Propaganda Minister Goebbels believed the Mickey shorts, featuring a heroic rodent, to be intended as pro-Jewish propaganda. (Copyright 1938 Walt Disney Productions; courtesy Buena Vista Releasing.)

Disney and the Jews
The Three Little Pigs (1933)
"Mickey Mouse" (character: 1928–present)
Der Fuehrer's Face (1943)

Walt's daughter Diane made her debut at the Las Madrinas Ball in Los Angeles. At the time, Jews were barred; they would be until 1967. One can interpret this (and many have) as Disney's uncritical acceptance of anti-Semitism. Another possible reading of the situation: Diane was the first child of *any* motion-picture-industry family to debut there. By fighting against restrictions—winning for his family in particular, show business people in general (many of whom were Jewish)—Disney forced open the doors to previously marginalized people.

Owing to his Midwestern upbringing, Walt always harbored "the small land-holder's justified prejudice against bankers."[18] This would be dramatized in diverse films ranging from earthy drama *(Those Calloways)* to musical comedy *(Mary Poppins),* both featuring portraits of bankers, along with other raw capitalists, New York–based money people in particular, as the least human members of modern society. This doesn't so much constitute prejudice (*prejudging*) as judgment derived from harsh personal experience. As a child, Walt's family was driven to distraction by bankers threatening to foreclose on them. As a young adult, the Charles Mintz Company brazenly stole Walt's first animated animal creation, Oswald Rabbit. Incredibly, though, none of the unpleasant bankers and/or businessmen in the films is ever identified as Jewish, though many of the people who drove Disney to distraction in fact were. Instead, bad bankers are identified as Old Money Anglo-Saxon types, precisely John Ford's approach in *Stagecoach* (1939) or Frank Capra's for *It's a Wonderful Life* (1946).

In that rare case when a Jewish actor is cast in such a part (Keenan Wynn in *The Absent-Minded Professor* and *Son of Flubber*), the character he plays is clearly established, by every element from name ("Hawk") to lifestyle, as *not* being Jewish. For the most part, Disney appears blithely unaware of or utterly unconcerned with the ethnicity of those who treated him poorly, blaming it on orientation and profession rather than racial identity. On the other hand, he remained acutely aware that, at least on one occasion, a Jewish banker had offered Walt a helping hand when he most needed it, even as bankers of the old Anglo ethnicity failed to come across. During his lifetime, Disney loved to tell the story, to pretty much anyone who would listen, of Joseph Rosenberg, a representative of the Bank of America. The two met at a moment of crisis when *Snow White* could not be completed in time for the 1937 Christmas season without a further advance of $250,000, then a heady amount of cash. Rosenberg spent an entire day with Disney, touring the studio and watching rushes of the incomplete film, before breathing deeply and, despite gnawing fears that the enterprise might yet bring them all down, agreeing to negotiate the loan.

This belies Richard Schickel's sweeping statement that "Disney appears to have shared, in mild form, some of the anti-Semitism that was common to his generation and place of origin."[19] Such a claim is easy to make, in Disney's case impossible to prove—either through anti-Semitic statements made during his lifetime (no hard evidence exists) or internal evidence in the movies. If anything, we sense a sharp contrast between Walt's assumed anti-Semitism and the overt anti-Semitic statements made at around the same time by Ezra Pound. Or the gross, caricatured portraits of Jews in the most acclaimed works of Ernest Hemingway (Robert Cohn in *The Sun Also Rises*) and F. Scott Fitzgerald (Meyer Wolsheim in *The Great Gatsby*). Those portraits do blatantly reveal that these major authors—both like Disney originally from the Midwest—did indeed share the anti-Semitism of their generation and place of origin, and openly passed it on to the nation's literate audience.

In films made more or less simultaneously, and targeted at the mainstream, Disney revealed no such tendencies. Schickel unashamedly claims that "at least once [Disney] presented a fairly vicious caricature of the Jew onscreen."[20] For the moment dropping any guise of objectivity to speak directly as a Jewish American, this scribe cannot begin to grasp what the phrase "fairly vicious" could possibly mean. A caricature is vicious or it is not; "fairly" appears to be a hedge word, implying something negative about Disney without quite committing to an honest, open insult. Later, Schickel refers to a sequence in *The Three Little Pigs* when,

> in the course of attempting to breach the solid defenses of the eldest pig's brick house, the wolf donned the robe, beard and glasses of the long-caricatured Jewish peddler. It was an unfortunate choice for a gag.[21]

The statement contains one glaring factual error. The pigs, as any child can attest, are triplets. The one inhabiting the house of bricks may be wiser, but is no older than the others. As to the purported caricature, all films need to be studied in the context of the era during which they were created and released.

In the 1930s, ethnic humor—however unpleasant we consider it today—was prevalent in all American culture, high-, middle-, and lowbrow. To seize on this gag as a means of indicting Disney, and Disney alone among Hollywood producers, is prejudicial. Besides, cartoons—with their extremely (and, for anyone who understands the medium, *necessarily*) broad form of portraiture—rely more heavily on caricature than any other cinematic form. With that in mind, we can closely consider what actually transpires in *Three Little Pigs*. The wolf does indeed disguise himself as a Jewish peddler. Again, this author, descended from just such immigrants, can attest to the fact that they did exist, as well as that, on the evidence of existing family photographs, this is precisely how such forebears appeared. Most notable is that the character of the wolf, *not* the filmmaker, "presents" such a stereotype. He does so to convince the pigs, quivering inside, that the wolf is gone. Now, they are being visited by a nice, harmless (and—oh, yes!—Jewish) fellow. Disney may have created the wolf, but it is the wolf—the film's villain—who invokes ethnic stereotyping. For a moment, the less intelligent pigs, relieved, are ready to throw open the door. The smart pig knows better, grasps this is not some likeable visitor (whom they apparently would welcome), but their adversary. Jews, by implication, are "good"; evil incarnate, trying to disguise itself, assumes the form of a Jew, someone who may be "different" yet can be trusted.

The Three Little Pigs offers a positive portrayal—a pro-Jewish employment of the existing cultural stereotype, invoked to ridicule the caricature—not the Jews. Otherwise, there are no Jewish characters, as such, in any Disney films. The worst charge that could be leveled against him is benign neglect. There are, though, numerous characters, all of a highly positive nature, played by Jewish actors, in particular, Ed Wynn. Disney revived the faded career of radio's onetime "perfect fool," awarding Wynn (who otherwise would have had difficulty finding work at this time) some of the best supporting roles in the studio's canon. These include the fire chief in *The Absent-Minded Professor,* the Toymaker in *Babes in Toyland* (essentially, a Jewish actor cast as a thinly disguised Santa Claus, something of a first), the agriculture commissioner in *Son of Flubber,* and the lovable Uncle Albert (inspiring a Paul McCartney tune) in *Mary Poppins.*

In *Those Calloways,* concerning big city money men who threaten a small town's integrity, both villains are played by Anglo actors, Philip Abbott and Roy Roberts. Wynn is cast as one of the old townsfolk, sitting around the proverbial cracker barrel. In Disney's vision, the Jewish actor (and, by implication, Jewish character) is fully assimilated into mainstream America. Other Jewish actors cast in roles that are notably nonstereotypical include three of the four leads in *20,000 Leagues under the Sea:* a macho seaman (Kirk Douglas), a sensitive intellectual (Paul Lukas), and a genial but loyal manservant (Peter Lorre). The fourth lead, James Mason (as Captain Nemo), may have been part Jewish. Jessica Tandy played the sympathetic colonial-era Anglo mother in *The Light in the Forest,* Jack Albertson a pleasant journalist in *The Shaggy Dog,* Lilli Palmer the dedicated mistress to an Austrian horse team in *The Miracle of the White Stallions,* Suzanne Pleshette an all-American contemporary wife in *The Ugly Dachshund* and a liberated lady of the Old West in *The Adventures of Bullwhip Griffin.* On rare occasion, when they proved to be the best

EXPANDING THE ACTOR'S HORIZON. Jews have been treated more sympathetically in Disney films than in those of any other studio. Walt allowed Ed Wynn, so often typecast in ethnic roles, to expand his range beyond such clichés in parts ranging from Santa Claus in *Babes in Toyland* (TOP) to a small-town cracker-barrel philosopher in *Those Calloways* (BOTTOM). (Copyright 1961 and 1964 Walt Disney Productions; courtesy Buena Vista Releasing.)

choices, Disney would cast Jewish actors as villains, including Eli Wallach in *The Moon-Spinners* and Walter Slezak in *Emil and the Detectives*. A rich verisimilitude to the roles assigned Jewish actors by Disney in itself defies any stereotype.

Film historian Patricia Erens has argued that the immediate onscreen identification of Jewish characters during the early years of American movies was accomplished not by bringing up the issue of ethnicity, but by having them played by actors (many, though not all, Jewish themselves) with notably large noses.[22] However horrific the practice of physical caricaturing may appear today, such racial stereotyping (for *all* minorities) must be accepted as a "given" for that era. The attitude of any one filmmaker ought to be assessed by close scrutiny of how positive or negative the portrayal of any minority is within the context of a then-abiding situation. The majority of the major studios were owned and run by Jews, as Neal Gabler documents in *A Kingdom of Their Own*.[23] Most Jewish characters in their films were genial immigrants, always characterized by large noses. In films released by non-Jewish producers (particularly those of Thomas Edison), Jewish characters, likewise identified by their large noses, were portrayed as Shylockian lowlives, interested only in money, willing to acquire it by dubious means.[24] Such is not, however, the case with Disney, whose greatest character is, according to Erens's concept, himself Jewish: Mickey Mouse.

Time magazine, among others, asserts that Mickey could most easily be distinguished by his "long, pointy nose."[25] In early short subjects, he is always the immigrant-outsider, trying to win a place in society, often by working as a street peddler. One essayist went so far as to compare Mickey (and suggest a direct blood lineage) with a beloved Hebrew character who—through luck, pluck, and faith—overcame great odds: "Mickey, kind of a little David, always wins against every Goliath."[26] The Mouse is, then, the ancient Jew, re-created as a populist hero for all of America in the twentieth century. He is also Disney's alter ego, Walt providing the voice of Mickey in all the early films. In essence, then, Disney—the eternal outsider—saw himself as a Jew on some occasions, even as Mickey's coloring makes clear he envisioned himself as black on others.

Another author insisted, in 1935, even as Hitler rose to power, that Mickey—like Germany's Jews—was the natural enemy of such despised "dictators and tyrants."[27] Hitler himself was horrified by the image and concept of Mickey, considering the Mouse to be the most degenerate piece of pro-Jewish propaganda ever to come out of America.[28] Hitler's own propagandists' most vicious ploy in their ongoing anti-Semitic campaign consisted of films, posters, and other visual items comparing Jews to vermin. This constituted a major effort by Hitler's propaganda machine to discredit Jews as "dirty." In Hitler's twisted mind, Disney employed Mickey as a means of countering all the anti-Semitic prejudices he—Hitler—had set out to further entrench. Mickey incarnated the Jew as a charming, clean do-gooder, the positive polar opposite of Hitler's negative vision of Jews. Walt's most direct assault against Hitler came with *Der Fuehrer's Face* (1943), in which the Anglo American, Donald Duck, initially accepts a life in a fascist state, finally realizing its implications, at which point he rebels. When he does, Mickey joins him in defiance—the white-bread middle American now aligned with the ethnic Jew against a common oppressing evil. As a pair of working journalists noted at the time, "No other weapon of propaganda can ridicule the Axis, expose its absurdities, as deftly" as Disney animation.[29]

Italian American
Lady and the Tramp (1955)

Like the Jews, Italian Americans are rarely if ever directly portrayed in Disney films. Moviemakers, like other artists, hail from a distinct background, ethnic or otherwise. Like other artists, particularly the most serious-minded, filmmakers early on sense that they must deal with what they know best to achieve authenticity. Obviously, Midwesterner Disney did not "know" Italian American culture any more than he "knew" that of Jewish Americans. Still, when his characters do brush up against ethnic minorities, the portrayal is never unpleasant. More important still, never does Disney reinforce any already existing negative prejudices.

A brief though notable sequence that conveys Disney's attitudes toward Italians is the romantic restaurant sequence in *Lady and the Tramp* (1955), in which Walt invokes an existing ethnic stereotype only to humanize it. The owner/chef and his chief cook at the spaghetti house are caricatured, though lovingly so. From the moment the two Italians appear, they are kind, hardworking, gentle, and incredibly generous. Despite their solid, industrious orientation, Disney's Italians feel great affinity for the outsider, Tramp, also openly accepting his uptown girlfriend, Lady. They are, when studied from our own politically correct position, multicultural Americans, happy to join the mainstream while maintaining their beloved heritage, and managing to maintain a delicate balance between the two. In other studios' films, Italians are portrayed as emotionally out of control, therefore constituting a threat, since such "excess is inappropriate to American society."[30] This is not true of these Italians. Though the dinner they serve Lady and Tramp is indeed stereotypical—spaghetti and meatballs—they remain free of the unpleasant stigmas that have surrounded Italian immigrants since the birth of American movies.

Such negativity precedes the invention of film. In popular literature written during the nineteenth century in England and America, a vision of the "Italian male and female as sinister sexual, ethical, and religious threats" to Protestant males predominated.[31] Such a vision existed not only in the passing fancies of penny-dreadful junk novels, but also in the elevated art of a Henry James or an Edith Wharton. Simply put,

> WASP America's obsessions and prejudices about "foreign influence" show up clearly in its images of Italians. . . . Like the earlier Irish immigrant, [the Italian] was a fearsome symbol of the alien Roman church; like the Jew from Eastern Europe, his features were in radical physical contrast to the pervasive Anglo-Saxon profile.[32]

Himself deriving in part from Irish ancestry, Disney had only positive things to say about his own people, as films like *Darby O'Gill and the Little People* make clear. But to defend one's own ethnic ancestry while either ignoring, or offending, other cultures—too often the case in popular films as in "serious" literature—qualifies as chauvinism, not enlightenment. How impressive, then, that Disney's sensitivity reaches out to include Jews, Italians, and other minorities.

As to the abiding cinematic cliché,

> The dominant portrayal of Italians in American film is within the gangster genre . . . the channeling of Italian-Americans into the gangster film effectively removes them from sentimental and domestic spheres of portrayal.[33]

Though there are many gangsters in Disney films, never once is a single such villain ever portrayed by identifiably ethnic Italian American actors—or actors of other ethnicities offering a burlesque of the deeply entrenched onscreen Mafioso. The most threatening mobsters on view (Alexander Scourby and Strother Martin in *The Shaggy Dog,* Don Ross and Charley Briggs in *The Absent-Minded Professor,* Neville Brand and Frank Gorshin in *That Darn Cat*) cannot in any way be identified as Italian American.

If the Italian male has too often been reduced in the cinema to a cliché gangster, the female of the species has been dichotomized into a pair of extremes: "the fiery, sensuous, outspoken willful 'Sophia Loren' image" or "the jolly, all-loving, naive rotund *mamma mia* image." [34] In essence, a woman who is either a slave to her passions (sexual and otherwise) or a nonsexual symbol of motherhood at its most subservient. In *The Rose Tattoo* (1955), Anna Magnani won an Oscar for playing the former cliché in the film's first half, the latter in the second. The same year that movie was released, Disney introduced his own Italian American star, Annette Funicello, on TV's *The Mickey Mouse Club.* Audiences discovered Hollywood's first significant challenge to two extreme stereotypes. Though she would swiftly emerge as the most popular of all Mouseketeers, Annette was the only member not picked at a traditional audition or during the nationwide talent search for young talent. Walt himself, having pretty much decided that the troupe of twenty-four juvenile performers was set, happened to catch Annette appearing as part of an amateur-night program at the Starlight Bowl in Burbank. [35] When fan mail proved Disney's instinct had been correct, he set about transforming Annette into the latest variation of America's Sweetheart—that beloved girl-woman who had been a staple of Hollywood since the silent days. Mary Pickford, Shirley Temple, Margaret O'Brien, Elizabeth Taylor, and Natalie Wood owned that title at one time or another. Annette's only competitors during the late 1950s and early '60s were white-bread blondes: Sandra Dee, Tuesday Weld, Carol Lynley, Yvette Mimieux. No Italian American young woman had been unofficially crowned as middle America's sweetheart until Disney broke the barrier.

Onscreen, Annette was never a slave to her passions, having more in common with Doris Day—the key blond symbol of onscreen virginity during the late fifties—than with any previous cinematic Italian woman. Loren, Magnani, and Gina Lollobrigida did embody the notion that Italian women were likely to fly out of control whenever the sex urge struck. Annette fended off the attentions, in Disney entertainment, of Tim Considine, Tommy Kirk, David Stollery, and Tommy Sands (and later, in non-Disney films, Frankie Avalon) with the same ferocity Day showed to would-be conquering males like Rock Hudson, James Garner, and Rod Taylor. Likely, the pairing of Frankie and Annette in the *Beach Party* films as *the* all-American couple might not have been possible had Disney not presaged that situation in *Babes in Toyland*. Funicello and Sands, both Italian American, played Mary Contrary and Tom Piper, portrayed in the earlier Laurel and Hardy film (as in most stage productions) by Anglo actors. Disney, through Annette (at Disney's insistence), pioneered today what would be called "color-blind" or "race-free" casting. Never once—in the second (1956) and third (1957) *Spin and Marty* serials or in the feature film *The Shaggy Dog* (1959)—was Annette cast in a role that in any way could be ethnically identified, avoiding the trap of ghettoizing her in ethnic parts.

In her own serial, *Annette* (1958), she was cast as one more of Disney's orphans. In the opening episode (of twenty), Annette arrives in a small town to live with her uncle and aunt. They, clearly nonethnic middle Americans, were played by Anglo actors Richard Deacon and Sylvia Field. Audiences were asked to accept Annette as their relative, and, in fact, the children and adolescents who watched happily did. In the lowbrow comedies *Merlin Jones* and *The Monkey's Uncle*, Annette played Jennifer, the college campus prom queen. This was the kind of role that, in the hands of other Hollywood filmmakers, would automatically have gone to a young June Allyson—blonde, white-bread, and more conventionally middle American. On television, Walt cast Annette in *The Horsemasters* (October 1 and 8, 1961; released theatrically in Europe) as Dinah Wilcox, an American daughter-of-privilege attending a prestigious English riding school, again refusing to typecast the Italian American actress.

Early in her career, Annette realized that she had the potential to remain a star after her Disney days were done. At that point, she considered, as had so many Italian, Jewish, and Irish performers, changing her name to play down her ethnicity. More or less casually, Annette suggested such a possibility to her mentor. It was the only time that the young actress ever recalled Disney growing visibly angry at her.[36] Walt disparaged that process, insisting that she had been born Italian, would always be Italian, and that she must do absolutely nothing to suggest anything but pride in her cultural identity. Rather than try and escape from her background to assimilate into the mainstream, they would together alter the way America's vast middle class saw ethnicity by inducing it to accept Annette, in films and TV programs, as the girl next door.

AMERICA'S SWEETHEART. Beginning with Mary Pickford, a "girl next door" invariably implied an Anglo star with natural blond hair. Disney countered that notion by casting an Italian American in wholesome if sexy roles; Annette Funicello went on to star in the *Beach Party* movies opposite Frankie Avalon. (Courtesy American International Pictures, 1963.)

This, Disney explained, would allow them to use what appeared to be nothing more than genial entertainment as a means of educating the audience toward a higher plane of enlightenment without being aware of it. Fortunately, Annette saw the wisdom of Walt's way and did not Anglicize her last name. This was the first case of such a decision proving workable, the initial challenge to Hollywood's long-held belief that an obvious ethnic could not possibly become a star. As a result of what Disney and Funicello achieved, performers of diverse backgrounds—Dustin Hoffman, Al Pacino, Barbra Streisand, Robert De Niro, et al.—were freed to maintain their names and true identities, without always being limited to stereotypically ethnic roles.

AMERICAN BANDSTAND. Before Disney challenged the stereotype, "good" onscreen women were asexual and recessive; in "All the Cats Join In," Walt positively portrayed teenage females with strong libidos and an admirable desire to take charge, even on the dance floor. (Copyright 1946 the Walt Disney Company; courtesy RKO Radio Films.)

4

Racial and Sexual Identity in America
Disney's Subversion of the Victorian Ideal

Sex, like dirt, disease, and death, is anathema to a country that treasures cleanliness above godliness and innocence above experience.

—MOLLY HASKELL, 1973

We'd been told that sex was dirty, dangerous, and powerful stuff. That nothing could touch it for pleasure and fun . . . was the best kept secret of our coming of age.

—BENITA EISLER, 1986

*O*pposition by reactionary forces to the civil rights movement in the polity of the 1950s was paralleled by an equally fervent opposition to rock 'n' roll music on the era's corresponding cultural landscape. The two ultraconservative agendas were essentially symbiotic, for both derived from an abiding fear on the part of the country's most narrowly traditional whites that ethnic and cultural minorities—most obviously, African American progenitors of the new American music—embodied a sensual freedom which threatened the very foundations of a society that had never entirely separated itself from either its Puritan origins or Victorian values. Even the titles of such songs as "Sixty Minute Man" and "(I Found My Thrill on) Blueberry Hill" proved frightful to a mind-set that wanted nothing more than to preserve an old Anglo sense of decorum that had already begun to disappear from the everyday American scene.

A massive postwar migration of African Americans to the North in search of new industrial jobs led to the creation of "race music" stations, once confined to the South, in places like Detroit, Chicago, and New York. Flipping the dial, Anglo youth—the first true American teenagers—discovered and instantly became enamored of a musical genre that appealed to them in a way their ever-more-conformist suburbanite parents' popular white-bread performers—Perry Como, Patti Page—did not. In 1956 white artists—Elvis Presley most prominent among them—also began performing in just such a manner. As Erika Doss has noted,

> Consciously courting black music, black musicians, and mixed audiences in the mid-1950s, Elvis participated in the creation of a powerful form of popular culture—rock-and-roll—aimed at crossing and even dissolving a racially divided post-war America.[1]

Elvis emerged, in the words of Trent Hill, as "the poor white messenger of poor black sexuality."[2] Not surprisingly, the same conservative adults who were already complaining about the full-force Negro integration of formerly all-white schools beginning in 1956 likewise denounced Presley's integration of black music (as well as black movements in his shake, rattle, 'n' roll gyrations) into his signature style. "It wasn't just Elvis's erotic style that riled 1950s critics," one social observer noted, "but the recognizably African-American sources of that style."[3] The crusade against Elvis and other early white rockers, often orchestrated by church groups, was implicitly hostile to integration of blacks—black people or black culture—into the era's vast though essentially white Protestant American mainstream. The key motivation, however implicit, had to do with human sexuality: a lingering hope—part Puritanical, part Victorian, all Anglo—to maintain an ever less tenable ideal of male courtliness and female virginity.

As one prominent film historian noted in 1973 about our collective heritage of repression, in everyday life and as expressed in popular art:

> To the degree that sex was the equivalent of the self, surrender to sex was to lose oneself, whereas abstinence would insure its safeguarding, if not its salvation. Our instincts were substantiated by the movies: The "virgin" was a primal, positive figure, honored and exalted beyond any [other] merits she possessed . . . while the "whore" . . . was publicly castigated and cautioned against—and privately sought by men.[4]

Such a conception of human sexuality was first challenged in the 1920s, then again in 1967, during what came to be called "the summer of love." Seemingly ironic to some, the key examples of modern sexual liberation hail from the Disney company. Progressive thinking—the wholehearted defense of free love, if not necessarily free sex—was preceded and predicted by Walt Disney, beginning with his earliest commercial and artistic output.

A Hint of Stocking
The Newman "Laugh-O-Grams" (1922)
Alice in Cartoonland (1924–1927)
Great Guns (1927)
The Mechanical Cow (1927)
Traffic Troubles (1931)
Mickey's Rival (1936)

Hints of the shape of things to come appear in Newman's "Laugh-O-Grams." These were the brief advertisements Walt and collaborator Ubbe Iwwerks (later shortened for professional purposes to Ub Iwerks) created in 1922 for a Kansas City department store, playing at theaters as preludes to the era's feature films. In addition to anticrime pieces and animated editorials on the need to clean up the corrupt local police, there were "Petticoat Lane" films—lingerie ads featuring scantily clad women in silk stockings. Mild "leg art" by today's standards, such short subjects provided a precedent for contemporary Victoria's Secret television commercials. In their time, these brief examples of sensuous cinema proved more than a tad shocking for that provincial city's middle-American audience. The onscreen images projected a ripe, unapologetic, healthily open attitude toward sexuality that would remain basic to the Disney formula after Walt and his brother Roy headed for California, shortly thereafter persuading Ub to join them.

When they arrived, the trio discovered that a striking dichotomization of the screen woman, which had been set in place shortly after the turn of the century, still drew upon the dictates of England's recently deceased (1901) Queen Victoria. Her attitudes persisted in the literature, in print and as plays, that had dramatized Her Majesty's scheme of values for the public at large. Such a morals system had been transferred to the embryonic movie divertissements with the introduction of Hollywood's first "bad" (man-eating vampire Theda Bara) and "good" (innocent, ever virtuous Mary Pickford) girls. Such a situation existed, if in slightly more sophisticated form, during the twenties, the first decade during which Disney produced films. Throughout the postwar period of short skirts, fast cars, and bathtub gin, newcomer Clara Bow—playing "the liberated working girl" and "boisterous flapper"—appeared as an alternative to "the Victorian valentine" embodied by Pickford's child-woman or Lillian Gish's "whispering wildflower."

Such prim, proper virgins were perceived by young audiences, relishing the relative freedoms of the Roaring Twenties, as a quaint throwback—an anachronistic reminder for older, more conservative audiences of their beloved (if fast-disappearing) "paragon of virtue, the old-fashioned girl."[5] Desperately needed (and notably absent), at least if the dichotomization of women were ever to be challenged, was a single, nonsimplified screen woman—able to project the daring idea that females who wore short skirts could balance such a progressive style with more traditional substance. Such an icon would express all the best values of the old-fashioned girl while somehow still enjoying the nouveau liberties automatically attendant on living as a flapper. Such a screen icon was nowhere so boldly in evidence as in Disney's first short subjects.

The concept for the *Alice* comedies was inspired by Max and Dave Fleischer's already successful *Out of the Inkwell* series, which had launched Betty Boop to cartoon stardom. Disney's diminutive girl-woman, however, was real. Like Betty, Alice wore short skirts; unlike her, Alice never simpered about, always walking and talking assertively. When attracted to a male, as she often is to her cat companion, Alice does not tease and flirt (in vogue at the time, always Betty's modus operandi). Alice, rather, approaches her targeted male outright, without any self-conscious game-playing. This was the case in *Alice's Auto Race, Alice's Monkey Business,* and most notably *Alice's Knaughty Knight*—that film every bit as risqué as its suggestive title, which sounds more appropriate for one of the era's forbidden stag films than a family-oriented cartoon. At the fade-out of each episode, Alice has the upper hand. Perhaps that explains why, in comparison to Betty's high heels, Alice prefers miniature dominatrix boots. Alice also wears provocative single-piece swimsuits, at a time when old-fashioned girls were still packed into modest two-pieces. Annette Kellerman, Australian swimming star, daringly pioneered the then-shocking one-piece, wearing such beachwear in the Hollywood film *A Daughter of the Gods* (1916). In *Alice Solves the Puzzle,* Disney's heroine was the first American female to follow suit.

Even before the birth of the Mouse, Disney dared to flaunt conventions of "respectable" filmmaking. Kissing was at this time particularly controversial, under heated attack since a seven-second 1896 Vitascope release immortalized a smooch from a popular Broadway play, *The Widow Jones.* This screen kiss caused one New York journalist to rail: "Such things call for police interference. . . . The [John Rice/May Irwin] kiss is no more than a lyric of the Stock Yards. While we tolerate such things, what avails all the talk of American Puritanism[?]"[6] Rules against lengthy kisses were set in place, with watchdogs at the newly created Will Hays Office for cinematic censorship insisting, for the next fifty years, no screen kiss could exceed three seconds in length. The idea that characters might possibly part their lips was all but anathema.

Yet in *Great Guns,* Oswald Rabbit, leaving for war, grabs his girlfriend and engages her in a kiss that lasts ten seconds. Mouths open wide, tongues become grotesquely entangled; an extended sequence depicts their harried attempts to release one another from oral embrace. As always, though, Disney got away with what others dared not try, because these were, after all, "only" cartoons. The very choice of a rabbit as hero, at a time when other animators (including Paul Terry) were opting for mice (which Disney would do later, out of necessity), suggests an inherent, if largely unconscious, interest in sex. No other animal has been so associated with reproduction in the history of popular culture, from ancient magicians pulling precisely this creature out of hats to the *Playboy* "Bunny." In *The Mechanical Cow,* milk salesman Oswald abandons his delivery job to flirt with a bunny of his own, after she's made it a point to reveal her underpanties, which have been barely covered up to this point by a short skirt.

When the Charles Mintz Company co-opted Oswald through legal maneuvering, Disney was forced to reimagine his hero as a mouse. *Traffic Troubles* and *Mickey's Rival* feature Minnie, a self-determined flapper, driving into the country with Mickey. The sexual revolution of the 1920s would have been impossible without the swiftly emerging car culture's alteration of the American lifestyle, allowing young people (like the animated icons offered here) to giddily slip away and be alone. Whatever the Mouse and his companion plan to do following the final iris-out, Disney apparently has no problem with it, for the tone remains lighthearted. In yet another "departure from tradition, Disney [early on] abandoned the strict moralism of nineteenth-century courting traditions to embrace a wholesome but more liberated idea of romance."[7]

Of Goddesses and Gold Diggers
Snow White and the Seven Dwarfs (1936)
Pinocchio (1940)

Any discussion of what Disney offered in the thirties must be set against its social and cinematic contexts. In the waning years of the jazz age, sex-and-drug scandals destroyed the careers of numerous popular stars, including Clara Bow, Wallace Reid, Mabel Normand, and Fatty Arbuckle, as well as director William Desmond Taylor. Though Hollywood's self-censoring organ, the Hays Office, had been created in 1924 (anything, producers believed, was better than outside intervention), the MPPDA Code was more forcefully applied to studio pictures following 1933, after the Legion of Catholic Decency had been formed by Joseph Breen. This organization, fully supported by Protestant groups, represented something of an inter-denominational breakthrough at a time when animosity among differing Christian sects still ran high. The demonized concept of sexuality, however, proved frightening enough to ally such longtime antagonists.

Simultaneously, the stock market crash added to the growing aura of conservatism in American life and letters. However free-living two years earlier, independent young women were transformed by financial disaster into Depression-era dollies, dresses once again were worn long. The Madonna/whore dichotomization of women, briefly challenged during the twenties, returned full force. No better onscreen example exists than George Cukor's film of Claire Booth's *The Women* (1939). The spirited comedy-drama pits loyal wife/demure mother Norma Shearer against predatory, carnal, scheming single girl Joan Crawford. That retro dichotomy, however, did not extend to Disney's "juvenile" pictures. *Snow White* argues, by implication, that progressive romantic inclinations and traditional moral attitudes were not necessarily at odds. The title character was transformed from the Grimms' eight-year-old child into the first of Disney's teen heroines, as a girl transforms before our eyes into a woman. And a natural woman at that, open to romance in the woods as her prince happens by. The contrast of Snow White with the wickedly beautiful queen is not the conventional dichotomy of *The Women,* but that "adult" film's polar opposite. Here, the "good" Snow White surrenders to her senses, while the "bad" queen remains cold, rigid, narcissistic—her beauty enjoyed alone, before the Magic Mirror.

Two years later, *Pinocchio* continued this all but revolutionary concept of overt sensuality and inner goodness as completely compatible. The Blue Fairy is a blonde goddess, what the term "blonde" represented having only recently been reversed in Hollywood's iconography. Fair-haired virgins (Pickford, Gish) and brunette vamps (Bara, Pola Negri) of late-Victorian films had given way to "good" brunettes (Shearer) and "bad" blondes (Jean Harlow, Mae West, Thelma Todd, etc.). Not Disney's Blue Fairy, though, who (hair color aside) appears wholesome, not hardened. This, despite the fact that she's bedecked in a sheer see-through gown, in the manner of a glitzy golden girl from a Ziegfeld extravaganza. The Blue

Fairy (the word "blue" had much earlier taken on a sexual connotation) may look like a gold digger, yet she gives rather than takes. Appearances, Walt implies, can be deceiving.

Disney's intended effect was achieved by the animators (with Marjorie Belcher serving as their model) after hearing Walt pronounce: "Although she must give the appearance of loveliness, she must not be [merely] a glamour girl."[8] Disney's injunction is highly important, for it implies that a gorgeous and sensuous woman can also be a person of substance—that, in essence, we must escape from the dichotomization of women as either attractive *or* serious. The resultant character provided a significant innovation: A cinematic female lovely enough to be a bewitcher, yet forever proving herself a nurturer. Bold beauty and inner badness do *not* necessarily go together—at least not in Disney films.

Ode on a Grecian Urn
Fantasia (1940)

The Production Code Administration, now run by Breen, meticulously scrutinized all Hollywood product, insisting that nonmarital sex should never "be presented in such a way as to appear attractive and beautiful," much less "right and permissible."[9] Nonetheless, Disney managed to further his own agenda. His envisioning of Beethoven's *Pastoral* Symphony reimagined the 1808 composition as a Greek myth, the figures on John Keats's literary urn freed from some Attican artist's "slow time." Centaurs, pans, and other mythic creatures slip from stark buildings, tepid outposts of Apollonian civilization, to visit more appealingly Dionysian surroundings. In nature's garden, they enjoy an orgy as fully visualized as in a Cecil B. DeMille epic. Disney shares none of that filmmaker's conventional qualms, however, which inevitably led to death and destruction for the revelers in *The Ten Commandments*, both in 1923 and 1956. Other than scurrying for cover when nature temporarily explodes with a spring storm, Disney's characters look none the worse for wear after, beyond the expected postcoital exhaustion.

In addition to recalling pagan myth and the early-nineteenth-century Romantic poets who revived it, the sequence looks ahead to an environment of sexual freedom unimaginable by most Americans during the 1940s and '50s. We must recall that this was an era when sexuality was still viewed by solid suburban types with "ignorance, fear and guilt . . . Of all the secrets of coming of age in the fifties, sex was the darkest and

"TRUTH IS BEAUTY; BEAUTY, TRUTH." The characters on the ancient vessel observed by John Keats can never consummate their passion, frozen in the "slow time" of traditional graphic arts. Disney and the contemporary cinema set such mythological creatures free to pursue and fulfill their "wild ecstasy." (Copyright 1940 Walt Disney Productions; courtesy RKO Radio Films.)

dirtiest." [10] Disney thumbed his nose at such a worldview, gleefully depicting his half-human, half-animal creations slipping off to make love in the forest. However sensuous, though, the sequence falls short of what Walt originally hoped for. Female centaurs were to have been topless African American beauties, freely sporting with Anglo males, thus breaking racial as well as sexual taboos. Disney's artists were animating the characters in such a manner until the Hays/Breen office announced that such stuff would not pass inspection, even in what was "merely" a cartoon. Reluctantly, Disney ordered his animators to (barely) cover the female breasts with delicate wreaths of flowers, though in fact several appealing and intriguing instances of total nudity remain, if only in subliminal form.

Disney's desire, we can deduce from what does appear onscreen, was to bridge the gap between primitive and pagan females and a future generation of normal though sexually liberated women. One film historian noted the "torsos and heads ... of these creatures"—though they had equestrian bodies below—"belonged to adolescent girls styled to resemble the teenager down the street." [11] In this, Disney's aim presaged that of

Hugh Hefner: to once and for all end the prevailing culture's limiting and lingering Puritanical attitudes. Particularly important was bringing about an end to the dichotomization of women by insisting, through visual example, that the nice, normal girl next door possessed full potential for human sensuality—this aspect of her being in no way diminishing her fundamental moral decency.

Disney entertainment, including *Fantasia,* consistently rejected "old-fashioned, rigid Victorian morality in the name of openness, optimism, fun, and personal happiness"[12]—that is, what came to be called "the new morality." Indeed, Disney even dared suggest, in this particular sequence's closing shot, a defense of anal sex. As two cupids pull a curtain over the romantic partners to allow them privacy, their derrieres commingle into a single heart as their asses literally kiss. Some twenty years later, Walt would revive this image for the animated closing sequence of *The Parent Trap.*

Twitter-pated
Bambi (1942)
Perri (1957)

In *Bambi,* Disney boldly announced his then-radical thesis: The inevitable arrival of sexuality, as one passes through adolescence, is not something we ought to fear, rather to enjoy and ultimately embrace as the positive core of life itself. As Bambi, Thumper, and Flower leave the innocence of childhood behind, they're warned by a wise old owl about becoming "Twitter-pated"—bewitched by some female of their respective species. Each insists this won't happen to him, as loyalty to the (male) group will remain dominant. Each, of course, is wrong. A sensuous female fawn, skunk, and bunny appear; one might believe Hefner was inspired to cast his club hostesses as "bunnies" owing to lingering memories of Thumper's wholesome yet flirtatious mate. Each male figure in time surrenders to the tender trap, and Bambi enters into a survival-of-the-fittest confrontation with a competing deer before he and Faline can mate. All in time enjoy sweet surrender, portrayed here as a natural (and innocent) continuation of childhood ramblings.

Adult-oriented films of the 1940s and '50s conversely conveyed "conflicting signals of sex as forbidden, dirty, dangerous, to be denied and lied about."[13] Understood in the context of its repressive era, *Bambi* can be read as a thinly disguised sex-education film, far ahead of its time in preparing impressionable young viewers to accept the erotic element of their upcoming lives as highly positive. This would be more obvious still in Disney's 1957 film of another Felix Salten novel, *Perri*. Since Disney always insisted on equality of the sexes, even as he did for races, *Bambi* would have been incomplete without audiences receiving equal opportunity to view nature's life cycles, particularly the sexual elements, from a female point of view. Not that sex is overemphasized among the squirrels studied in *Perri*. As in other effective examples of sex education, Disney portrays this part of life as one aspect of existence, perhaps central, offensive only when overly emphasized or unnecessarily repressed.

We meet Perri at birth, follow her through precarious survival and on to maturity, when sexuality becomes as natural for her as it was for Bambi. As Maltin notes:

> Though the word "sex" is never uttered, and the mating season is referred to as "Together Time," the film still takes a healthier and more open view of the mating ritual than any other contemporary film aimed at children, as well as a good many supposedly made for adults in this preliberated screen era.[14]

"Preliberated" is, in fact, putting it mildly. Lest we forget, as late as 1965, America's abiding Comstock Laws held that for a doctor to provide contraceptive information to a female patient (including a married one) constituted a felony, punishable by a jail term. Most purveyors of popular entertainment righteously subscribed to the attitudes embodied in these laws. Disney alone dared to differ—as always employing animals, Aesop-like, to comment on the human condition. When Perri and her mate Porro dart about, literally dancing through the woods, there's little question (as in the ancient art of terpsichore) that their movements are meant to suggest joy, happiness, and wondrous sensuality. True self-realization is impossible, Disney films suggest, without a full, unashamed acceptance of one's sexual side.

The Freudian Head of Sex
Donald's Diary (1954)
The Three Caballeros (1946)

One way to reveal the uptightness of white-bread Americans was to present such types in contrast to healthier foils. These include people from other cultures who appreciate what, during the 1960s era, would finally be hailed and accepted in America (by Dr. Alex Comfort) as the joy of sex.

THE SEX LIVES OF SQUIRRELS. At a time when most mainstream films expressed an uptight Eisenhower-era attitude, Disney employed his seemingly innocuous family entertainments as sex education films. *Perri* taught children about the joy of sweet surrender through together time in the Animal Kingdom. (Copyright 1957 Walt Disney Productions; courtesy Buena Vista Releasing.)

This, Disney achieved in *The Three Caballeros.* Donald Duck, the filmmaker's symbol of the shallow suburban conformist, journeys to Latin America, where he meets numerous attractive women of color. Like so many renowned literary conceptions, from those in Mark Twain's *The Innocents Abroad* (1896) to Henry James's title character in *The American* (1877), Donald appears embarrassingly naïve in contrast with the more sophisticated (sexually speaking) society he encounters. Shortly, he surrenders to his senses, apparently for the first time.

Back home, in the company of fiancée Daisy, Donald automatically slipped into the expected role of gentleman. In films like *Donald's Diary* (1954), he squired about town the woman he would someday marry. One real-life counterpart, a male survivor of the fifties, recalled his own extended stay in sexual purgatory:

> I felt that if I were sexual with someone, that indicated that I didn't respect them. I could be sexual with someone I didn't care for, but

not with someone I did care for. The fact that I was never sexual with anyone is because I never dated anyone I didn't care for.[15]

Daisy, conversely, appeared to fully accept the era's role-playing—"the rules" of dating as they existed in the 1940s and '50s for a savvy if unquestioning woman:

> If you go all the way with someone, he'll leave you and marry a "nice" girl. At the other end of the scale, a reputation of promiscuity was the equivalent of inciting panic—or wholesale dumping of market shares. In any market situation, value is the perception of value . . . market psychology [in the fifties] described a woman's sexual favors in terms of "giving it away" or "saving it."[16]

Daisy calculatedly (as we grasp from the look in her eyes) "saves it." Perhaps this at least partially explains Donald's regular outbursts of crazed temper.

Now, though, Latin America enraptures the heretofore Puritanical Duck with its sensual aura. The lyric presentation of coastal "Baia" features soft images of water and mountains, set to a relentlessly erotic beat. This so captivates Donald that he dives headfirst into the melee, joining old friend Joe Carioca (from 1943's *Saludos Amigos*) as Donald's conventional restraints give way to an overpowering libido. He's intoxicated by the sway of the samba, as performed by a lush, captivating, yet sweet, street dancer (Aurora Miranda). Trying (with little success) to divest himself of Anglo uptightness, Donald competes for her attentions with local boys, as tambourines and drums further heighten the ever intensifying atmosphere. After Donald loses her, Donald, Joe, and new friend Panchito head for Mexico. "Pretty girls," Donald mutters over and over again, enjoying new (for him) erotic sensations. Shortly, he's the era's Ugly American incarnate, pursuing with embarrassing abandon the bikini-clad bathing beauties on Acapulco Beach. One shocked critic noted: "Sex rears its pretty but definitely Freudian head" as Donald Duck "becomes a very lusty Drake as well as a girl-chaser to rival Harpo Marx."[17]

Donald's hysteria reaches its height when he surrenders to the jarring beat of the Jesusita. Carmen Molina, in drag, appears coolly butch in her skintight leather vaquero outfit. The breathtaking dominatrix employs a black whip to subdue, with calculated cruelty, a stultified Donald. Around them, phallic cacti, objective correlatives for the Duck's rising maleness, explode upward every time she slaps down her whip, much to

Donald's masochistic delight. About this sequence, one reviewer fussily complained:

> A somewhat physical romance between a two-foot duck and a full-sized woman, though one happens to be a cartoon and the other pleasantly rounded and certainly mortal, is one of those things that might disconcert less squeamish authorities than the Hays office. . . . A sequence involving the duck, the young lady, and a long alley of animated cactus plants would probably be considered suggestive in a less innocent medium.[18]

The New Yorker is considered sophisticated, particularly in comparison to Walt's supposed brand of "innocent" family entertainment. Yet Disney openly embraced a daring sexuality, contrasting with the critic's elitist sniffing.

Enjoying the Body Beautiful
Make Mine Music (1946)
Melody Time (1948)

Sociologists concur that audiences of the late 1940s weren't "ready for the joy of sex, or even the body beautiful."[19] Whenever a gorgeous woman—Lana Turner, Rita Hayworth, Ava Gardner—appeared onscreen in the era's film noirs, she was likely to be both "cunning and destructive."[20] As always atypical, Disney projected a more enlightened attitude, as sequences from the era's feature-length anthology-films reveal.

Make Mine Music begins with "A Rustic Ballad,"[21] Disney's variation on the legendary Hatfield/McCoy feud, the families here redubbed the Martins and the Coys. Adult filmmakers proceeded from more conventional premises. The physical love of young people escalates the bloodshed in *Roseanna McCoy* (1949) and actually causes the feud to begin in *The Hatfields and the McCoys* (TV, 1975). Disney, on the other hand, portrays sexual attraction as socially curative, much as Shakespeare had in *Romeo and Juliet*. When the young people from each camp meet, fall madly in love, and then marry (in Walt's version if not in Will's), the feud abruptly ends. Twenty years after this film's release, hippies would insist: "Make love, not war!" The phrase underscores Disney's viewpoint, as spirits from deceased feuding members of both families drift up to the clouds, forced to peer down in consternation as young Henry and Grace couple.

In "A Jazz Interlude" (aka, "All the Cats Join In"), Disney graphically displayed the female anatomy in a manner no other Hollywood filmmaker of that time would have dared attempt, much less been able to realize on-screen. A pretty teenage girl receives a phone call from her boyfriend, asking for a date at the malt shop. The camera follows her upstairs, where in her room she undresses with pagan abandon. Her body is on full display as she showers, then slips into tight clothing, heading off to meet him. Such actions on the part of a young female, in more typical 1940s films, always indicated "a bad girl." Moral without being moralistic, Disney presented the sexual young woman as a healthy role model.

Melody Time went further still. "Blame It on the Samba" reunites Donald and Joe Carioca, frustrated following their failure in the previous film to find mates. The boys are painted blue, the color here symbolizing both of its pop-culture associations, sadness and sexuality. Panchito arrives and all three enjoy an immense cocktail. Alcohol, if not overdone, is always acceptable in Disney entertainment. Disney's studio was, in fact, the only one in which beer was openly served at the commissary.[22] In this segment, the drink contains a beautiful woman (Ethel Smith) playing piano. The boys leap into the concoction to "dance" with her. At sequence's end, all appear ready to take the attraction to another level.

By far, though, the film's most memorable story is "Pecos Bill." A natural man, the happy-go-lucky redheaded cowboy rides on his horse Widowmaker to varied violent adventures. Until, that is, Bill's first glimpse of Sluefoot Sue, gliding down the Pecos River on the back of a giant fish. Sue's abbreviated outfit rivals any 1960s Carnaby Street miniskirt. Part Venus on the half shell, part Vargas girl, while also providing a prelude to the *Playboy* centerfold, Sue is the sensuous woman as sexual adventuress, but not, significantly, the conventional sexual predator. "Pecos Bill" can be read as Disney's deconstruction and decimation of the old myth, propagated by endless B-Westerns aimed at preadolescents, that in the final fadeout, a cowboy would rather kiss his horse than the girl. Bill does indeed kiss Widowmaker, but that occurs early on in the film, before he catches his first glance of Sue and falls into a fit of "mad love" that, even by today's standards, appears remarkably vivid in its vision of sexually induced hysteria.

Moreover, Walt diminishes another myth. Numerous sociologists have written about an "age-old sexual injustice, the male burden of performance, with all its attendant ego risk."[23] Eustace Chesser—the era's per-

AN ALTERNATIVE TO ALFRED HITCHCOCK. The most famous shower scene in film history occurs in *Psycho* (1960), as a beautiful woman is violently assaulted while most vulnerable. The Disney Vision does not include any such attacks on sensuous women, joyfully celebrating their naturalness. (Copyright Walt Disney Productions; courtesy Buena Vista Releasing.)

ceptive analyst of then-predominant and utterly unliberated male-female relations—noted that the man was expected to "educate his wife, one step at a time, in the art of joyous mating." He had better perform that task well, Chesser continued, owing to a "strange intuition of woman" that "warns her against the nervous lover. . . . He is among the enemies of women."[24] A problem for most men and women of the forties and fifties, perhaps, both in real life and on the screen, though never in Disney. When Bill, despite overt machismo, proves unable to take the initiative, she (clearly sophisticated about sex) seizes his arms, silently, sweetly, and sympathetically (in a totally nonthreatening manner) shows Bill what to do. When Disney's men prove naïve, sexually (which is most of the time), the women—knowing, sophisticated, yet never criticized in any film's context for their full understanding of sexuality, whether it's the result of prior experience or natural instinct—take charge. Bill responds, though initially he cannot control his excitement, coming all too soon—this

THE NEED FOR SEX EDUCATION. Pecos Bill, overwhelmed by Sue's sensuality, experiences implied premature ejaculation via his "guns" (TOP). She then administers a sweet sexual education in one of the first Hollywood films to depict a woman of experience in a highly positive light (BOTTOM). (Copyright Walt Disney Productions; courtesy Buena Vista Releasing.)

symbolized by phallic pistols that hop out of their holsters and fire full wads into the air.

In time, tragedy is precipitated by Sue's unfortunate subscription to an abiding dictum: "Sexy women were called 'bombshells,' but were expected to tame their fleshy bodies inside Bestform bras and Lovable latex girdles."[25] Sue makes the mistake of wearing a grotesque bustle on her wedding day, signifying that side of her female psyche which has not broken with conventions for women. Still, Sue is a forward-looking female who insists on proving equality by riding Bill's horse. Her untenable combination of conflicting values destroys everything. While liberated Sue easily subdues the bronco, traditional Sue's bustle begins bouncing, sending her flying off toward the moon.

Blondes Have More Fun
Cinderella (1950)
Adventures in Music: Melody (1953)

Disney's first animated fairy tale of the 1950s featured his first blonde heroine. Cinderella was the original among the decade's blondes, presaging even Monroe, if not onscreen (Marilyn debuted with a bit in 1948's *Scudda-Hoo! Scudda-Hay!*), then at least as popular icon. "The blonde" was about to again alter in meaning. Except for rare occasions when she played an outright villainess (1953's *Niagara*) or equally rare good girl (1955's *The Seven Year Itch*), Marilyn's most memorable "loose girl" roles—*The Asphalt Jungle* (1950), *All about Eve* (1950), *River of No Return* (1954), *Bus Stop* (1956), *The Misfits* (1961)—redefined women by eliminating any easy dichotomizing. Morally flawed, inwardly troubled, yet inherently decent, the blonde of the 1950s emerged as a person with real problems and myriad failings, all the while harboring a deep desire to do the right thing. But if blondes had more fun, they usually ended up alone. 20th Century Fox followed *Gentlemen Prefer Blondes* (1953) with *Gentlemen Marry Brunettes* (1955), the title of Anita Loos's sequel underlining the era's attitude. However "preferred" a blonde may have been (before marriage as trophy girlfriend, later as trophy mistress), the brunette—conservative, traditional, respectable—remained the great icon of marriageable material. Suburbanite Kirk Douglas might stray with the seductively trampy Kim Novak in *Strangers When We Meet* (1959); in the end, though, he quietly returned to soft-spoken, classy wife Barbara Rush.

Disney challenged all that. "In contrast with the girlish appearance and prepubescent sensibility of earlier [female] protagonists such as Snow White, Disney's animated females in the 1950s also began to display a noticeable, if wholesome, sex appeal."[26] Hardly platinum, Cinderella is a natural blonde. Indeed, *everything* about her is natural, in the most positive (and philosophically Romantic) sense of that term. In the opening, Cinderella rises from bed, utterly at ease with her nude body in a way that no other positively portrayed screen woman was at that time. Her casualness induces the uptight audience to likewise relax about sexual matters. Cinderella opens wide the window, allowing every aspect of nature—sunlight's warmth, birds singing—into the "civilized" (corrupt) house she shares with her unpleasant stepmother and stepsisters.

Such an openness appears considerably less shocking today. It's important to note, then, that in "the fifties—hard as it may be to recall in the era of [the] organic—*natural* was a dirty word."[27] Not, though, in Disney's lexicon. His heroine's naturalness, even more than her beauty, is what attracts the prince. At the ball, every other woman tries to outdo the next with forced shows of sophistication. She wins him by simply being herself. The prince's father, a Disney addition, is hardly the older man as blocking-character, interfering with the interests of the young. Unabashedly, the king insists on sexuality as an important part of one's mental and physical health. He wants a grandchild, which is why, in Disney's retelling, the ball is staged. Not (as in the Perrault and Grimm sources) to produce a ceremonial marriage, rather a coupling based on the bedroom—rare for 1950s films in general, unheard of for a family film.

If the passage of years makes Disney's scenario seem less daring, we must consciously recall there was

> a larger moral panic about sexual control and identity in postwar America. This was, after all, an era when novels from Vladimir Nabokov's *Lolita* (1955) to Grace Metalious's *Peyton Place* (1956) were threatened by censorship, when saucy little sex comedies like Otto Preminger's *The Moon Is Blue* (1953) were tamed for moviegoers by the removal of obscenities like "virgin" and "seduction," and when Cincinnati businessman Charles Keating (later indicted for his role in the savings and loan scandals in the 1980s) started Citizens for Decent Literature and declared holy war on *Playboy*.[28]

As a one-man woman, Cinderella balances her natural qualities with a traditionalism that endeared her to 1950s audiences. But Disney also insisted that less substantial blondes likewise ought to be treated with respect.

In *Adventures in Music: Melody,* Professor Owl conducts his treetop schooling for birds. He attempts to discover the inner inspiration of each pupil, advancing Disney's vision of the ideal educator, and notably radical at a time when society dictated that teaching ought to propagandize then-current modes of conformity. For some class members, the inner self proves intellectual; for others, emotional. Susie Sparrow, the school flirt, finds hers in romantic love. Rather than portray her as a negatively trashy foil to the rest and, as such, the butt of cruel humor, Disney renders her situation with obvious affection as Susie bounces from one beau to the next. She may be the resident slut, but that hardly qualifies her for condescension or condemnation in Disney's more enlightened value scheme.

Tinker Bell as Centerfold
Peter Pan (1953)

Disney first dared to do what Hugh Hefner, in *Playboy,* would shortly become (in)famous for: the demystification of sex, particularly the female body. Parallels between the two empire-builders are as striking as they are surprising. Each hailed from a middle-class, relatively rural background (Disney's in Missouri, Hefner's in Illinois). Each in his time traveled to a metropolitan center (Kansas City and Chicago, respectively), taking various jobs in art, entertainment, and advertising. Each conceived and created an actual place (Disneyland, the Playboy Club) where fans could come in contact with beloved fantasy creations. In the early days of television, each personally hosted a TV series based on his already-existing "world"; later, each inspired a pay-cable channel, recognizable by either man's personal logo, in each case a pair of animal ears.

Hefner's decision to bedeck his hostesses in rabbit ears takes on new meaning when we recall Disney's original conception for his own corporate insignia had been Oswald. How interesting to note, then, that when ABC broadcast *Wonderful World of Disney: 40 Years of Television Magic* (December 10, 1994), tributes to Walt's lasting impact, offered as expected by veterans of Disney entertainment (Fess Parker, Debbie Allen, Tom Hanks), were interspersed with what must have struck most audience members as incongruous comments from Hefner. "What was really special about Disney," he explained, "was that he gave us a magic kingdom at Disneyland, and also 'a magic kingdom of the imagination.'" To a degree, Hefner seemed to be speaking about himself. In the realm of adult entertainment, he in fact presented precisely that. "[Disney] represents some of the best of [what is in us as a people]: The dream, and the sheer pleasure, of being a child." There's certainly something childlike and innocent (if also adolescent in the arrested sense) about "Uncle" (as more than one former centerfold girl refers to him) Hef's own vision, a criticism that, in less sexual terms, has also been directed at "Uncle" Walt. "Like most American boys, I grew up with Mickey Mouse," Hefner continued. "The early comic strips . . . were real cliff-hangers. [Disney] had a big influence on me when I was a kid."

That influence can be seen in the manner that Hefner achieved for the grown-ups what Walt had for kids. Each presented his audience with an image of sexuality as wholesome and healthy, contradicting abiding attitudes of the 1950s. In this context, the ultimate connection between Disney and Hefner is Marilyn Monroe. Her own career was certainly paradoxical. Last of the old-fashioned Hollywood glamour girls, Marilyn—however incongruously—was also first among a new breed of sexual pioneers. Nude photographs of the legend-to-be, dating back to her financially distraught prestardom period, had been making the rounds of bus-station men's rooms (as "calendar art") for years. However much that helped publicize a more open sexuality, the déclassé context served to keep sex sleazy. As one social observer succinctly put it: "The 1950s were profoundly conflicted about the body and sexual display: *Playboy* was first published in December 1953 (with the era's other sexual icon, Marilyn Monroe, as its first centerfold offering), but sex itself was viewed as something dangerous and explosive."[29] As to Marilyn, in her earliest incarnations, "For the average, confused American male during this transitional period, the image of Monroe could be conceived as an update of the old vamp concept: Something to be at once desired and dreaded."[30]

Playboy would not receive widespread acceptance until the early 1960s, when its views increasingly reflected a nation's rapidly changing attitudes. For the time being, sexual panic remained the order of the day during the 1950s. "Don't use the word 'naked,'" literary agent "Bradley Holmes" tells a young protégée in Grace Metalious's scandalous first novel, *Peyton Place*. "Naked has the sound of a rock being turned over to expose maggots."[31] Hefner's aim was to change that. He believed that a glossy, upscale publication including mild eroticism (in moderation, presented amid a context of literary elements) could make nudity respectable. Simultaneously with

"PUT JUST ENOUGH CLOTHES ON HER SO WE DON'T GET BUSTED." Cementing the relationship between Disney and Hugh Hefner, Walt's Tinker Bell in *Peter Pan* was modeled on the same nude photograph of Marilyn Monroe that would be used as *Playboy*'s first centerfold; film and magazine appeared simultaneously. (Copyright 1953 Walt Disney Productions; courtesy Buena Vista Releasing.)

the first edition hitting newsstands, Disney's *Peter Pan* arrived on movie screens, introducing a Tinker Bell who appeared anything but the traditional ball of light. Walt himself admitted he'd instructed his artists to use the nude photographs of Marilyn as their model. Several Disney illustrators later confided that he had implied they ought to "put just enough clothes on her so we don't get busted." [32] The overt sexuality hardly went unnoticed. *Newsweek* reported that Tink "not only throws off star dust in the proper tradition, but she is also a particularly endearing little vixen compounded of blond hair, feminine curves, and a pout," resulting in a party doll who proves "just a little too bosomy to squeeze through an oversized keyhole." [33] The reviewer could have easily been describing the first *Playboy* centerfold—and, when one considers the Marilyn connection, in effect was.

A Natural Woman
The Sword and the Rose (1953)

Even in the mid-fifties, when a retro-Victorian standard dictated conventional relationships among suburbanites, "for both Mickey and Minnie Mouse and Donald and Daisy Duck," Disney offered a forward-looking vision of "an awkwardly defined relationship [that] suggested cohabitation but explicitly rejected marriage."[34] This, in opposition to the general attitude:

> In its repressed way, the Fifties were the last days of the Garden of Eden—after the fall, to be sure, but before Masters and Johnson, before Ruth Westheimer, and *Good Sex* on cable TV. Ignorance may not have been bliss, but with little experience, few expectations, and no sense of the entitlement that would come a decade later, invidious comparisons had to be rare.[35]

In truth, sex—the act, if never openly (or healthily) spoken of—ran rampant in the fifties. The motor hotel (later, shortened to "motel") was created in and for postwar car-culture America. This travel innovation hit its peak when forty thousand new properties were built during the fifties—not all employed for vacation or business purposes. Likewise, drive-in movies, originally conceived as outdoor entertainment facilities for families, soon became known as passion pits, frequented by newly mobile teenagers.

The unmentionable reality of sex was particularly obvious in the second installment of Disney's British trilogy, following *Robin Hood* (1952) and predating *Rob Roy* (1954). Despite top billing going as always to Richard Todd, the focal role was its female lead. By focusing on Glynis Johns as Mary Tudor, sister to Henry VIII, Disney reimagined English history to comment on the role of women in contemporary society. Sixteenth-century Britain, though visualized with an admirably painstaking attention to accuracy of detail, serves as an objective correlative for America in the fifties. Mary herself appears as a sexual revolutionary against the staid system. Her first onscreen act consists of manipulating her seeming friend Buckingham (Michael Gough) into a bout with a French wrestler, which Buckingham wins. Despite Buckingham's obvious fascination with Mary, she has eyes only for a visitor, Charles Brandon (Todd), "a gentleman without title," as such Disney's common-man hero.

A WOMAN OF SUBSTANCE. Feminist historians perceive Mary Tudor as a seminal protofeminist, daring to stand up against Henry VIII's patriarchal notion that an aristocratic woman ought to be married off for political purposes. No male Hollywood filmmaker considered the story of Mary's "free love" with a commoner worthy of cinematic treatment except Walt Disney. (Copyright 1953 Walt Disney Productions; courtesy RKO Releasing.)

Representing a new breed, Brandon plans to relocate in the New World, implying Disney's conception of this historical character as the American spirit in embryo.

Shortly, Brandon is manipulated by Mary into a match with Buckingham. After he wins, Brandon is recruited as captain in the palace guard.

Mary is fascinated (and sexually aroused) by this fellow's lack of pretension, particularly when he treats her abruptly.

> LADY MARGARET: I have never seen the like!
> MARY TUDOR: Neither have I. He acted like a *man!*

The real woman—assertive, independent, intellectual, potentially sexual—can only be drawn to a man worthy of her. Not according to rank, station, or birth, but in a typically American sense: proving his worth through positive action. What seemed a simple sporting event actually invokes a sense of survival of the fittest at work in the human sphere. Like those male animals who win females through a combination of brawn and brain in Disney's nature films, Brandon proves himself superior.

The conflict between Henry's wife, retro woman Catherine of Aragon (Rosalie Crutchley), and the modern, liberated heroine erupts over Princess Mary's upcoming ball. Numerous nobles haven't received invitations, which outrages the queen. Mary takes gleeful pleasure in small transgressions against the "correct" order. Not surprisingly, then, she invites her new captain of guards, flaunting another convention by allowing a virtual commoner to attend and expressing Disney's ongoing ideal of a future society without classes. A true romantic, Mary cannot achieve her seduction of Brandon within castle walls. They must be alone, and alone *in nature.* During a hunt in the forest, she arranges to have her horse dart away at the perfect moment, when no one but Brandon is nearby. Shortly, she and her rescuer embrace in the woods. What they discover is not a Classicist's heart of darkness but a Romantic's Eden recovered—the perfect place for pastoral romance.

As always in Disney, she initiates sexual contact, insisting on a first kiss. He responds, like the hippie youth to come, by picking wildflowers for her, insisting that these constitute his entire fortune.

> BRANDON: The only wealth that I may ever hold are these flowers in my hand.

Disney's role model for young women, Mary makes clear that money and title mean nothing to her. She wants him to compose a love sonnet, the equivalent of requesting he write a soft-rock song expressing his love. Aretha Franklin could have been speaking of Disney's Mary, and her relationship to Brandon, in 1967:

You make me feel
Like a natural woman!

With no intention of accepting her brother's plan to marry her off to the aged king of France, Mary goes so far as to use her blossoming sexuality to deflect such an arrangement. After she retires to her rooms, avoiding Gallic ambassadors, Henry huffily brings them to see her. Naked under a sheet, Mary dangles a shapely leg in defiance of aristocratic decorum. Uptight males hurry away when she threatens to rise and parade herself au naturel. The filmmaker takes obvious delight in her charming naughtiness, as does the audience. Later, when a fully dressed Mary is cornered, she speaks her piece:

MARY: It's time you all understand that Mary Tudor will marry a beggar if she chooses!

The Mary Tudor of Disney's imagination serves as predecessor not only to Hefner's call for the sexual liberation of women, but also to the subsequent popularization of women's rights, and the liberation of their souls and psyches as well. Though Disney would appear, from what we see on-screen, to agree with Hefner's belief in the beauty of the female body, he far surpasses that other significant influencer of popular culture by also addressing issues involving the emotional, intellectual, and spiritual liberation of women.

THE YOUNG AND THE RESTLESS. Disney films, it is generally believed, offered impressionable audiences perfect role models of teenagers who were less sexual than their counterparts in the era's youth-exploitation films. Not true, as *The Light in the Forest* makes abundantly clear. (Copyright 1958 Walt Disney Productions; courtesy Buena Vista Releasing.)

5

"If It Feels Good, Do It!"
Disney and the Sexual Revolution

The mystical Fairy with the Blue Hair of *Pinocchio* turns out to be Marilyn Monroe, blonde hair and all.
—DOROTHY SAYERS, 1953

The message of *Sleeping Beauty*: what may seem like a period of deathlike passivity at the end of childhood is nothing but a time of quiet growth and preparation, from which the [female] will awaken mature, ready for sexual union.
—BRUNO BETTELHEIM, 1975

*P*aradoxical as it may at first sound, all revolutionaries are at heart reactionaries. Their various rebellions—cultural and political, intellectual or emotional—would never occur without the stimulus of whatever came directly beforehand. For the social as well as sexual revolutionaries of the 1960s, all their attitudes and behavior existed as an explosive response to the fifties, most notably the Eisenhower era's mainstream celebration of a conformist ideology. As one keen observer noted about that period: "The 1950s in this country were a decade far more obsessed with the horrors of bodily secretions and smells than the nineteenth century."[1] Self-help books written to educate average people held that the all-but-unmentionable act be contained in a society that strove for a morality more rigid even than that of the Victorian era, parents now responsible for what others previously oversaw. One such tome insisted:

In a world of chaos and in an era in which national and international integrity have fallen to a low level, there remains only the solid structure of the home to form the basis for the re-establishment of the ancient standards of virtue.[2]

Any gains made toward sexual enlightenment during the intense period of sexual revolution that characterized the 1920s were gone and virtually forgotten. Unconsciously obeying the Marxist dialectic, the pendulum had swung back the other way, if to a more fierce extreme.

There was, however, an unofficial "underground." The Beats—or, as they were derogatorily referred to, Beatniks—had been scoffing at such straight values while living in the cocoon of a counterculture, celebrating freedom from constraint in such places as New York's Greenwich Village and San Francisco's Haight-Ashbury district. Novelist Jack Kerouac celebrated their lifestyles in novels like *On the Road* and *The Subterraneans*. The Beats' vision and style would never make the kind of inroads into mainstream America that would occur when the hippie movement became (albeit briefly) the very epicenter of fashion and thought between 1967 and 1970. Still, they were noticed, at least by impressionable youth. The virtually overnight embracing of rock 'n' roll by teenagers in 1956–1957, its big beat affronting their parents, can be read as an acceptance by suburban youth of the Beat Generation's views on sexual liberation—as such, an intended slap in the face to the strict and rigid code of their suburban parents.

As always, Walt stood with the rebels. Parents may have been, by this point, programmed to believe that Disney represented the last refuge from what they considered a threatening new order of things. Understandably, they breathed a collective sigh of relief whenever one of his films appeared at the local theater. Here, they assumed, was "safe" entertainment. What those kids encountered, however, provided their initial entry into an alternative vision that rejected the era's mainstream conservatism, providing a liberal/progressive mind-set on all issues, particularly those relating to society's sexual mores.

Cinematic Sex Education
The Vanishing Prairie (1953)
Secrets of Life (1956)

"The Big Lie" of the fifties was that "if nobody was doing it, nobody had any responsibility to instruct us."[3] Adults continued to believe (or pretend they believed) the preposterous notion that teenagers weren't engaging (or even interested) in sex. Why, then, consider sex education? Disney saw things differently, instructing young people by offering a commonsense vision of the facts of life, in most cases skirting censors by doing so under the guise of harmless nature documentaries, the *True-Life Adventures*.

While spending two years capturing images of the American West, N. Paul Kenworthy Jr. and a team of naturalist-photographers amassed more than 120,000 feet of 16 mm film. This they delivered to Disney and James Algar, whom Walt had assigned to transform an excess of riches into a compact film. In the process of reducing the footage to 30,000 feet, Disney and Algar became captivated by one sequence. Accidentally, Kenworthy and company had captured the birth of a buffalo calf. The censors, however, had other ideas, and not only in Bible Belt locales. Incredibly, in "sophisticated" New York, the state censorship board refused to permit *Prairie* to be screened until the offending sequence was excised. As one film chronicler reflected:

> That Walt Disney, the purveyor of the screen's finest family entertainment, should ever have censorship problems was the target of many a snicker in 1954—and a cause of considerable embarrassment for the New York board of censors.[4]

Fully understood, the controversy reveals the distinction between Disney as perceived and Disney as he really was. The filmmaker himself defended his decision to include the sequence: "The birth scene would never have appeared on the screen if I believed it might offend an audience," and he wryly noted that "it would be a shame if New York children had to believe the stork brings buffaloes, too."[5] Disney had reinforced the old stork myth in *Dumbo* (1941). Now, he forsook reassuring fairy tales, conveying the realities of life to children in a judicious, sensible manner that would not threaten impressionable psyches. The board relented, though only after the American Civil Liberties Union—scorned by the then-powerful McCarthy element as defenders of communists, Negroes, and other supposedly "dangerous" elements, Disney now included in their number—lodged a complaint. *The New Yorker*'s reviewer noted that, much like the buffalo calf in the film, censors "must at one time have been born," adding: "I lived through the scene, and I suspect you will, too."[6] Happily, the facts of life were left intact.

Arguably, *The Facts of Life* is what Walt would have liked to call one subsequent film, released under the less incendiary title *Secrets of Life*. "This is an authentic story of nature's secret world," the opening crawl tells us, "of her strange and intricate designs for survival . . . and her many methods of perpetuating life." Other nature films included the concept of sexual reproduction; *Secrets* focused almost exclusively on it. Reproduction among every living element, from plants with throbbing buds to bees fashioning the honeycomb and ants scrambling through tunnels toward their queen, was entertainingly catalogued. Time-lapse photography transformed the excited, extending stems of plant-forms into G-rated phallic symbols, each "obeying the ancient urge to propagate its kind."

For the grand finale, volcanoes were filmed and edited in such a manner as to appear orgasms of the earth, satiated only after making contact with their female counterpart, the sea. Women's roles, as always, are fully depicted, the drones' worship of the queen bee culminating in the wedding flight. A quarter century before Bo Derek would, in Blake Edwards's *10*, surrender to sensuality while listening to Ravel's *Bolero*, Disney employed that musical piece for the same purpose while chronicling the sex life of plants.

"We Wear Short-Shorts!"
Disneyland/Walt Disney Presents (1954–1961)
The Mickey Mouse Club (1955–1958)
The Hardy Boys (1956)

When Disney unveiled his first television series, a scantily clad Tinker Bell swept about, whisking away cartoon curtains for the host to appear. TV was at the time a considerably more conservative medium even than motion pictures. As reruns endlessly reveal, Desi Arnaz and Lucille Ball, a long-married couple in real life while playing one on *I Love Lucy* (1951–1957), were not permitted to utter the word "pregnant" (much less allow Lucy to "show") when she was with child in fact *and* fiction. Lucy and Ricky, like all other supposedly typical (in truth, grotesquely idealized) TV married couples, slept in separate beds. The only exception could be found in Walt's TV work. On the Disney hour, Davy and Polly Crockett didn't bother to slip into the single bed in their room of the log cabin, instead making impassioned love on the hardwood floor before a roaring fire during his brief leave from the Indian wars.

Disney's incarnations of Davy and Polly, ostensibly living in 1813, had apparently read Eustace Chesser. All but forgotten today, she provided a voice crying out in the fifties' sexual wilderness, shockingly insisting that in a marriage, both partners must always be "frankly aspiring to become perfect lovers."[7] In the *Crockett* series, Davy never recovers from the death of his wife, Polly; in real life, the coonskin congressman was remarried within the year.[8] Disney improved on the Crockett shows by pushing for ever greater realism about adult marital (and sexual) matters in *Tales of Texas John Slaughter*. Following the untimely death of his first wife, John remarries and fathers more children with the second Mrs. Slaughter. They share—not surprisingly considering that this is Disney, though shockingly in terms of television depictions of adult couples at that time—a single bed at his Arizona ranch.

On afternoon TV, during the children's hour, Disney might have been expected to pull back a bit. The opposite proved true, as Disney dared to push all the then-dangerous buttons. A huge hit with the small fry, *The Mickey Mouse Club* introduced an ensemble of twenty-four child performers. One emerged as a star, Annette Funicello becoming an overnight sex symbol for millions of young boys (and not a few fathers) out there watching in televisionland. The hundreds of adoring letters that adolescents mailed in each week had more to do with Annette's physical attributes than any skills she may have had at dancing, singing, or acting.[9] Adult observers noted that Annette displayed "the classic Latin features—a creamy velvet complexion, lustrous eyes, naturally wavy hair."[10] As Annette matured during the following seasons, journalists noted that her "full-busted" quality helped explain why boys reacted to her precisely as their dads, if in secret, did to *Playboy*'s centerfolds. Again, Disney and Hefner shared a conception of the nondichotomized woman as displaying "innocent sensuality."[11]

In the summer of 1956, a fashion innovation known as short-shorts appeared, revealing more of a woman's leg than had ever been seen in public. Not surprisingly, much of the country reacted with outrage, imposing a "banned in Boston" mentality. Short-shorts were outlawed as obscene not only in the rural South, but in such seemingly cosmopolitan places as White Plains, New York, where women who failed to comply with restrictions were arrested.[12] Rock 'n' roll, the musical voice of an emerging rebellious youth, responded by defending the fashion statement. As the Royal Teens defiantly announced:

> Who wears short-shorts?
> *We* wear short-shorts!

But their defense would not hit the airwaves until 1958.

Disney, always siding with youth against the Establishment, was the first to positively respond by legitimizing the phenomenon in the least likely medium. In the fall of 1956, he premiered (as part of *The Mickey Mouse Club*) *The Hardy Boys,* an afternoon serial based on Franklin W. Dixon's perennially popular books for young readers. In the Disney Version, Iola (Carole Anne Campbell) is a twelve-year-old girl living down the street from the title heroes. She regularly roller-skates by the Hardy home, wearing the shortest of short-shorts. This does not qualify her as a dangerous local Lolita, however—only a typical, healthy (and sexy) teenage girl.

Appearing on any other show, the image might have provoked outrage. Contained within Disney entertainment, the opposite occurred. Swiftly, the controversy abated. Importantly, then, Disney championed not only a freer sexuality for men, but also women, an absolutely radical position in the fifties. Lest we forget,

> if one believed what one read in the second Kinsey Report (and most middle-Americans did indeed assume this the be-all and end-all on sex, as irrevocably etched in stone as the Ten Commandments), women (that is, decent, normal, everyday suburbanite women) were, by their very nature, repulsed by men's bodies. Moreover, they (as compared to the cheap, trashy prostitute mutant form of woman, dismissed as a genetic throwback on the evolutionary ladder) had little or no interest in sexual activity, other than for its reproductive importance.[13]

More Victorian even than the Victorians, at least in theory and principle, the American fifties middle class accepted what now seems an absurd myth: If any such woman were to become excited during sexual activity, even with her husband in the process of trying to create a baby, there was something seriously wrong with her. Depending on her degree of shame afterward, such a woman might secretly attempt to deal with her "problem," or sneak off to visit a psychiatrist (more likely than not, male), who would attempt to "cure" her of such a sickness. Before women could move on to other forms of liberation—intellectual and emotional, financial or social—they had to achieve sexual liberation, in spirit as well as body, accepting that in this sphere, they had the same rights as men. Few elements of mainstream culture dared to advance this idea. One of the rare places that such then-outrageous notions were promoted was, surprisingly enough, in the context of Disney's "family" entertainments.

Call of the Wild
Pollyanna (1960)

All at once, the Eisenhower era was over, the pendulum about to swing once more in the opposite direction. From their opening hours, the 1960s offered a dialectic to '50s thinking and behavior. In 1960, the first contraceptive pill, Enovidone, was created and marketed. Shortly, middlebrow entertainment, in the form of the James Bond series, portrayed casual sex as not only acceptable but enviable. Though *Playboy* had been around since 1954, Hefner's publication had not immediately been understood as something entirely other than such preexisting sleazy girlie magazines as *Swank* and *Titter*. Now, and virtually overnight, all-American college boys openly enjoyed the magazine, often claiming to buy it for the quality articles and fiction. Many mothers purchased subscriptions for their sons as Christmas presents. More notable, "nice" girls, including respected A-list movie starlets and coeds at posh universities, posed nude for the magazine, where they were identified by their real names. Young men who gazed at their glamorous images did not perceive them in the same light that men of the 1950s had ogled Bettie Page and her contemporaries in sleazy pulp publications: i.e., as threatening objects of dark desire or nervous derision. These were the girls they hoped to meet, date, marry.

A complete turnabout in values had occurred in popular culture and the mainstream ideology that it both reflected and helped to create. The sixties were to the fifties what England's Romantic era had been to the Age of Reason, the Roaring Twenties to the late Victorian age. But while Disney entertainment paved the way, the filmmaker never approved of casual abandonment to the pleasure principle. In the context of the Disney canon, *Fantasia's* orgy sequence served less as a suggestion of what we ought to emulate, in place of Puritanical posturing, than a necessary corrective to the opposite extreme. Long overdue was a healthy, sensible Golden Mean. This represented precisely what all great thinkers, beginning with the ancient Greeks, had proposed and what Disney always conveyed. Like Shakespeare's Romeo and Juliet, Disney's role-model lovers in his 1960s films opt, at the woman's insistence, for the sanctity of marriage before the couple consummates their romantic relationship. This may sound like the opposite of sixties-era hipness, though in truth the youth-rebellion generation swiftly moved beyond the free-sex ideal of the decade's early years, toward a free-love reality as the seventies approached.

As Paul Stookey, who like Walt sensed the need for maintaining traditional values if in a progressive context, postulated in "The Wedding Song":

> Well, the man shall leave his mother,
> And the woman leave her home.
> They shall travel on together
> Where two are joined in one.
> As it was at the beginning,
> It will be until the end.
> Woman draws her life from man,
> And then gives it back again.

Such a sensibility proves identical to Disney's. In *Pollyanna*, however attracted Aunt Polly's Swedish maid, Nancy (Nancy Olson), may be to George (James Drury), she will not let him go "too far" until she's certain that he wants a companion for life, not merely a Playmate of the Month. Nancy's decision in no way implies she's uninterested in sex (clearly, she's excited), which would qualify her as a Victorian-era image of the American woman, one who embodies the period during which the film is set. That isn't the case, nor is Nancy playing games (she makes her values clearly known to George). This distinguishes her from the supposedly "cute" teasers so prevalent in post–Production Code films. Nancy resembles Juliet, the strong-willed young woman—wise beyond her years—who, in the balcony scene, makes certain that Romeo is totally committed:

ROMEO: Would thou leave me so unsatisfied?
JULIET (concerned): What satisfaction would thou have tonight?
ROMEO: The exchange of thy true-love's vows for mine.
JULIET (relieved): Thou hadst *that* before thou asked for it!

Similarly, Nancy demands (and, as a result, receives) total commitment. This includes a solid dose of sexuality, which, in its proper perspective, will complement all other aspects of a full and lasting relationship.

Still, Nancy regularly slips away from the mansion (civilization) to the garden (nature), secretly embracing her working-class fiancé. The healthiness of Nancy's shift toward the Dionysian—as long as it comes to a halt at the Golden Mean—is compared to Aunt Polly's stultifying Apollonian extreme. The contrast is highlighted by one early confrontation between the two. Aunt Polly (Jane Wyman), learning that Nancy has been slipping off, scolds the girl:

> AUNT POLLY: Conduct yourself properly and modestly!
> NANCY: I assure you, George has been a perfect gentleman!

Perhaps "perfect" is stretching the truth. George openly gropes and kisses Nancy, even in front of impressionable Pollyanna! Still, Nancy remains in control, forcing George to control himself. If less than modest (in the superficial "keeping-up-appearances" value scheme of a Victorian extremist like Aunt Polly), Nancy emerges as a natural woman *without* abandoning herself to Dionysian wantonness. Again, she resembles Shakespeare's Juliet. Nancy is progressive enough to demand a marriage of like souls rather than a coldly arranged one, yet traditional enough to believe that marriage—altered from its previous patriarchal form reducing the woman to a commodity lacking her own will—remains the best possible way to create a lasting couple.

Likewise, Disney is often written off as the purveyor of simplistically goody-goody entertainment. Yet he defends lying and manipulation when they are employed for the sake of a healthy relationship, even as the Bard excused such things for precisely that purpose in *Much Ado about Nothing*. When Aunt Polly insists Nancy break off the romance, she agrees (to save her job), but goes on seeing George anyway. Pollyanna (Hayley Mills) regularly twists the truth, lying outright to cover for Nancy and George—with the audience encouraged to root for her.

When Pollyanna encourages the latent romance between Aunt Polly and Edmond (Richard Egan), what occurs is intensely sexual without becoming antifeminist. Disney, all but alone among male filmmakers of his time, did not subscribe to the stereotype that a woman must surrender to a man, as in the D. H. Lawrence view, if she is ever to experience fulfillment. That notion would be incarnated in hundreds of "adult" Hollywood romantic films, *Gone with the Wind* (1939) and *Spellbound* (1945) among the most memorable. But in Disney's equally romantic yet more enlightened view, gender has nothing to do with sensuality in relationships. A person, male or female, who has bought into society's rules must acknowledge the call of the wild, though that does not necessarily entail giving in to it. Aunt Polly isn't expected to rush off into the woods, where Edmond likes to camp. This would entail transforming into a Constance Chatterley by sexually surrendering to him as her Mellors, in hopes of being "saved" by doting on the male member. Edmond is, for the most part, relatively civilized himself. A doctor, he's happy to live in society, so long as he can escape on Sunday afternoons to the fishing hole, keeping in touch with his primal sympathy. Disney's ideal, then, is the character (male or female) who combines the best of both worlds.

Those holding extreme positions are, like Lady and her Tramp, expected to meet midway. On her first night in the house, Pollyanna asked Aunt Polly if she might kiss her goodnight, the older woman reacting in silent horror. There was not the slightest hint of sexuality in Pollyanna's request; Polly's fear, not specifically sexual in nature, is of the more generalized notion of physicality in human relationships. Aunt Polly, we learn, destroyed her one chance for happiness by rejecting Edmond, who hoped to shower Aunt Polly with kisses of, granted, a decidedly sexual nature. As Pollyanna plays Cupid, the kiss she now hopes to engineer between Aunt Polly and Edmond is, then, not *exclusively* sexual. A better term would be "sensuous," alive with a pantheist's cognition that the physical (natural) best conveys the religious (spiritual). This essential truth, Pollyanna instinctively senses, knowing also it is what her aunt desperately needs.

On some repressed level, at least, Aunt Polly knows it, too, though she has given herself over too fully to rationalism to ever admit this without help. As Pollyanna and Edmond before her, Aunt Polly must learn to enjoy the experience of kissing. Or, more correctly (and in a Wordsworthian sense), must *un*learn the Classicist constraints of an uptight society and relearn the Romantic ideal of the naturally inclined individual. Following Pollyanna's accident, Aunt Polly finally confesses her inability to love, crumbling in Edmond's arms. The scene's effect is less the sexist cliché of a weak female surrendering to the strong male than a person liberating herself from constrictive attitudes by learning to love—and physically join together with—another person. It means little, in Disney, whether the object of her affections is a grown man, a little girl, or humanity itself.

We the audience grasped that Aunt Polly would complete this inner journey. At mid-movie, she reached her point of no return, revealing a potential for reclamation of her natural self. Visually, this was signified by Polly's letting down her overcoiffed hair, something Edmond and Pollyanna begged her to do. The natural woman, however repressed, had never been entirely absent. Long hair—in Disney as for the Woodstock Generation—represents a rightful rebellion against stultifying convention.

A WOMAN OF THE BOULEVARDS. During the early sixties, prostitutes were positively portrayed in arthouse imports; Hollywood movies offered negative images of such women. The exception was *Bon Voyage*, in which American Fred MacMurray meets a highly admirable streetwalker (Françoise Prevost). (Copyright 1961 Walt Disney Productions; courtesy Buena Vista Releasing.)

The Generation Gap
Bon Voyage (1962)

In response to the growing differences between middle-aged Americans and their offspring in terms of music, manners, and morals, a new term entered our language. "The Generation Gap" implied the ever-expanding chasm between the way grown-ups and young people perceived the world and their place in it. To illustrate this, Disney relied on a device he regularly returned to: contrast heartland hicks with the freer lifestyles of other cultures. *Bon Voyage* concerns a family from Terre Haute, finally making a long-planned trip to the continent. Harry Willard (Fred MacMurray) and his wife Katie (Jane Wyman) bring their children along on the grand tour: pretty Amy (Deborah Walley), just turned twenty-one; teenage son Elliott (Tommy Kirk); and little "Skipper" (Kevin Corcoran), a nonfantastical Puck, the perennial mischief-maker.

Harry undergoes a life-altering experience, introducing the middle-aged American male to the sexual revolution's reality. This was the film in which Disney openly acknowledged the swinging lifestyle that had developed in postwar Europe, immortalized by Federico Fellini in *La Dolce Vita* (1960). Shortly, the sexual revolution would likewise make itself felt in America. Essentially, such a transition began in 1962, the same year that this film premiered. So in *Bon Voyage,* we meet Disney's first onscreen prostitute. At a café on the Champs-Élysées, Harry encounters (and quickly comes to like, admire, and respect) a Parisian day-lady of the boulevards (Françoise Prevost) who attempts to pick him up. What qualifies the unlikely sequence as Disney-esque (in the best sense of that term) is the noncondescending portrait.

Ordinarily, a family film that included such a scene (the notion in and of itself highly unlikely) would have simplistically contrasted the good, simple American male with a jaded, devious Frenchwoman. This would result in a smarmy, superficial scene, the filmmakers winking to their middlebrow audience while smirking at another nation's sexual conventions even as they exploited the heartland's secretive interest in such stuff. That doesn't happen here. Harry, however typical he appears, turns out to be that rarest of rarities, an enlightened American male, also serving as Disney's role model for the mature male element in the audience that would identify with any character played by the genial star of TV's *My Three Sons.* Harry turns the young woman down not because he believes himself, or his values, to be morally superior. Far more appealingly, his reason is that he happens to be madly, truly, deeply in love with his wife. Likewise, Katie is pursued by a professional gigolo (Ivan Desny). No Mrs. Dodsworth, offering superficial pretenses of middle-class respectability while secretly enjoying the flirtation, Katie is, like her husband, the real thing, discouraging (and meaning what she says) the gigolo's attentions.

Disney contrasts the adults' activities with the romantic misadventures of their grown children. Amy becomes involved with Nick (Michael Callan), an early screen example of what would come to be called Eurotrash. Educated at Yale, armed with a degree in architecture, Nick is devoid of any values other than living for the moment as he kicks around the continent. If Disney seems square to some for putting down such a lifestyle, it's worth noting that, two years earlier, Fellini criticized rather than celebrated what he tagged "the sweet life." The two filmmakers share moral outrage at the modern notion of living without meaning, though their ultimate philosophies are at odds. Fellini's pessimism is clear at *La Dolce Vita*'s end. His equivalent to Nick, Marcello (Marcello Mastroianni), meets an innocent young woman, with whom he might escape his own shallowness by returning to a simpler, more satisfying life in the presence of an unspoiled peasant woman whose warm folk songs signify the opposite of the decadent pseudosophistication the film's antihero wallows in. Marcello fails to take that option. He is—tragically, in Fellini's view—lost forever in an amoral abyss. Disney, ever the guarded optimist, ends his film with the opposite implication. Inspired by Amy's decency and simplicity, Nick turns his back on the fast life, determining to work hard and establish himself in New York.

There is no easy happy ending here. Amy doesn't promise to join him; the two will likely never see each other again. Still, she—and the traditional love Nick discovers still existing in her functional family unit—turns him away from the cynicism that formerly overwhelmed him. Elliott emerges from being an uptight teenager at the beginning, constricted by heartland values, into a protohippie. First, he enjoys a shipboard romance with a beautiful young Indian woman, Shamra (Ana Maria Majalca). Significantly, Elliott finds Shamra appealing not only because she's exotically beautiful. He's fascinated too with Eastern religions and their alternative approach to life's spiritual side. Elliott embodies what one observer noted as the youth movement's "Romantic flight to the East" owing to the "claim of Indian philosophy to embrace the primitive unity of Being,"[14] expressed in the Beatles's fascination with the Maharishi Mahesh Yogi and the sudden popularity of Ravi Shankar's sitar music.

This also allows for full expression of Disney's antiracist attitudes. The issue of color is never raised, either by Elliott's father or mother. Interracial dating is presented as a perfectly natural part of a young person's experiences, a generally accepted idea today, if a notable departure from attitudes contained in non-Disney movies of the early sixties. As always, Disney makes clear that it is indeed a small world after all. The young woman's father (Hassan Khayam) is clearly as protective of his beloved daughter's virginity as Harry is of Amy's. In diversity, Disney discovers a universal chord. Shamra's father closely follows Elliott and Shamra around the boat, precisely as Harry does Amy and Nick. After disembarking, Elliott buys a beret and grows a mustache, heading for Paris's Left Bank, where he mixes with the youth culture he discovers there. Elliott dates an Englishwoman, played by Carol White, several years later to incarnate the 1960s Brit "bird" in Kenneth Loach's *Poor Cow* (1967). On the French Riviera, Elliott meets a young Frenchwoman (Marie Sirago), whose virtue he despoils. Perhaps surprisingly, for those who cling to the vision of Disney as ultraconventional, this occurs without any horrific long-term consequences. Though at movie's end we do not learn what Elliott will do with his life, it's doubtful he can go home again. Having been exposed to an emerging lifestyle, Elliott would likely enter college, becoming a part of the new youth that emerged in the mid-sixties.

In *Bon Voyage*, Disney also achieved the same legitimacy for the bikini that he had won several years earlier for short-shorts. Throughout the 1950s, this bathing suit had been the controversial choice for swimming attire of such European sex kittens (a decade ahead of their American counterparts) as Brigitte Bardot. Any moviegoer hoping to view such near-nudity had to head for an arthouse, the true bikini remaining as absent from American movies as from American beaches. Even in the more liberated early sixties, a partial ban remained in effect. Ursula Andress, first of a new decade's European sex symbols, was forced to wear a modified compromise between the true bikini and a conservative two-piece suit in *Fun in Acapulco* (1963). Even the first of the *Beach Party* films (1963) featured only modified bikinis. Then, Disney entered the fray. Deborah Walley's all-American girl unashamedly models the wildest bikinis (including one composed of faux leopard skin, what there was of it) to appear in an American commercial film. In true Disney fashion, this shocking abandon in no way impinged on her wholesome image or reputation. Immediately, things changed—the mainstream as always following Walt's lead. One year later, Walley was again wearing just such swimwear (the stigma having been erased by Walt) in teen-oriented films that now boasted titles like *Bikini Beach* (1964). Shortly, women across America were donning the swimwear that initially was associated only with such California girls.

"SHE WORE AN ITSY-BITSY, TEENY-WEENY BIKINI." In the late 1950s, the bikini bathing suit, still considered scandalous in America, could be glimpsed only in imported European movies. When wholesome Deborah Walley donned such a suit in a Disney film, the negative stigma immediately disappeared. (Courtesy the Deborah Walley Estate and the late Ms. Walley.)

Into the Sixties
Moon Pilot (1962)
The Moon-Spinners (1964)
The Ugly Dachshund (1966)

We can chart the progress of the sexual revolution in the titles of sequential books written by a single author. First, America needed to be assured that sexuality was not necessarily a bad thing, at least when confined within traditional institutions. *Creative Marriage* (1961), by Dr. Albert Ellis, insisted on the need for enjoyable sex on the part of legally wed couples. A mild concept today, this constituted something of a radical notion at the time, constituting as it did an early-sixties reaction against fading 1950s values. In 1967, Dr. Ellis took a giant leap further, publishing *The Art of Erotic Seduction,* in which he notably chose to ignore whether or not the enjoyable sex was being practiced by a married couple. Finally, in 1972, he offered *The Civilized Couple's Guide to Extramarital Adventures,* assuming that most Americans were now involved in adultery. Perhaps they always had been—the difference being that, for better or worse, participants no longer bothered to be so secretive or guilt-ridden about it.

As *Bon Voyage* made clear, Disney could never condone adultery, which remained antithetical to his essentially traditional values. Yet his films do favor great sex within a lasting relationship, in itself a progressive notion when first advanced, particularly considering the context in which his family films were created and received. Nurturing relationships—free love with the single person whom one truly does love, a commitment including but not limited to an intense sexual bond—formed the basis of Disney's 1960s comedies, light enough on the surface but with serious subtexts.

Perhaps no single image so completely conveys his attitude than the final shot of *Moon Pilot*. One more uptight American, Richmond Talbot (Tom Tryon), has been approached by an exotic female, Lyrae (Dany Saval). The Gallic actress, then being hyped as "the next Bardot" (apparently, she forgot to wish upon a star, for her dream didn't come true), made her American debut in a Disney film. Talbot is an astronaut, Lyrae a girl from space who arrives on a mission of peace, determined to keep him from being killed. Her people realize that Talbot's spacecraft will explode upon takeoff, owing to a failure in its construction. Initially, Talbot can't grasp his attraction to someone so different from the uptight American women he's always dated. When he eventually gives in to his romantic

AND GOD CREATED WOMAN. During the early sixties, French sex kitten Dany Saval was trumpeted as "the next Brigitte Bardot." Though she never became, like "B.B.," a household name, Saval did incorporate the ultracontemporary sensuality of a Gallic sex symbol into a family-style comedy when Disney cast her in *Moon Pilot*. (Copyright 1961 Walt Disney Productions; courtesy Buena Vista Releasing.)

feelings, he's saved in more ways than one, for only then can Lyrae convince him to correct the craft's flaws in time. When Talbot is successfully launched into space, the earthbound control team is shocked to hear giggling emanating from the craft. Their communications system then goes dark. Lyrae has stowed away; she and Talbot make love onboard. Their coupling is anything but superficial. In Disney, as with Shakespeare, the Romeo and Juliet characters eventually consummate their relationship, initiated by physical attraction yet expanding to something considerably more spiritual. The man gradually comes to accept the woman's mature wisdom as superior to his own.

That theme underlies *The Moon-Spinners,* essentially "Pollyanna comes of age." Hayley Mills had turned eighteen, and Disney had no plans to extend his star's reign as America's Sweetheart. Instead he offered her a vehicle that paved her way to more mature roles. This diverting exercise in Hitchcockian suspense (a variation on 1938's *The Lady Vanishes*) cast her in an intense tale of young love. No wonder that, in his *New York Herald-Tribune* review, Robert Salmaggi noted the once "bubbly" child-star was "now grown up and sexy at 18."[15] Film historian Leonard Maltin added that "in the film, she is something of a man-chaser," and "rather worldly, even capable of wearing a dress with some decolletage."[16]

Based on a best-selling novel by Mary Stewart, the film opens on Crete. Two Englishwomen—one mature (Joan Greenwood as Aunt Frances), the other a teenager (Mills as Nikky Ferris)—check into an isolated hotel. The owners (Eli Wallach and Irene Papas) initially refuse to acknowledge their reservations, suggesting that something illegal is going on. Undeterred, Nikky quickly becomes involved with a handsome young Englishman, Mark (Peter McEnery). When her overprotective aunt suggests caution, Nikky—a member in good standing of the sixties youth culture—informs Aunt Frances that she's already experienced. At one point, she states outright, "I'm not all that innocent," predating Britney Spears's identical statement by thirty-seven years.

The fadeout is shocking for anyone who insists on clinging to the cliché that Disney's final films served as a last bastion of conservatism in a shifting sea of ever more sexual cinema. What the teenagers exchange is no sweet, simple, innocent kiss, as in most other teen-oriented movies of the decade's first half. The embrace of Nikky and Mark is a notably passionate one. Once the crime has been solved, the villains brought to justice, Nikky and Mark are not merely heading off to hold hands by the sea.

In *The Ugly Dachshund,* the sex drive is again presented as something other than the Eisenhower-era conception of a superficial (and potentially dangerous) attraction. As in all Disney films, a strong physical attraction makes the individual characters, particularly the males, "better" in the most substantive sense. Brutus, a Great Dane raised with a litter of dachshund pups, is initially unable to function when his master, Mark (Dean

POLLYANNA A-GO-GO! Most producers attempt to keep their female child stars cute and in-nocent for as long as possible. Disney provided the notable exception, insisting that Hayley Mills act her age in *The Moon-Spinners,* playing a "twisting" British "bird" of the Beatles era. (Copyright 1964 Walt Disney Productions; courtesy Buena Vista Releasing.)

Jones), enters him in a dog show. Despite formidable size, Brutus acts like one of his cute little "sisters." Then, Brutus spots a comely female Dane, also in competition, and everything changes. His identity, ambiguous up to this point, alters. To impress her, Brutus acts like a Dane, winning a blue ribbon. Learning from his pet, Mark comes to see that his success as an artist derives from the influence of wife Fran (Suzanne Pleshette). This allows Mark, like his pet, to arc, appreciating her and the magic of sexual attraction ("twitter-pation"):

FRAN: Do you think that's why [Brutus] won, Mark? Did a female make the difference?

MARK: Honey, females *always* make the difference!

Beyond the Sexual Revolution
Lt. Robin Crusoe, U.S.N. (1966)
Monkeys, Go Home! (1967)

A woman's freedom to choose, in terms not only of sexual identity but *every* aspect of life, is as essential to *Lt. Robin Crusoe, U.S.N.* as it earlier was to *The Sword and the Rose,* despite a contemporary slapstick tone. The title character (Dick Van Dyke), castaway on a South Sea island, is joined by his own Friday, a lovely native woman (Nancy Kwan) whom he nicknames "Wednesday." The film chronicles the attempts of Robin, engaged to a girl back home, to balance his waning commitment to a typical suburbanite while sharing a makeshift shack with the immodestly costumed Wednesday. That their sensual relationship develops as the story progresses is obvious, if implied. Wednesday warms to the American, eventually addressing him as "Admiral Honey," a term he doesn't mind. The natural setting does wonders for this previously uptight Establishment type, who grows ever more at ease with his own sexual self.

This erotic situation, incidentally, was not the brainchild of one of those independent producers who regularly came up with projects for Buena Vista. The story credit reads "Retlaw Yensid," Walter Disney spelled backward. The movie that finally brought the sexual revolution home to the family-film audience was Disney's own highly personal project. Just as personal was Disney's insistence on moving beyond the expected smarmy sex farce, which might have seemed "liberating" during the mid-sixties but appeared sexist only a few years later. Such films were typified by *The Swinger* (1966), with Ann-Margret, in which her character pretends to be sexually profligate to turn on an attractive male (Tony Franciosa), while actually remaining purer than the new-fallen snow. This is simply an updated variation of what had occurred when, beginning in 1934, the Production Code for Hollywood films quickly ended onscreen portraits of flappers who felt free to seek sexual liberation. In their place, films now

THE SWINGIN' SIXTIES. *Lt. Robin Crusoe, U.S.N.* offers an updating of Daniel Defoe's hapless hero as an uptight American suburbanite who loosens up with female companion "Wednesday" (TOP); later, he enjoys (implied) group sex with her "sisterhood" (BOTTOM). (Copyright 1965 Walt Disney Productions; courtesy Buena Vista Releasing.)

offered "the tease," considered "cute" when she presented herself to a man as free-spirited, then darted away at the last possible moment.

Moving beyond eroticism, Disney allows Wednesday to emerge as a person, not just a male's sex fantasy come to life. Wednesday, we learn, was cast away on this island by her father, Chief Tanamashu (Akim Tamiroff). He had (like Henry VIII in *The Sword and the Rose* and Mary Tudor) insisted that Wednesday marry a man she didn't care for. Although refusing to conform to patriarchal power, Wednesday did at the time assume there must be something wrong with herself, since none of the other girls minded such a system. Robin explains to her that in America, women have begun to rebel against living their lives in male-directed ways. This amazes Wednesday, who suddenly realizes she was not crazy but right on. Summoning other native women to the island, she forms an army of Amazons. When Tanamashu and the men arrive to retrieve them, his warriors are greeted by feminist protestors, carrying signs demanding women's rights. At the end, the male hierarchy has been toppled, the women have won, and things are better in the South Seas.

One year later, such a situation would be replayed in a different setting, as the opening of *Monkeys, Go Home!* makes clear. One more uptight American, Hank (Dean Jones), arrives in a provincial French town to claim his inheritance, an olive farm. He arrives, suitably, in a Volkswagen, the car of choice for so practical a person. Hank spots the female lead driving into town: Maria (Yvette Mimieux) arrives on a motorcycle. Significantly, this marks the first time that a biker babe was portrayed as a positive character in an American film. Such women had consistently been depicted as sleazy ever since *The Wild One* (1954). In France, however, women were allowed to embrace motorcycles without surrendering a respectable image. Several of Brigitte Bardot's most popular posters featured her in black leather, on a bike. Significant, then, is the fact that shortly before this Disney film went into production, actress Mimieux had been hailed by the media as America's answer to Brigitte Bardot. Posing in revealing bikinis on California beaches, including a *Life* magazine cover story,[17] Mimieux had a wholesome sexuality that made her a key (if brief) symbol for mainstream America's belated acceptance of the new sexual freedom—clean-cut as Sandra Dee though as sensuous as "B.B."

The actress ordinarily associated with surfer-girl roles here convincingly affects a Gallic accent. At times, we almost forget that we're not watching Bardot herself. The movie, at least in terms of subtext, is "about" a typical American falling under the spell of a Bardot-type Frenchwoman.

THE BIKER BABE REDUX. Beginning with *The Wild One* (1954) and running through *The Wild Angels* (1966), female motorcyclists were portrayed as sleazy lowlife stereotypes. Disney reconsidered that image, casting wholesome yet sexy Yvette Mimieux as the American screen's first positively portrayed biker babe. (Copyright 1967 Walt Disney Productions; courtesy Buena Vista Releasing.)

Initially frightened by his own attraction, he soon realizes the liberated lady can, if he passes beyond his restricting worldview, exert a positive influence. Hank is enraptured by her blond beauty and what, for him, is a decidedly unconventional way for a lady to arrive on the scene. He follows Maria when she steps into the butcher shop. Gazing in the window,

Hank is shocked to see her in the arms of the butcher, Marcel (Bernard Woringer). Assuming Maria must be a "typical" French girl (in the eyes of an American abroad, i.e., sexually promiscuous), Hank turns away, disappointed. In Disney, however, characters hailing from a country associated in our popular mentality with some form of behavior are never "typical." The films deprogram us from such stereotyping.

Marcel, we learn, tried to force himself on Maria, a virgin who will have none of it. This might initially seem a cop-out, in terms of Disney fully embracing the sexual revolution. It's important to recall, then, that in 1967, several of the young women who posed nude for *Playboy* insisted, in their biographical sketches, that they were virgins. Acceptance of their own bodies as sensuous vehicles did not, the magazine implied, empower the male viewer with a right to make any assumptions about the woman's sexual proclivities or experiences. Disney's view on this subject is strikingly similar to Hefner's: Do not make assumptions about an individual based on any specific aspects of her lifestyle. That is, do not dichotomize women into "good girl" and "bad girl" polarities by making snap judgments based on appearances, which may have nothing to do with reality. Hank wins our admiration only after learning to accept the woman he's attracted to as an individual. Like Disney's Mary Tudor, Maria—unconventional when it comes to flouting society's sillier restrictions on women—is anything but promiscuous.

Knowing less than we know and guilty of false assumptions, Hank is shocked, on his first morning at the villa, to wake up and find the lovely girl preparing his breakfast. This is not what an American girl would do, and reaffirms his false impression from the previous day. Maria, in fact, is a serious young woman in search of a lasting relationship. Only upon becoming convinced this is what she and Hank share does Maria put her traditional, self-confessed "religious" restrictions on sexuality aside for a roll in the hay (quite literally) with Hank. This doesn't occur at the end, as would be the case in most American "romantic" movies—lovemaking put off until the final credits are ready to roll. Maria and Hank consummate their relationship midway through, she—like so many previous Disney females—gently teaching him the art of love.

From that point on, they operate as a team. Hank's attempts to make the olive farm a going concern would fail if not for his new partner. Men are complete, in Disney films, only when they share with the woman all aspects of life: the business venture, mundane elements of everyday exis-

IF ONLY WE HAD BRAS, WE'D BURN THEM. In the early 1970s, feminism emerged as a cause celebre, though mainstream Hollywood all but ignored women's protests. The exception was Walt Disney, who as early as 1965 depicted such activity in *Lt. Robin Crusoe, U.S.N.*; significantly, it is the male patriarch (Akim Tamiroff), not the feminist leader (Nancy Kwan), who is cruelly caricatured. (Copyright 1966 Walt Disney Productions; courtesy Buena Vista Releasing.)

tence, and—fully accepted, if in its place—the bedroom. As in *Lt. Robin Crusoe, U.S.N.*, what began as a sixties study in sexual revolution concludes as a precursor to the 1970s call for women's rights.

With such an attitude, Disney moved beyond the limiting margins of the sexual revolution and into the larger and greater issue of feminism. By the mid-sixties, pro-civil-rights and antiwar demonstrations were essential to the emerging sensibility of a new American youth. Virtually ignored during the ever-louder, ever-more-disruptive demonstrations was the women's movement. The counterculture's attitude could not even be dismissed as benign neglect. Toward the decade's end, feminists attending a Students for a Democratic Society (SDS) convention were appalled enough by the blatant chauvinism there that they staged a walk-out.

Hippiedom's retro masculine point of view was vividly articulated in *Getting Straight* (1970). Playing an edgy college professor living with a flower-power grad student (Candice Bergen), Elliott Gould at one point angrily rails at her for daring to disagree with him on some minor issue. "We shouldn't be burning our draft cards," he screeches. "We should be burning women's *library* cards!" More or less simultaneously with the film's release, the Guess Who hit the Top Ten with what may be the most unabashed antifeminist anthem in music history:

> *American woman, stay away from me!*
> *American woman, Mama, let me be!*
> *Don't come hangin' around my door;*
> *I don't want to see your face no more.*
> *I got more important things to do*
> *Than hang around, growin' old with you!*

Not content to merely attack American women for wanting committed relationships, in which they would be treated as sexual beings rather than accept their male-dictated roles as sexual objects, the rockers also blamed the female of the species for atrocities—most notably, war of an imperialistic nature abroad, virulent racism at home—that had been created by a male-dominated social structure:

> I don't need your war machines;
> I don't want your ghetto scenes!

Then, with the winding down of the Vietnam War and successes in the civil rights field, a new cause celebre was required. Jane Fonda's abrupt haircut in *Klute* announced that her days as Barbarella were over. A sizable portion of American womanhood fell in line with her new image, opting for similar styles. The Helen Reddy pop recording "I Am Woman" was accepted (if not necessarily intended) as a feminist anthem. Gloria Steinem's *Ms.* magazine appeared and, during its initial run as a commercial venture, proved highly successful with women whose consciousness had been transformed. Movies, of course, would shortly respond as well, with the release of such films as Martin Scorsese's *Alice Doesn't Live Here Anymore* (1974), John Cassavetes's *A Woman under the Influence* (1974), and Paul Mazursky's *An Unmarried Woman* (1978). And, belatedly, films about women that were actually written and directed by women arrived.

The point here, though, is that as always, in terms of a male artist who appreciated diversity before that term became a byword, Disney had been there first. Moreover, he had—far ahead of his time—offered an enlightened vision as part of his worldview, without calculation or box-office considerations. Walt—and Walt alone among Hollywood's men—presented such portraits because, unconsciously, it came naturally to him and, when he did think about such stuff, it seemed the right thing to do.

ALTERING THE AMERICAN MOVIE ICONOGRAPHY. Previous makers of Western films depicted subdued women riding in wagons while strong men march out front as their protectors. Early in "Johnny Appleseed," Disney forever changed the visual rhetoric of Hollywood by depicting women in every possible role. (Copyright 1948 Walt Disney Productions; courtesy Buena Vista Releasing.)

6

Our Bodies, Ourselves
Disney and Feminism

I realize now I've been living in a doll's house!
—HENRIK IBSEN'S NORA TORVOLD, 1878

Why, it looks just like a little doll's house!
—WALT DISNEY'S SNOW WHITE, 1937

*I*n 1961, while most Americans waxed euphoric over the election of John Kennedy, Parisian intellectual Simone de Beauvoir attempted to inform everyone that the latest First Lady ought to be recognized for brains as well as beauty: "The male amuses himself with free flights of thought . . . but women's reveries take a very different direction: she will think about her *personal appearance*." [1] In 1963, Betty Friedan's *The Feminine Mystique* insisted that women "are living with their feet bound in the old image of glorified femininity . . . Encouraged by the *mystique* to evade their identity crisis." [2] Eventually, Germaine Greer noted that "Woman must have room and scope to devise a morality which does *not* disqualify her from excellence." [3] Hollywood filmmakers responded by removing previously unquestioned, now obviously sexist, sentiments from scripts while presenting strong images of independent women.

I Am Woman: Hear Me Roar
The Story of Robin Hood and His Merrie Men (1952)
Alice in Cartoonland (1924–1927)
Plane Crazy (1928)

Soon, dialogue such as the following flourished, as, in a costume film, England's ruler leaves for the Crusades:

KING RICHARD I: Don't worry, mother. Prince John will be here to take care of you.

ELEANOR OF AQUITAINE: I raised two sons on my own after my husband died. I can take care of myself now.

This exchange, one might guess, occurs in a postfeminist revisionist film version of the Robin Hood legend. In fact, it's from Disney's 1952 version—the *only* Robin Hood movie to include the queen mother as a key character. Always, Disney's attitude toward women emphasizes strength of character in pursuit of excellence and self-fulfillment.

His first screen character was the live-action heroine of the *Alice* shorts. Unlike Max and Dave Fleischer's Betty Boop, always surrounded (and in due time rescued) by male characters, Disney's Alice is most often on her own. Though played by a child, Alice owns her own home and car in *Alice Rattled by Rats,* and her own business, an egg-producing farm, in *Alice's Egg Plant.* In *Alice's Orphan,* she adopts a lost cat, proving herself a worthy if diminutive mother figure. Yet she nurtures even while continuing to pursue her own personal interests.

While Alice is not uninterested in men, Disney's character differs significantly from most of her female onscreen contemporaries—animated and live—by projecting a commonsense wisdom beyond her years. At the end of *Alice Solves the Puzzle,* her constant companion, a macho tom cat, sidles up along her, flexing his muscles—a caricature of the traditional macho male. Alice notices, nods her head in mild appreciation of his physique, then asks if he has the brainpower to solve a crossword puzzle. When he fails, Alice shrugs, loses interest in him, and completes the task herself. Alice may, like Boop, always appear enticing. For Alice, though, there's no incompatibility between feminine attractiveness and feminist attitudes.

What a difference here from other films of the era, which presented women as either serious or sexy, never both. As Molly Haskell noted in 1973:

> Just as the serious and political "Apollonian" side of the current women's movement seems often opposed to the hedonistic and sexual "Dionysian" side, so the "emancipated woman" of the twenties was either a suffragette or a flapper, depending on what she wanted and how she chose to get it.[4]

It's interesting to note that the only New York distributor who took any interest in the initial Alice short, *Alice's Day at Sea,* was a woman. Margaret Winkler responded—as a woman as well as an industry professional—to something special that she perceived in Disney's conception.

IN PRAISE OF OLDER WOMEN. Every film of the Robin Hood legend eliminates Eleanor of Aquitaine except the live-action Disney version. Walt not only included the Queen Mother (Martita Hunt) but made her a central figure, joining with Locksley (Richard Todd) as full partner to fight fascism. (Copyright 1952 Walt Disney Productions; courtesy RKO Radio Pictures.)

In that first film, Alice visits the seashore, goes out boating, and falls asleep. When she wakes, Alice is surrounded by menacing figures: Fanged fish, an octopus, swooping birds of prey. Rather than scream out for a male hero to rescue her, de rigueur for screen heroines of that time, Alice handily deals with the problems herself, solving them through a combination of brain and brawn. She then makes her way back to shore on her own. Between 1924 and 1927, fifty-six Alice cartoons were produced, the originals starring Virginia Davis (with whom Walt had worked in K.C.). Margie Gay and Lois Hardwick each in turn assumed the role. Viewed in retrospect, they present a startling set of attractive possibilities for women in the brave new social landscape of post–World War I America. If the Fleischers suggested that inside every seemingly sophisticated flapper there beat the heart of an overgrown child, Disney conversely implied that inside every supposed female child, there existed in embryo an intelligent and capable woman, eager to emerge.

Alice served as a forerunner of such flapper stars as Clara Bow and Joan Crawford. Perhaps most significantly, in comparison to earlier Theda Bara vamps, obsessed with carnal knowledge, or Mary Pickford virgins, mortally terrified of it, what has been written about Bow applies equally to Alice:

> She was no ordinary sex symbol—indeed, she described herself as a "tomgirl" who "doesn't care particularly about men" [though she] knew precisely how to use her body, how much of it to expose and, more important, which portions of it to cover alluringly.[5]

Also, Disney was the first Hollywood filmmaker to condemn in his work, through dramatic illustration of the consequences, chauvinistic behavior on the part of men. Even his beloved mouse had to learn such lessons the hard way. In *Plane Crazy* (the first Mickey cartoon ever made, though third to be released), Mickey is inspired by Charles Lindbergh's then-recent transcontinental flight to build his own plane, certain this will impress Minnie. No sooner does he get her up in the air than Mickey attempts to put the make on his inamorata, certain there is nothing she can do to stop him at such dangerous heights. Stunned to realize the venture was designed to reduce her to a sexual object, Minnie fervently rejects Mickey's advances. She's then inspired to use her pantaloons as a parachute, returning to earth. His attempt at seduction a failure, Mickey is reduced to a laughingstock in the last shot—the implication being that his actions were wrong. He even laughs at himself, arcing as he rejects chauvinism.

Still, the feminist consensus has always been to dismiss Disney's portrayals of women as superficial images of helpless princesses, subserviently trusting males to carry them off and live "happily ever after" in a retro world of postmarital bliss. Images of women in the Disney canon may, in the words of one female essayist, be seen as serving the male status quo, thanks to brainwashing females at an early age with

> the illusions of romance—created to foster her obedience to the courtship system and pandered to by cheap fiction and media advertising. . . . Her reveries of falling in love, of being swept off her feet, her depictions to herself of marvelous tales whose farthest limits in her imagination were reached on a glorious triumphal wedding day.[6]

Still, a close examination of Disney's female-oriented fairy-tale trilogy reveals something notably different. Each film appeared at or near the end of a decade during which the role of women in America had drastically altered, owing to political and cultural changes in the social fabric.

Such characters as Clever Grethel, the Goose Girl, and Rapunzel had no appeal for this filmmaker. Far from arbitrary, the selection process was determined by the degree to which any ancient fable allowed Disney to dramatize his contemporary yet highly individualistic worldview. He carefully picked from the plethora of female fairy tales in Grimm and Perrault three stories all but identical in premise: A young woman of aristocratic birth or bearing, humbled by her current déclassé station, fulfills a singular destiny thanks to a characteristically American approach to adversity—coupled with what, on close consideration, can only be considered a mainstream feminist outlook. This in no way negates femininity. Women can, Disney early on insisted (and Germaine Greer later reaffirmed in *The Female Eunuch*), have it both ways, though only if, like Disney's role-model characters, they firmly believe in themselves—as individuals and as women. Since each incarnation offers a unique variation on this theme, the essential similarity implies, to paraphrase Joseph Campbell, that what we encounter is the heroine with a thousand faces. This concept lived on, long after Disney's death, in *The Little Mermaid* (1989), Belle in *Beauty and the Beast* (1991), *Pocahontas* (1995), and *Mulan* (1998).

"Jo Heck with the Men"
Snow White and the Seven Dwarfs (1937)

During the twenties, a sense of liberation (albeit a superficial one) had been achieved by the country's first generation of working women, on their own in the big city. Hemlines had shortened while Victorian morality frayed. Still, as Una Stannard noted in "The Mask of Beauty":

> The modern woman's liberty to expose her legs and most of her body does *not* signify women's liberation. . . . Women are "free" to start wearing padded bras at the age of nine and to spend forty-eight million dollars annually on eye make-up alone . . . Women are not free *not* to be sexy.[7]

Economic woes have a way of deflating hubris. As Fay Wray's first scene in RKO's *King Kong* (1933) revealed, yesterday's carefree flappers stood in breadlines after the stock market crash of 1929—desperate for work, too proud to return to the farms and small towns they'd made a mass migration from a decade earlier.

Seemingly set in a Ruritanian kingdom from European folklore, Disney's *Snow White* immediately introduces us to just such a situation. As her beautiful stepmother stares down from a castle window, the title character—dressed in rags identical to those worn by her Steinbeckian sisters—labors below. Disney emphasizes an element only suggested in the source.[8] Snow White is scorned by the "vain and wicked stepmother" owing to her fear that this girl's emerging beauty will someday dwarf her own. "Who is fairest of all?" the Queen demands of the magic mirror. The face of a slave in the mirror insists Snow White's *natural* good looks outshine any self-conscious attempts at beauty. "Women in our society," a feminist leaflet from 1968 proclaimed, are "enslaved by ludicrous 'beauty' standards we ourselves are conditioned to take seriously."[9] Though considered extreme in the freewheeling hippie era, such a statement articulates the theme of Disney's *Snow White* as postulated in the film's opening iconography.

The Queen—eyebrows arched high—resembles the two reigning European imports who dominated 1930s screens, Greta Garbo and Marlene Dietrich. Such stars caused a revolution in fashion, owing to their harsh—indeed, "ludicrously" so—glamour, which became a "standard." As a result, ordinary women—including middle-class housewives—felt compelled (if they could afford it) to buy crimson lipstick and ghostly mascara. Sophistication edging toward decadence emerged as haute couture. On the other hand, Snow White—in her total lack of self-consciousness about appearance—recalls the period's most popular American star, Shirley Temple. Engagingly innocent, Snow White appears in an iconographic dialectic with the beauty-as-artifice approach of the Queen. "A man's love is beauty deep," Una Stannard would complain in her early-seventies essay, adding: "Doesn't a man always say 'you're beautiful' before he says 'I love you'?" [10] Often—but not always, and never in Disney films. *Snow White,* thirty years ahead of its time, can be "read" as a protofeminist cautionary fable, implicitly criticizing what in time would be attacked as "the beauty trap." "Rags cannot hide her gentle grace," the mirror's Slave informs her majesty. True beauty, Disney insists, is not applied from the outside but grows from within, and has less to do with a woman's physical appearance than her personality.

In this case, inner beauty—effectively represented within the context of a musical movie by her warm, loving, sensitive voice—is what draws the birds and other animals to Snow White, then Prince Charming as well. What served only as a plot element in Grimm was transformed into a resonant theme—introduced at the outset, then powering the film. Though much of the old fairy tale is excised, Disney retained what the brothers Grimm insist is the essence of Snow White's appeal: the colors red (lips), white (skin), and black (hair). This, not coincidentally, is the essential color combination for Disney's greatest original creation, Mickey Mouse. Similarly, his Snow White will express, in female form, the same set of values that turned a simple cartoon rodent into a populist icon.

Prince Charming's fascination with Snow White—his ability to at once see beyond the drab surface of her current existence, appreciating her greater appeal as a person—qualifies him as an early rendering of Disney's ideal male. He is enlightened in outlook and possesses total integrity. Though the most extreme (and highly verbal) radical feminists of the early 1970s would come to consider man as "the enemy" by virtue of his essential nature, others—more mainstream—adamantly argued otherwise. As, for instance, that night when radical feminist Susan Brownmiller announced on TV's *The Dick Cavett Show* that all men "oppress us as human beings." Another guest—Grace Slick of the rock group Jefferson Airplane—struck back:

> Some [men] are great, some are crummy. Why do you have to form a theory? Some of them look at you as sex objects . . . [but] the ones

who like to *make music* and talk to you and go to bed with you and write, whatever you do—draw?—you do all those things with. I don't see where the problem is, because I don't see what you're talking about.[11]

The first thing Disney's prince attempts to do is, in Slick's words, "make music" with Snow White by joining in her chorus. Far from saying anything about her looks (pleasant but unremarkable), he attempts to learn more about her *as a person:* who she is, where she comes from, etc. This approach—the one Slick called for—is, as we shall see, what makes this young man "princely," rather than any worldly kingdom, which—so significant in Grimm—does not exist in the Disney film.

Indeed, the very idea of his wandering by at this moment is noteworthy, implying a sense of destiny not present in the original. (The source's Snow-white is a mere seven years old when she first flees.) Disney's male hero appears less a conventional fairy-tale prince than a troubadour of old, or one of the twentieth century's young men in search of truth and self—what Jack Kerouac tagged as the dharma bums. Either way, he's drawn by her poetry as a total person, *not* her physicality. This enrages the Queen, observing from a tower that isolates her from life itself. Narcissism gives way to agoraphobia; she never leaves this place until transformed into an entirely other persona. The irony is that, by such self-containment, the Queen denies herself any possibility of fulfillment. According to one aspect of feminist thinking, the true tragedy is that woman is "an object not only of lust and ego but *vanity* as well—not only a conquest and a possession but needed *to be seen* as a conquest and a possession in the eyes of men."[12] The Queen's anger appears absurd, since her positioning of herself keeps the prince from ever seeing her.

As in Grimm, the huntsman assigned to murder Snow White cannot bring himself to do so. But while the Grimms' huntsman is moved only by Snow White's appearance ("she was so *lovely* the huntsman had pity on her"), Disney's burly fellow—like the slender prince—is moved by Snow White's *personality:* her innocent approach to life, her concern for others, her essence as a human being. That essence is, in a word, "natural." Aretha Franklin's 1967 soul classic, "A Natural Woman," could be added to Disney's sound track.

In Grimm, Snow-white accidentally discovers the dwarfs' home. Disney's Snow White, led there by animals who sense a oneness with this radical innocent, shares her thoughts with them. "You don't know what

I've been through," she sighs upon realizing they—and the natural world itself—constitute no threat. "And all because I was afraid," she adds. This admission is Snow White's first step on her journey toward self-realization as a woman. Like America's then-current president, she believes we have nothing to fear but fear itself—an attitude that will become both her greatest strength and near-fatal weakness.

Then follows one of the famous musical numbers, "With a Smile and a Song." However pleasing (and necessary as an interlude between the abject horror that precedes it and the warm comedy to come), the lyrics thematically express Disney's vision. "I'll get along somehow," she insists, despite the difficulty (indeed, apparent impossibility) of her current position. Her guarded optimism will eventually be rewarded. First, though, she enters the cottage and proclaims that the residents must be "seven little children." Snow White draws this conclusion after observing a general untidiness: clothing strewn everywhere, dirty dishes piled high, filth on the floor. Nothing could more directly contrast with the Grimms' description: "Everything there was very small, but as pretty and clean as possible. There stood the little table ready laid, and covered with a white cloth." Beds, adjoining the kitchen rather than upstairs as in Disney, are neatly decked "with clean white quilts." Disney's decision to reverse the Grimms' description may largely be due to plot possibilities. The subsequent cleaning sequence (Snow White, assisted by woodland animals, whistles while she works) is charming. However engaging Disney may be as mass entertainer, though, always we sense an artist's ongoing sensibility at work—his unique vision of the universe, vividly rendered in a singular style.

In the world according to Walt, men—even the best of men—are (as in films by such diverse cinema artists as Griffith, Ford, Bergman, and Fellini) naturally inclined to chaotic behavior. Women, conversely, offer an organizing principle and sharp common sense. Or, as Disney himself put it when speaking of the public's reaction to his work:

> Women are the best judges of anything we turn out. Their taste is very important. . . . If the women like [a new film], to heck with the men. . . . We get advance reaction to our movies at previews and if the women's reaction is good, I feel fine. If it is adverse, I begin to worry. I feel women are more honest about [their reactions] than men.[13]

Not surprisingly, then, the world (the microcosm of this cottage, the macrocosm surrounding it) qualifies as a mess until a right-minded woman takes charge.

The mistaken notion that the residents must be children has no place in Grimm, where the dwarfs' behavior is consistently mature. Like good males in all retro drama, they protect Snow-white, who fails to heed men's wise words. Disney's Snow White, on the other hand, is essentially correct in her judgment, since these dwarfs *do* qualify as children—if not in age, then in attitude. Or, in contemporary terms:

> The hatred of the youth culture for adult society is not a disinterested judgment but a terror-ridden refusal to be hooked into the, if you will, ecological chain of birthing, growing, and dying. It is the demand, in other words, to remain children.[14]

Not, significantly, in the best sense (Dylan's belief in remaining "forever young," at least spiritually) but in the worst: refusing to achieve maturity after reaching adulthood. This precisely describes the dwarfs—until, that is, Snow White arrives and they fall under her positive influence.

Disney consistently undermines the old tale's unquestioning acceptance of male superiority. While the child-men (particularly Grumpy) may initially resist, only by a gradual but full acceptance of a female leader do they become "men" (that is, adult persons) in the truest sense. The Grimms' dwarfs, as has often been noted, possess no distinct personalities, each a virtual clone of the next. The personalities of Disney's dwarfs—Grumpy, Sleepy, Doc, Bashful, Sneezy, Happy, Dopey—constitute caricatures of each and every type of traditional male behavior. They exist as modern equivalents of Elizabethan "humour" characters. Each serves as an archetype, some single personality trait entirely dominating everything the fellow says or does. Snow White, on the other hand, is the film's only three-dimensional character, her complex personality enhanced by the fact that she, and she alone, was closely modeled on a human being: Adriana Caselotti, who provided Snow White's singing and speaking voices.[15] The impact here is to focus on a real woman's coming to terms with each limited possibility of the unenlightened male. When the Grimms' dwarfs first enter, they sound like the three bears, discovering Goldilocks: "Who has been sitting in my little chair?" Without fear, they discover Snow-white asleep. Well meaning but incurably conventional, they decide not to wake her, instead guarding the vulnerable girl all night. Disney's dwarfs, noting that their domain has been invaded, fall into fits of terror.

Compared to the Grimms' solid community of little men, the film offers seven rugged, if immature, individualists. Earlier, glimpsed working in their mine, they did not collaborate, keeping separate from one another, each hammering away at his own diamond (gold in Grimm) pile. Now, Disney's dwarfs cringe in fear, aligning only when they force Dopey—most vulnerable (even feminine) among them—to approach the perceived "monster" sleeping across three beds (the Grimms' Snow-white, still a child, occupied but one). As Dopey cautiously approaches, we see Snow White from his point of view; struggling to sleep under sheets, she does appear to be a goblin. In fact, that is how the female principle appears to men who have not learned to accommodate themselves to a woman's presence and potential, thereby relinquishing childish male be-havior for true maturity. "Let's kill it," one dwarf shouts, "before it wakes," expressing an all too typical male reaction: Eliminate, through violence, anything you don't understand. Then comes the realization that this is a girl. Though that relieves their fear, it hardly ends male anxiety, expressed by the arch-male Grumpy: "She's a *female*, and all females is *p'isin*," full of "wicked wiles."

When another dwarf, after first mindlessly agreeing, asks what "wicked wiles" are, Grumpy—ignorant as he is bigoted—replies: "I don't know, but I'm *ag'in* 'em." Grumpy represents the extreme reactionary male po-sition. His eventual conversion to Snow White's most wholehearted fan signifies not only his arc, but—Disney apparently hopes—his audience's, or at least the male portion of it. "Why, you're little *men*," Snow White remarks upon waking. True, but so was her earlier deduction. All men are overgrown children until sanitized and sensitized, a process only a woman can manage. Snow White determines each dwarf's name by close observation, establishing her intelligence and powers of perception. Also possessing a keen sense of humor, she kids each without ever becoming patronizing or condescending—a neat trick!

At this point, the story—Grimm or Disney—moves in a direction that can only anger radical feminists. For Snow White takes on a role they condemn: That of "nurturer," attacked (at least during this period, now referred to as "First Wave Feminism") as the basis for women's "victim-ization" within "the domestic prison-house" in which she's expected to labor.[16] Snow White will become, in the words of one prominent 1970s feminist, part of "the largely unpaid, largely female labor force that does the daily work."[17] But while there may be no resolving the polarity of housework and liberation for the most extreme radicals, even during feminism's Third Wave, mainstream feminists—then and now—ought to appreciate Disney's rewriting Grimm so as to empower his heroine. Snow White proposes that she work in return for bed and board ("Let me

THE REDEMPTION OF HOUSEWORK. Mainstream feminists insist the true "enemy" is not housework but a mind-set that perceives such labor as inferior to working outside the home. Disney set the pace for this: Snow White suggests the arrangement rather than having it dictated to her by "the little men," as in Grimm. (Copyright 1938 Walt Disney Productions; courtesy RKO Radio Films.)

stay; *I'll* keep house for you, cook . . ."). How different from the source, in which "the dwarfs said to her, 'If *you* will keep our house for us, and cook, and wash . . . you may stay.'" There, men determine an arrangement; the woman passively agrees, the very thing mainstream feminist Greer condemned.

As James R. Petersen noted, Greer always attacked "the ancient role of the passive female."[18] Disney, however, transformed his Snow White into the active character. Likewise, antifeminist Midge Decter, in *The New Chastity*, defended women's continuing (so long as it was by choice) in the role as nurturer: "As a special being, her true fulfillment lies in the exercise of her special capacity for sustaining and refining and enriching the materials of everyday existence."[19] Though she performs the same work as will be done in the Disney film, the Grimms' Snow-white incarnates the retro woman, given no choice but to assume a domestic position. Walt's Snow White makes her own decisions, redeeming housework from mere drudgery—less a description of housework itself than the proper way to define housework if it is imposed on the person doing it.

Clearly, Disney would agree with those members of the National Organization for Women who stand in

> opposition to the idea that men are the enemy. They do not seek to sever relations with men . . . only to alter them. They do not . . . seek to liberate women [from men and/or marriage to men] but to liberate men *and* women from [an unbalanced] system . . . that does danger to both.[20]

What must be acknowledged by the man (or, in this unique case, men) in a woman's life is that housework is equal in value to any labor performed "in the world"—that, in fact, the home *is* a part of that world, and the work done there equal in validity to anything achieved in an office.

Though Snow White does indeed cook, she's anything but their servant. Hands on hips, she is a take-charge woman who unrelentingly insists they wash (thereby eliminating dirtiness, a key vestige of the immature male) before sitting down. Grumpy's reaction is precisely what we expect: "Women!" In no way, though, does Disney defend this, or any of Grumpy's other proclamations. He is the only dwarf we laugh *at* rather than *with*. The redneck male who must be won over, Grumpy does possess an essential goodness that ultimately allows him to overcome a lifetime of narrow thinking. In due time, he will come to see a woman in charge is not necessarily a bad thing. It all depends on the individual woman who holds that position.

For contrast, Disney then cuts from their meal to the Queen's castle. The film's two women serve as foils for each other, highly complex positive and negative (rather than simple good and bad) extremes of the female principle. If the positive is based on natural inner beauty radiating outward, then the negative derives from neurotic, obsessive dwelling on one's physical attributes, appearance as image. Yet Disney, no male basher, does not blame men for this neurosis. However unconsciously, he takes umbrage at what's now often viewed as the "*male*-inspired process of turning her [face and] body into a *thing* to be prized."[21] The key male character before Prince Charming's arrival—the Queen's husband, Snow White's father—never appears in the film, though he plays a significant role in the Grimm and Perrault sources.

This Queen's tragedy is self-absorption. Confronting the mirror once again, she learns that Snow White lives still. At this point we encounter

Disney's most significant alteration. The Grimms' evil Queen "painted herself and dressed like an old pedlar woman, so that no one would know her," before setting out for the dwarfs' cottage. Disney's mixes "a formula to transform my beauty into ugliness." Nowhere is it implied that, if and when the Queen does succeed in eliminating Snow White, she can return to her former beauty. This qualifies her decision as abject madness. The image of a crone, grinning and without irony cackling, "I'll be the fairest in the land," is implicitly one of the great artistic condemnations of the Beauty Trap. Now, every other woman in the land is fairer than she.

A true foil for Snow White, the queen-crone taunts her nasty pet bird. Snow White's oneness with nature was conveyed by her warm relationship with a sweet bird. Though "beauty is as beauty does" may be a tiresome cliché, it's one we now accept as an enlightened outlook. The Queen—initially far more beautiful than Snow White, physically speaking—makes herself hideous by bad behavior. What a difference between her cruel domination (the huntsman lies dead in a cell, a skeleton arm stretching for water) and Snow White's always positive "domination" over the dwarfs. Though Snow White, as we already know, possesses a lovely voice, she joins the dwarfs only at the end of their choral performance, via a single note that, ribbonlike, ties their individual voices together into communal song. Yet her continued presence creates a positive bonding among the men notably missing from their earlier scenes. They failed to function as a group, until a woman entered their lives. Rather than de-emphasizing their masculinity, she helped little boys become, finally, adult persons.

Snow White is formidable. Dopey must climb up on Sleepy's shoulders to dance with her, visually implying that the strong woman is worth any two men. Snow White remains, however, as feminine as she is feminist. The delightful kissing sequence—the dwarfs anxiously file past Snow White on their way to work next morning—makes clear that Snow White is aware of, and willing to positively exploit, the power of her sensuality. Each dwarf receives a kiss on his bald head. She, however, remains in clear control. Dopey rushes around the building for an additional kiss. Though his first transgression is tolerated, his second is not. Incessantly, he tries for a kiss on the lips, yet willingly accepts one identical to what his comrades receive. Grumpy, after feigning disinterest, submits to a kiss, and is transformed. After experiencing this female's "white" (as opposed to the

PROMOTING INTERRACIAL LOVE. The once potent stigma of miscegenation was at the heart of most racist thinking, and Disney films were among the first to discard such outdated ideas by offering positive images of interracial love to impressionable young people. Anglo boys who identified with Peter Pan were charmed by his happy romance with Princess Tiger Lily. (Property of Walt Disney Productions; reprinted courtesy of Buena Vista Releasing.)

INITIATING AN INTEGRATED AMERICA. When the government hired Disney to produce educational shorts about modern health issues, Walt added an anti-racist subtext by insisting (over objections from some officials) upon including among the children a centrally situated, non-stereotypical African in *Defense against Invasion* (1943). (Property of Walt Disney Productions; reprinted courtesy of Buena Vista Releasing.)

THE USES AND MISUSES OF CARICATURE. Racial caricaturing within a work of art is always abhorrent when employed to imply the inferiority of any one ethnic group or when any one such group is singled out for negative caricature while, in contrast, the Anglos are more fully developed. Disney takes the other approach: The Indians in *Pecos Bill,* though certainly caricatured, are no more exaggerated than any of the grotesque whites encountered in the story (TOP). Likewise, the five black crows in *Dumbo* are *positively* caricatured, being the only characters (other than Dumbo's mother) who—like the brown mouse—reveal true and selfless humanity (BOTTOM). (Property of Walt Disney Productions; reprinted courtesy of Buena Vista Releasing.)

DEFYING THE PRODUCTION CODE. Though nudity was banished from films following Joseph Breen's 1933 crusade to "clean up" Hollywood, Disney alone managed to slip subliminal images of healthy sensuality into films like *Fantasia* (TOP); in that same movie (BOTTOM), he defended "the orgy," depicting such an event as harmless fun for positively portrayed characters, whereas conservative directors like Cecil B. DeMille used open sexuality to identify villains who would in the end die horribly. (Property of Walt Disney Productions; reprinted courtesy of Buena Vista Releasing.)

THE INCEPTION OF DIVERSITY. Ten years ahead of his time, Disney cast ethnics in anti-clichéd roles. Creating a symbol for the typical American farmer in *Food Will Win the War,* he chose an African American (TOP); as signifier of our common pan-American heritage in *The Grain That Built a Hemisphere,* Walt picked a notably nonviolent Native American (BOTTOM). (Property of Walt Disney Productions, 1942, 1943; reprinted courtesy of Buena Vista Releasing.)

THE "STRAFING" OF ACAPULCO BEACH. Politically correct critics attack Disney for allowing Donald Duck and friends to sweep down on Latina women in *The Three Caballeros,* claiming it is both racist and sexist. They fail to take into account the moral context. The Duck and his pals are portrayed as embarrassing jerks, while the women are all shown in a highly positive light. The film (and the filmmaker) criticize rather than celebrate such outrageous activity, qualifying the sequence as both anti-racist and anti-sexist. (Property of Walt Disney Productions; reprinted courtesy of Buena Vista Releasing.)

THE SECRET LIFE OF A MACHO MALE. Disney films imply that extreme macho posturing may be an attempt to cover up and compensate for deep-seated insecurities about one's gender identity. Tough, abusive Sgt. Pete is such a character. In *The Vanishing Private* (1942), when he believes no one is around, Pete dances with pink flowers (TOP). In *The Old Army Game* (1943), Pete slips into bed with blissfully oblivious draftee Donald (BOTTOM). (Property of Walt Disney Productions; reprinted courtesy of Buena Vista Releasing.)

A KISS IS STILL A KISS. A male-to-male kiss was all but unheard of in Production Code Hollywood. Disney alone circumvented such rules. Chip 'n' Dale in *Two Chips and a Miss* (1944) are among many male characters who embrace and, to their surprise, enjoy it. (Property of Walt Disney Productions; reprinted courtesy of Buena Vista Releasing.)

Queen's "black") magic, Grumpy will never be grumpy again. Disney's dwarfs fulfill, in the words of Michelle Wallace in *Ms.*, the hope that

> men must be made so uncomfortable by the lunacy of sexism that they feel compelled to do a few things males seem rarely to do—explore their motivations and become suspicious of their desires in regard to women.[22]

For economy's sake, Disney eliminates several attempts by the Queen to kill Snow-white. While an unpleasant incident involving attempted strangulation may have been excised for the sake of family entertainment, another appears cut for a thematic purpose. The Grimms' Queen tempted Snow-white with a poisoned comb, which so attracted the girl that she opened her door. By implication, then, Snow-white is, in the source, as vulnerable to vanity as her antagonist. Disney's Snow White allows the crone to enter only because she carries an apple, which the heroine hopes to bake in a pie for her friends. The Grimms' greedy, selfish girl wanted to devour the apple all by herself. The original Snow-white endangered herself by superficial self-interest; Disney's Snow White, by her desire to please others who, having treated her well, deserve recompense.

The Grimms' Snow-white appears an absolute airhead, allowing the same tricky pedlar woman into her home three times. Disney's Snow White slips only once, in accordance with her construction as an intelligent if imperfect being. As in Grimm, Disney's dwarfs warn her about strangers. Here, though, she appears less dumb than naïve, admirably vulnerable to an old woman's protestations. In Disney, not only the dwarfs but also the animals sense danger, though Snow White—still the radical innocent—does not. However strong an individual Snow White may be, there comes a time when only community effort will suffice. Animals (nature) and dwarfs (men) align themselves for the first time, owing to a now-shared belief in the positive female principle. Together, they rush (too late) to rescue their dearly beloved, as Snow White bites into the poisoned apple. Though this might appear to cut across the film's incipiently feminist grain, the opposite proves true. Were Disney to present Snow White as perfect, she would not qualify as a feminist heroine, only an old-fashioned male's placement (in art) of his ideal woman on a pedestal. Few things prove more damaging to healthy relationships between women and men than dichotomizing women as saints or sinners. Despite a descent into evil and madness, even the Queen is hardly a cliché. Rather, she embodies a warning against an all-too-true type of self-defeating female behavior. Likewise, Snow White—however good and honorable—is a fine, decent, though flawed, woman who can learn as much from men and nature as she can teach them.

A complaint can be lodged about the way in which everything ends happily—and with that harbinger of Hollywood happy endings, a traditional marriage. Even here, Disney improves on the original and, in the process, proves himself progressive within his essentially traditionalist context. The Grimms supply no foreshadowing of salvation; their Snow-white was dead, so her revival seems only a dubious deus ex machina. Disney adds an earlier line in which even the Queen is made aware that Snow White—kept in a glass coffin by the adoring dwarfs—can rise from the dead upon "a true love's kiss." So Prince Charming arrives, having searched for the girl he briefly loved and lost.

Had Disney followed the letter of the original, his feminist fable would have been spoiled. The Grimms' prince covets Snow-white not out of love, but rather because, in his words, "I cannot live without *looking* at Snow-white." Since the 1970s, feminists emphasize the importance of "liberation [for a woman] from the *eye* of the [male] beholder."[23] Critic Laura Mulvey's conception of "the male gaze" has become a staple of feminist film criticism. The least enlightened of males, the Grimms' prince is obsessed with her physical allure rather than, as in Disney, truly in love with a person.

The modern American woman, like the Grimms' Snow-white, is, in the words of Shulamith Firestone, "haunted by fears that [an attentive man] doesn't love the 'real' her—and usually she is right."[24] Usually, but not always—and never in Disney. The Grimms' Snow-white awoke when, being moved by the prince to a place where he could daily adore her, a piece of poisoned apple fell from her mouth. Her reward was to become a walking, talking beauty-object rather than an immobile one. "I would rather *have* you than anything in the world," The Grimms' prince informs Snow-white. Disney's prince makes no such possessive pronouncement. He and Snow White ride off as equals, arm in arm. There is no retro depiction (which many viewers recall, though this never appears onscreen) of her being carted away in the prince's arms. They are, as Caroline Bird expressed it in *Born Female*, prototypes of the modern, enlightened couple that emerged in the seventies, married or cohabiting, who always "think of themselves [first and foremost] as companions."[25]

Disney adamantly defends heterosexual marriage. The traditionalist in him would have been horrified at Kate Millet, WITCH, Daughters of Bilitis, and other organizations that called for the total abolition of this institution. On the other hand, Disney's progressive side caused him to break new ground within male-dominated Hollywood cinema by insisting, via his film's subtexts, on equality between woman and man in a reformed and redeemed marital situation. In the final image, Disney's Snow White is not glimpsed (as in the source's ending) in the castle of the prince's father—a trophy-wife possessed by men with power. Rather, she heads toward distant clouds, which gradually take on the shape of a castle . . . though only in the moviegoer's mind . . . and, perhaps, Snow White's. Her prince may not be an aristocrat after all, possibly cannot offer his new bride a physical castle. That, as this Snow White knows and Disney implies, doesn't matter. A man's home is his castle. Any woman who *shares* such a place *as his equal* is a queen in the fullest and finest sense. No Ibsenesque doll's house for Disney's Snow White. She will never play at being a wife, inhabiting like Shakespeare's disappointed Portia only the suburbs of her husband Brutus's "good pleasure." This Snow White will stand alongside her husband, living a thoroughly revised definition of what we mean by the term "happily ever after."

Mother of the Bride
Cinderella (1949)

During World War II, women were portrayed as patiently waiting for their men in sentimental, propagandistic movies. In the postwar years, they were—in the altered, cynical context of film noir—envisioned as beautiful, betraying bitch goddesses. However brilliant individual films may have been—*Double Indemnity* (1944), *Out of the Past* (1947), *The Lady from Shanghai* (1948)—their collective attitude can hardly help but draw criticism today. On the other hand, Disney's *Cinderella* appears enlightened when contrasted with the more generalized cinematic conception of women from that time. Most "adult" movies of the late forties play as bitter indictments of the female. Disney's—despite a family orientation—offer a more complex view.

An element of female empowerment appears even before the story begins. As an old book opens and viewers see the "Once upon a time . . ." intro, an unseen narrator's voice reads the words aloud. Significantly, it's a *female* voice—warm, resonant, and intelligent. However normal now, the employment of a woman in this capacity was, in the late 1940s, as unlikely as a female news anchor being hired for a radio or TV broadcast. The long-held prejudice that a man's voice sounded more "objective" and "rational" held sway. Disney alone broke that gender barrier.

As in *Snow White,* in the previous decade, this film early on warns against the Beauty Trap. The orphaned Cinderella's stepmother and half sisters, Drusilla and Anastasia, are "bitterly jealous" of the girl's "charm and beauty." Disney turns his back on the source, where the sisters were themselves "beautiful and fair in appearance." The Grimms' Cinderella appears nondescript until adorned with a magical makeover that briefly conveys an appealing if artificial surface—allowing her to "catch" the prince by calculatedly exploiting the male gaze. Disney's shrewish sisters have sufficient motivation to be jealous: this Cinderella is indeed a beauty. Significantly, though, she's a *natural* beauty whose loveliness shines through her rags, thereby reversing the source's conception. The Grimms' notion of Cinderella as unattractive owing to her clothing, becoming gorgeous after receiving a "gold gown," is justly deserving of the feminist dismissal of a certain kind of artificial beauty as dehumanizing. Disney reverses such attitudes.

The essential concept—an outright attack on the fallacy of judging women by appearance only—emerges as this film offers a variation on *Snow White*'s theme. Cinderella is completely unimpressed with (if not oblivious to) her physical attractiveness. She cannot be faulted for being born with good looks any more than Gloria Steinem. It would be wrong to dismiss a woman of brains *and* beauty so long as she keeps the latter in perspective. As Disney heroines, Cinderella and Snow White are sisters under the skin. If Snow White brought woodland animals into the dwarfs' home, then Cinderella hides her household's vulnerable animals from the wicked people who run this place.

Structurally speaking, *Cinderella* emerges as *Snow White* turned inside out, providing a perfect complement to the earlier movie. That notion is enhanced by Disney's sense of cinematic geography. Whereas *Snow White* opened with the Queen on high, gazing down from her tower's window at the young woman below, this film begins with an upward camera movement toward just such a tower, Cinderella up on high and inside. Still, certain elements, essential to his ongoing vision, do not alter. For Cinderella, as for Snow White, marriage is the end-all, suggesting there are indeed limitations to any feminist interpretation. Again, though, there's a farsightedness to Disney's presentation of marriage. This is enhanced here by Disney's portrayal of the prince's father, broadly caricatured as a well-intentioned yet foolish old king who literally daydreams about the grandchildren he doesn't have but desperately wants. For this reason, he grows ever more anxious for his son to take a bride. This satiric (if never savagely so) vision presages the contemporary feminist point of view that "marriage had been the invention of men to . . . take control of [women's] capacity for reproduction—in order to lay claim to the rights of property."[26] In contrast, there's the prince, who, like *Snow White*'s indistinguishable male hero, signifies the emerging enlightened American male, here wandering less to look for medieval romance or chivalric adventure than searching for a sense of self.

The ball, in Disney's version, is held to celebrate the return of a prodigal son. In the source, the less ambitious (and less interesting) prince never left his father's kingdom. In Disney, the invitation list is open to *all* "available maidens," including ones as unattractive as Cinderella's stepsisters. In the source, only "*beautiful* young women" (emphasis added) were allowed entrance, so the prince "might choose between them." The institution of marriage would shortly emerge as a key Hollywood theme, most notably in Vincente Minnelli's *Father of the Bride* (1950). In such a context, *Cinderella* appears considerably foresighted in comparison to that celebration of capitalist excess. The title character (Spencer Tracy) prepares for an elaborate ritual in which his daughter (Elizabeth Taylor) will cease to be his little girl, emerging as an American Nora—a trophy-wife living in the Ibsenesque home of her husband (Don Taylor). Such portrayals were also evident in most other marriage-minded movies of the Eisenhower era, running the gamut from *Seven Brides for Seven Brothers* (1954) to *Gentlemen Marry Brunettes* (1955).[27]

While the source's prince unquestioningly does as told by his father, Disney's modernist hero scoffs at the notion of a certain time when anyone—male or female—"ought to" get married. Serving as the filmmaker's spokesman, this prince never damns (any more than he dreams of) the institution itself. He'll marry, happily and without hesitation, at that moment when he meets a woman who impresses him as an individual, rather than in the service of a conservative social convenience. As a foil, there's his father, forever muttering things like "There must be one who would make a suitable mother . . . wife."

In the introduction to their anthology *Woman in Sexist Society,* Vivian Gornick and Barbara K. Moran complain that as long as unenlightened, patriarchal males call the shots,

> woman shall remain a person defined not by her brain or her will or spirit, but rather by her *childbearing* properties and her status as *companion* to *men* who make, and do, and *rule* the earth. [Emphasis mine.][28]

By favoring the son, Disney makes clear whose side this auteur is on. Disney comes down squarely in favor of the feminist position expressed, some twenty years later, in *The Dialectic of Sex:* "the *patriarchal family* . . . defined woman as a different species due to their unique childbearing capacity" (emphasis added).[29]

Cinderella, of course, will prove to be the prince's right woman. In Grimm, however, the prince is single-mindedly (indeed, simplemindedly) attracted to the way she *looks* after donning her magical gown. In Disney, he isn't drawn to Cinderella's pleasant physicality so much as to her overall essence. Likewise, Disney's Cinderella undergoes a confusion not present in the source. For this Cinderella never realizes she's danced with the prince, but is mistakenly convinced she's fallen for an ordinary man—ordinary, at least, in the world's eyes. She, then, projects the new American woman who would assume center stage during the second half of the twentieth century.

That famed theme song of all Disney heroines—"Someday, my prince will come!"—is well illustrated here. What attracts her to the young man ("*my* prince" rather than "*the* prince") is his rightness for *her.* That is why she falls in love, not (as in the source) the potential of "marrying up." "Bride," Cinderella sighs, articulating a perfect balance between old (still subscribing to marriage) and new (redefining marriage for a new age). Other women in the film likewise present positive images of women who "take charge." The fairy godmother was nonexistent in Grimm, wherein a magic tree does the job. But if Disney planned to include an evil old stepmother, then for fairness's sake, there must also be a fine older lady as her foil—a positive female pole for full moral compass.

Cinderella will, receiving inspiration from her fairy godmother after the darkest moment, reassert her power of fiercely tested positive thinking. This too connects Disney's film to the later women's movement: "One of the curious and interesting things . . . is [the feminists'] discovery of Mother," Decter noted. "Several volumes of the movement's literature are dedicated to the author's mother," for whom the feminist writer has during her own life's journey gained new respect.[30] All the while, Cinderella's determination is mirrored by the little mice who create, in Disney's delightful addition, a makeshift gown. Though wiseguy Jacques initiates this project ("Cinderelly, Cinderelly, we can help our Cinderelly") while slow-minded Gus-Gus performs most of the grunt work, a female mouse assumes full control of the operation. Under her knowing guidance, the task is properly performed by male subordinates. Orchestrating the work of animals cleaning the house, she resembles a miniature Snow White. Only when a woman is in charge do men perform menial jobs properly.

In the Company of Women
Sleeping Beauty (1959)

Marriage is here again a central issue, though the filmmaker's approach is even more questioning than in the earlier films. Freely inventing from material in both Grimm and Perrault, while effectively pacing the picture to Peter Tchaikovsky's *Sleeping Beauty Suite,* Disney's team chose to begin their version with the announcement of an arranged marriage. The recently born Princess Aurora (Rosamond in the original) is betrothed by her parents to five-year-old Prince Philip, heir-apparent in a neighboring friendly country (Philip doesn't exist in the source). Only after establishing this impending situation does Disney introduce the essential plot device. Furious at not being invited to the betrothal ceremony, a witch (here called Maleficent) decrees that the princess will die after pricking herself on a spinning wheel. In Grimm, this will happen at age fifteen, Rosamond in her final days of childhood. Disney shifts the date to a year later, when, at sixteen, Aurora, every bit a teenager, will be torn between childlike loyalties and adult instincts.

Initially, Disney follows the source, having a good fairy (twelfth and last in Grimm, her number here reduced to third) alter the curse to sleep rather than death—an indeterminate time in the film, one hundred years in the original. The king's only solution (in both versions) is to destroy all the kingdom's spinning wheels in a great bonfire, interpreted by Disney as a well-intentioned male's drastic (and notably unsuccessful) response to the problem. Here, Walt breaks from the earlier conception by having his three wise women/fairies spirit Aurora away. They will live together, as a community, in the woods—precisely that sort of women's commune numerous feminists experimented with throughout the seventies. "There is a fear on men's part," Anne Koedt warned, "that women will seek the company of other women on a full, human basis . . . [and thereby] threaten the heterosexual institution" of marriage.[31] Disney, based on internal evidence in his work, reveals himself as that rare male *not* threatened, and obviously admiring such an approach. The drama that follows makes clear that marriage is indeed not threatened, but in good time salvaged, by just such a community of women. His mother figures/female mentors raise their foundling close to nature, leading to another of Disney's admirable "natural women"—beautiful without makeup.

Aurora (now called Briar Rose) becomes, like Snow White and Cinderella, linked—in the film's visuals and its music—to gentle birds; the villainess/foil, like her predecessors, is accompanied by a menacing raven. The good fairies (their names, including Flora and Fauna, make clear they, too, are *natural* women, if elderly ones) blessed the girl not only with outward beauty but also inward spirit. Once again, this positive personality is effectively expressed in the unique context of a movie-musical—in Disney, "song" always symbolizing a sweet yet fiercely independent spirit. As in the earlier films, song first attracts the prince to her. Another of Disney's young wanderer figures, Philip likewise overhears the girl singing in the woods to animal friends. He's irresistibly drawn to the source of that wondrous sound. We really do believe that, were he to discover a woman less physically perfect than the one he encounters, he would still fall in love with her.

Likewise, she falls in love with him. "Women are in no position to love freely," one 1970s feminist posited. "About the only discrimination women are able to exercise is the choice between the men who have chosen them."[32] But in Disney films, each heroine chooses for herself—a reversal of what occurs in Grimm and Perrault. These two teenagers, though consistent with earlier Disney incarnations of young people discovering true love, also reflect the period during which *Sleeping Beauty* was created. "Why do they still treat me like a child?" Aurora/Briar Rose complains of the three good fairies. Her precise words were, four years earlier, spoken by Natalie Wood's Judy in *Rebel without a Cause* about her parents. Shortly, Prince Philip has strong words for his dominating parent: "Father, you're living in the past!" He then storms out of the castle, rejecting the patriarch's carefully formulated future plans, riding off to the woods to meet his true love. With similar words, *Rebel*'s Jimbo (James Dean) rushed out of his father's house, hopped into his car, and headed for a wooded—i.e., "natural"—spot to meet Judy.

Finally, Disney brings one of the most significant plot elements from the earlier films to full fruition. Like Snow White and Cinderella before her, the princess has no idea she's fallen in love with a prince. She responded to the man as an individual, as—importantly—he did to her. Now, though, in an ironic turn of events, the prince likewise does not know he has met, and fallen in love with, the very princess he's promised to. Each, aware of but unconcerned with his/her royal station, would affront the social order by marrying a peasant. Like earlier Disney couples, though more adamant and insistent, Aurora and Philip would willingly defy an outdated structure were it to stand in the way of true love.

Whenever possible, Disney diminishes any element in the source that might inadvertently create what we today would tag as a sexist tone. The Grimms' princess, on the eve of her birthday, discovered the spinning wheel when

> the king and queen rode abroad, and the maiden was left behind alone in the castle. She wandered about into all the nooks and corners, and into all the chambers and parlours, as the fancy took her.

Rosamond proved a second cousin to Pandora—the heedless, immature female who surrendered to whimsical curiosity and opened the wrong box, loosing evil upon the world. Disney's mature, complex, emotionally torn young woman—weeping alone, Juliet-like, divided between duty to beloved parents (promised marriage to a royal man) and to herself (desired marriage to the man she truly loves)—is instead cast in a spell that draws her unwillingly toward the wheel.

The Grimms' prince (arriving a century later, after countless others tried and failed to break through walls of thorn hedge), did so for the most superficial of reasons: "I do not fear to try, I shall win through and *see* the lovely Rosamond" (emphasis added). His only desire is to fulfill a male compulsion by getting a good *look* at this girl's legendary beauty. Conversely, Philip fights his way through all barriers to rejoin his "one true love," the girl—make that "woman"—of his dreams. The prince in Grimm is, simply, lucky. As the hundred years have passed, thorns fall away so he has no trouble entering unscathed. The prince in other earlier versions does hack his way through the barrier, allowing ample opportunity to display considerable—and conventional—machismo. Disney alone feminizes the situation. His Prince Philip, locked away in a dungeon by Maleficent, cannot perform his princely duties without help from the three good women.

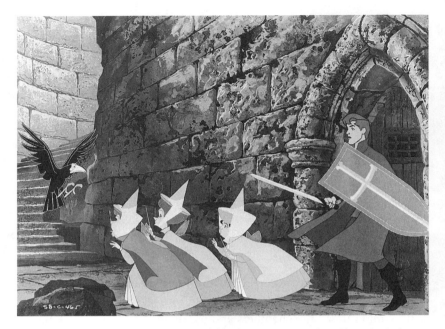

THE FEMINIZATION OF FAIRY TALES. In Perrault's *Sleeping Beauty*, Prince Charming is the traditional male hero who single-handedly rescues the helpless virgin. Disney's version transforms that macho parable into a feminist fable, as he merely follows a community of strong women. (Copyright 1958 Walt Disney Productions; courtesy Buena Vista Releasing.)

It is *they* who break his chains, *they* who provide a bridge for him to escape over a dangerous moat, *they* who cut away the thorn hedge, and *they* who finally transform his ordinary sword into a magic weapon, able to conquer the dragon barring his way. Without a team of capable, clever women accompanying him across dangerous ground, Disney's hapless prince would not succeed. When he does, it is at reawakening the woman he deeply cares for with true love's kiss. For Grimm, "when he saw her *looking* so *lovely* in her sleep, he could not turn away his eyes; and presently he stopped and kissed her" (emphasis added). What we encounter in the old tale could today be viewed as sexual victimization of a woman by a man obsessed with her physical beauty but uncaring about her person—imposing himself upon her without permission.

Disney even adds, through a gag, one final notion of the ever-present importance of women—and not only young, conventionally beautiful ones. Two of the good fairies have agreeably argued throughout as to whether Aurora's wedding gown ought to be blue or pink. The couple dances together, first in the castle and then amid clouds. All the while, the two good (if slightly mischievous) fairies employ their magic wands to constantly change the dress's color, back and forth. Though the lovers remain oblivious, we are kept very much aware of women who have, throughout the preceding events, controlled the story's situation for positive purposes. Even when at odds with one another, they continue to do so—seemingly forever. It is a fitting way to end not only this individual film, but the trilogy by which Disney transformed patriarchal old fairy tales into contemporary feminist fables.

Herstory

So Dear to My Heart (1948)

Old Yeller (1957)

Davy Crockett, King of the Wild Frontier (1954–1956)

Tales of Texas John Slaughter (1958–1961)

The Story of Robin Hood (1952)

Rob Roy, the Highland Rogue (1954)

The Sword and the Rose (1953)

Lady and the Tramp (1955)

The African Lion (1955)

Jungle Cat (1960)

Perri (1957)

The early articulation of feminist thinking evident in the fairy-tale trilogy was hardly confined to animated classics. Strong women, including nonglamorous females, handily compete with men in the world of business or manage a home, this always a matter of the female's choice. In *So Dear to My Heart*, set in heartland America during the early twentieth century, Grandma (Beulah Bondi) is first glimpsed doing the plowing on her farm. Where her "man" is (having deserted, now dead) is never mentioned. Disney apparently didn't consider an explanation worth the effort. The same holds true for Westerns. Dozens of filmmakers told the tales of post–Civil War Texans, heading up the trail to Kansas cowtowns. Only Disney focused instead on the frontier woman left behind to maintain a household, as incarnated by Dorothy McGuire in *Old Yeller*. Even when the focus remains on a relatively traditional male hero—frontiersman Davy Crockett (Fess Parker), cattleman John Slaughter (Tom Tryon)—

VEIN OF IRON. In the historical novels of Ellen Glasgow, frontier women were portrayed as stronger than the men, an image that rarely appeared in movies. Disney offered the exception; females old *(So Dear to My Heart)* (TOP) or young *(Old Yeller)* (BOTTOM) are most often seen working behind a plow, the children required to help with the chores. (Copyright 1946 and 1958 Walt Disney Productions; courtesy Buena Vista Releasing.)

Disney emphasizes the relationship of the man to his wife, particularly the equality of their relationship.

The same holds true for the British historical films. *Robin Hood* and *Rob Roy* concentrated, as their titles indicate, on legendary male outlaw heroes. Even here, though, Disney's image of women is impressive and, by today's standards, enlightened. Maid Marian does not, as in the more famous Warner Brothers version (1936), serve as Robin's aristocratic trophy-wife after arriving in Sherwood. Disney's Maid Marian becomes a full member of the revolutionary force, trading in her elegant clothing for the rough green outfit worn by the Merrie Men. She then volunteers for the most hazardous mission of all, spying on Prince John and his ruling-class thugs. Without her, Robin and his men could not pull off their final daring mission. Likewise, Queen Eleanor of Aquitaine—though elderly—physically joins in the fight against her oppressive son.

In Disney's depiction of the Highland Rogue, Rob Roy's mother and wife both join in the Scottish rebel's fight against tyranny. More significantly, they invoke a feminine, and incipiently feminist, principle by—after proving their equality as worthy combatants—convincing the righteous outlaw to give up violence and find more peaceful ways to solve political problems. Only when he listens to this advice—advice that proves to be correct—is a just peace at last created. All's well that ends well, and, in Disney, things "end well" only when the men allow the will of women to override their own violent inclinations. This concept was furthered still in Disney's version of Charles Major's novel *When Knighthood Was in Flower,* a historical romance based on incidents from the reign of England's Henry VIII. The book's title indicated male domination of the period. To make the material more in line with his ongoing vision, Disney scuttled that concept, suggesting an equality between men and women when he named his movie after a symbol for each: *The Sword and the Rose.* While the sword of hero Charles Brandon (Richard Todd) dominates in the film's early portions, the rose of heroine Mary Tudor (Glynis Johns) wins out at the finale.

Animated films were released intermittently with such live-action dramas. There's a touch of feminism in *Lady and the Tramp.* When several male dogs kid Lady about her obvious pedigree, a rough-hewn female, Peg, comes to Lady's defense. For Disney, sisterhood exists even among *les biches.* A sensitivity to women's issues can be found in the *True-Life Adventures.* In *The African Lion,* the female of the species is seen dragging a gazelle's carcass to her hungry cubs. During the hunt, Disney

THE SWORD OF SHERWOOD FOREST. In Disney's version of the Locksley legend, Maid Marian (Joan Rice) is not, like Olivia de Havilland in the more famous Warner Brothers movie of two decades earlier, a papier-mâché helpless heroine, waiting for Robin Hood to rescue her. A flesh and blood woman, she can wield her lover's sword when necessary, or employ it as a phallic symbol when he is absent. (Copyright 1952 Walt Disney Productions; courtesy Buena Vista Releasing.)

emphasizes her ingenuity and courage. Constantly, there are crosscuts to the male, seen lazily yawning, much to the audience's amusement. *Jungle Cat* similarly focuses on the female of the species, her mate reduced to a supporting role. The title character in *Perri, a True-Life Fantasy,* is a female squirrel, her mate Porro seen strictly in relationship to her primacy.

Into the Sixties

Pollyanna (1960)
The Absent-Minded Professor (1961)
A Tiger Walks (1964)
Follow Me, Boys! (1966)

As the sixties emerged, Disney's live-action comedies and dramas presented portraits of liberated women freeing the minds of men heretofore locked in constrictive worldviews. When, in *Pollyanna,* we see an old-fashioned band playing at an evening carnival, the drummer is a female, a fact emphasized in close-ups. Not a stunning young woman, to lend the scene sex appeal, but an older, unglamorous lady, clearly chosen owing to her talent. In *The Absent-Minded Professor,* Betsy (Nancy Olson)—is presented as a protofeminist heroine: self-sufficient, working at the college not because she has to (proposals come to her constantly), but because she wants to, flatly refusing to marry to satisfy social convention or for financial security.

In *A Tiger Walks,* Pete the sheriff (Brian Keith)—a traditional "man's man" in the John Wayne mold—is forced to choose between two value systems: the natural love of women—represented by his daughter (Pamela Franklin) and wife (Vera Miles)—and the unnatural ambitions of men (symbolized by a jaded coterie of local political leaders, uptight middle-age Anglo men in business suits). At the moment of decision, Pete moves in opposition to what the stock Western hero would do—deciding to stand with the women and attempt to rescue an escaped circus animal rather than use guns to kill it. By absorbing female values, Pete saves himself from the macho mentality that threatened to destroy him in their more enlightened eyes.

Likewise, Disney's approval of what would shortly emerge as feminist values is in evidence in *Follow Me, Boys!* as Vida (Vera Miles) makes her choice between retro male Ralph (Elliott Reid) and iconoclastic Lem (Fred MacMurray). Though Ralph owns a new car and can chauffeur Vida around, while Lem is unable even to afford new shoes, attitude—not social status—attracts this enlightened woman. Vida isn't necessarily sure that she wants to marry at all, and has refused to do so for conventional reasons. She will marry if, and only if, she finds a man worthy of sharing her life.

When, on the open road, the three accidentally come into contact (Vida and Ralph are picnicking, Lem out camping with his scout troop), Ralph

"YOU DON'T OWN ME!" A song with that title, performed by Lesley Gore during the early sixties, is often considered the first feminist rock 'n' roll record; Disney championed such an attitude in *Follow Me, Boys!* His heroine threatens to break off the relationship if her fiancé ever again "orders" instead of "asking" her to help. (Copyright 1965 Walt Disney Productions; courtesy Buena Vista Releasing.)

makes the mistake of ordering (rather than asking) Vida to step back into the car. Outraged, she prefers to walk back to town with the scouts, later breaking a dinner date with Ralph to attend a movie with Lem. He, however, almost loses Vida, for reasons similar to Ralph's macho-mentality blunder. While Lem is trying to teach the boys to be self-reliant in nature,

Vida shows up with chicken dinners for everyone. Lem is insistent that she remove the food at once, so that they can learn to survive on their own.

Vida has no objection to Lem's concept but questions his tone of voice:

> VIDA: Is that an . . . *order?*
> LEM: No, a suggestion.

She can live with this answer, so they enter into a debate as to whether the boys ought to be allowed to eat the dinner. Suddenly, though, Lem reverses his position.

> LEM: All right, it's an *order!*
> VIDA: Now, you sound like *Ralph!*

Though Lem is far more attractive than Ralph, that does him no good whatsoever. To win the Disney woman, a man must first set aside what she fumingly refers to as "male pride." In time, Lem backs off his patriarchal position, something Ralph proved unable to do.

> LEM: All I did was ask you to get rid of the chicken.
> VIDA: No, you didn't. You said: "I forbid you." Huh! "Master of the Universe."

There's little question whose side Disney is on. The male-as-master is an offensive notion, throughout his work in general, in this film in particular. In time, Lem and Vida will become Disney's vision of the enlightened couple, existing in a state of total equality—the ultimate onscreen expression of Disney's enlightened attitude.

BEWITCHED, BOTHERED, AND BEWILDERED. Practitioners of Wicca (commonly if incorrectly referred to as "witches") have been more maligned in motion pictures than any other minority group. Disney alone humanized such people; in *The Three Lives of Thomasina*, a minion of the moon (Susan Hampshire) teaches a man of science (Patrick McGoohan) that there is more to heaven and earth than dreamt of in his philosophy. (Copyright 1963 Walt Disney Productions; courtesy Buena Vista Releasing.)

7

Something Wiccan This Way Comes
Walt's Wonderful World of Witchcraft

Most Wiccans know the goddess as three aspects, corresponding
to the three stages in life. These are the maiden, the mother, and
the crone.
—SCOTT CUNNINGHAM (1988)

Everybody's feeling warm and bright;
Such a fine and natural sight.
We don't bark, and we don't bite,
Dancin' in the moonlight.
—KING HARVEST (1973)

By the mid-1970s, most women appreciated that their screen image
was finally being presented with more sensitivity than had been the case in
earlier Hollywood films. If there was a single notable exception, however,
it was Wiccan woman, who—in the traditional guise of the evil witch,
be she an ugly old crone or a desirable young seductress—inevitably appeared onscreen as a menace. In society itself, however, the cultural revolution of the sixties had initiated a reconsideration:

> The youth movement . . . rebelled against rigid social codes and Chris-
> tian based ideals. Some young persons turned to Buddhism, Zen, and
> other Eastern teachings. Others became enchanted with . . . spells,
> charms, herb magic, tarot cards, amulets, and talismans. . . . Today,
> the resurgence begun in the late 1960s has produced a generation
> [intrigued by] channeling, psychic healing, herbal medicine, sen-
> sory deprivation, holistic consciousness, crystal work, vegetarianism,
> neuro-linguistic programming, meditation, and Eastern teachings.[1]

Or, in a phrase, the New Age movement, which cut across three millennia
of Judeo-Christian thinking, as well as the scientific dictates of modern-
ism, to revive primal faiths in ancient gods.

In prehistorical times, the Great Goddess (like the earth, which she represented) signified a primitive gestalt in which nature, if occasionally dangerous, existed as a benign force to revel in, not revile. The earliest civilizations revered woman as "free, independent, and wise," implying (in today's terminology) a feminist bias to all the Old Religions—in societies as diverse as the Minoan Greeks and the ancient Egyptians, running through the dictates of Druidism to the credo of the Celts.[2] Such thinking has, for three thousand years, been considered alien to inherently patriarchal visions of God (Zeus, Jehovah, etc.), leading to the persecution of Wiccans, or, as they came to be popularly called, witches.

If mainstream Hollywood films have been consistently insensitive in their treatment of such figures, Disney's as always proved the exception. His films portrayed a more enlightened image of witches and their male counterparts, warlocks, both demystified in the shorts and feature-length films.

Knowing the Oak Tree
Melody Time (1948)
Johnny Tremain (1957)
Pollyanna (1960)
In Search of the Castaways (1962)

For early people who worshiped nature, the tree emerged as most revered of all natural forms. The very term "Druid" constitutes a variation on the ancient notion of "Drui," signifying "a knowledge of the Oak tree."[3] When forces of the Holy Roman Empire conquered what they considered to be the primitives in northern Europe, imposing Christianity on defeated peoples, those who converted under threat of death retained one beloved tradition—bringing a tree into the home during winter. They thinly disguised a pagan rite by decorating the tree with holy icons from the New Religion, thereafter referring to them as "Christmas trees," the very concept—when seriously studied—utterly paradoxical.

The Disney worldview, when closely considered, appears strikingly close to the pagan vision of life:

> a religion of magic and mysticism, and its followers were both spiritually and intimately connected to the sacredness of nature. To the Celts, trees, rocks, streams, mountains, and rivers were sacred places.[4]

Similarly, Disney has admitted:

> I have learned from the animal world, and what everyone will learn
> who studies it is: A renewed sense of kinship with the earth and all
> its inhabitants.[5]

Flora as well as fauna, as the love of plants, notably trees, is an essential
and recurring motif. The anthology *Melody Time* includes two notable
salutes to trees. First appears an animated depiction of Joyce Kilmer's
poem "Trees" (1913), concluding with the famous line that pantheistically
connects true religion with nature: "Only God can make a tree!" In the
"Johnny Appleseed" episode, Disney pays tribute to the nonviolent pioneer who, instead of fighting Indians, spent his entire life planting trees
that would thereafter provide humans and animals with a food source. At
the end, John Chapman is embraced by God for his good work. The brief
glimpse we have here of heaven—Disney's only significant image of that
place—is notably better when it becomes more *natural*, Johnny recruited
by an angel to add trees, the single missing ingredient.

In her novel *Johnny Tremain*, author Esther Forbes allows no indication of what Boston's rebels did following the famed Tea Party. Disney's
film vividly depicts their possible activity in a way that neatly characterizes
the auteur. Johnny (Hal Stalmaster) and his compatriots march through
the streets, singing; the communal concept of a chorus has been portrayed as redemptive in Walt's films since Snow White first taught the
seven dwarfs to sing as a group rather than as so many individuals, nothing more than a lonely crowd. The rebels congregate at the fabled Liberty
Tree, barely mentioned in the book yet central to the Disney Version, in
which this single spot of nature within the city becomes a spiritual rally-
ing point.

Trees, most often oaks, continue to offer the possibility of spiritual redemption in the films that follow. In *Pollyanna*, the title character (Hayley
Mills) and her long-haired, protohippieish companion (Kevin Corcoran)
despise traditional church services, but commune with God, as well as
one another, by climbing high into the branches of the town's largest tree.
In Search of the Castaways features Mills as another young woman who
convinces her companions to seek safety in the branches of an immense
tree, magically sprouting from the ocean, where they (and various animals as well) create their own variation on the concept of nature as heaven
on earth.

Today, Walt's notion of trees as portholes to spiritual enlightenment is carried on in films by the current Disney company, the Tree of Life in *The Lion King* (1994) being the most notable example. Even as Walt always employed the theme parks as places where his ideal world could be actualized, the current Animal Kingdom in Florida has, as its centerpiece, a Tree of Life. Also furthering the tradition is Tim Burton, who began his career as a Disney animator, and in his own (not unlike Walt's) eccentric way furthers the original Disney vision. In films as diverse as *The Nightmare before Christmas* (1993) and *Sleepy Hollow* (2000), the characters experience true enlightenment, as well as the metaphysical, by entering into portals of time and space existing within the cores of memorable trees.

The Familiar
Pluto's Judgment Day (1935)
Lady and the Tramp (1955)
The Great Cat Family (1956)
That Darn Cat (1965)
The Cat from Outer Space (1978)

Long before the birth of Christ, Hebrews railed against the worship of animals in general, cats in particular. As a long-lasting pop-culture artifact, Cecil B. DeMille's *The Ten Commandments* (1956) regularly reminds mainstream audiences (via ABC's annual broadcast of the film during the Passover/Easter season) of an anticat bias in Judeo-Christian thinking. Stalwart Moses (Charlton Heston) faces off against a sensuous, earthy Pharaoh (Yul Brynner), surrounded by immense statues of feline deities. As Lady Jane Wilde noted in her *Ancient Legends of Ireland,* circa 1880, the salutation upon entering an Emerald Isle home remained, for the better part of a millennium, "God save all here, except the cat." She continued:

> It is believed that the devil often assumes the form of these animals. The familiar of a witch is always a black cat. . . . They are endowed with reason, can understand conversations, and are quite able to talk if they considered it advisable and judicious to join in the conversation.[6]

An untold number of cats were burned along with more than 100,000 women and men accused of practicing the black arts in medieval and Renaissance Europe.[7] Ironically, their absence allowed the rat population to multiply, resulting in the Black Plague. Nonetheless, literature and film, ranging from Edgar Allan Poe's short story "The Black Cat" (1843) to Edgar G. Ulmer's deliciously perverse 1934 film of the same name, furthered a negative notion. Disney, and Disney alone, attempted to alter and diminish such prejudice within his medium of choice.

In *Pluto's Judgment Day* (1935), Mickey's beloved canine companion chases cats around the neighborhood with gleeful abandon. In a dream, he's dragged before a panel of cat judges, arrayed beneath immense cat-god statues from ancient Egypt. Pluto cowers as the feline jury forces him to realize that continuing such behavior will, in their view, damn him to an eternity in hell. He had better mend his ways while there is still time. No fool, Pluto (after waking) hugs and kisses Figaro, onetime companion to Pinocchio, now the familiar of Minnie Mouse. Shortly, Figaro would be transformed from sidekick to pint-size hero in a series of seven cartoons.

There was the occasional lapse. The twin Siamese cats in *Lady and the Tramp* have no redeeming value. But Disney the dramatist needed some villains to oppose his canine hero and heroine. Besides, these are the exceptions rather than the rule, the villainous felines necessary to offset what would otherwise have been undue romanticization of the cat. In Disney's vision, there are good and bad in any species. Without the twins, the full spectrum of feline possibilities would not be revealed. As if to compensate, Disney offered a revisionist view of this misunderstood animal with his broadcast of *The Great Cat Family* (originally televised September 19, 1956). The hour-long show proudly traced the cat's history back to its status as an Egyptian deity, offered much evidence that the stigma of felines in Christianized Europe was based on fallacies, and, finally, defended the studio's decision to make a series of movies portraying cats in a positive light. However entertaining, the show also served as an educational film, in the best Disney tradition, by deprogramming a viewer from some common prejudice that had come to be accepted as fact.

Rather than attempt to counter such groupthink by eliminating the age-old stigma of a metaphysical element, Walt retained this quality while implying that it should not rule out the cat as equal to the dog as loving companion. In *That Darn Cat,* a seemingly lighthearted comedy with serious implications, sisters Ingrid (Dorothy Provine) and Patti (Hayley Mills) Randall live alone for the summer while their parents are away. The older of the two, Ingrid has settled into an ultraconventional life, working a nine-to-five job. She dates the impossibly epicene boy-next-door,

Gregory Benson (Roddy McDowell), for no better reason than that, as a lawyer, he'll eventually make a great deal of money.

Patti, on the other hand, is typical of the emerging 1960s woman. Mills's English accent, always left intriguingly unexplained in her American contexts, heightens this quality during the period of the British Invasion (1963–1967) in popular music. In sharp contrast to her sister, hippieish Patti dates a surfer, Canoe (Tom Lowell), whom she entertains unchaperoned, after hours. Hard as it may be to believe today, this was all but unthinkable in middlebrow suburbia of the time, at least for a decent woman—though in the film's context, Patti's free living is always defended. But her actions drive a guardian of conventional morality, neighbor Mrs. MacDougall (Elsa Lanchester), crazy with wild thoughts about what must be "going on." In fact, nothing is happening. Though Patti cares naught for appearance, she's unswerving in her personal morality, making the choice not to have sex, which Canoe dutifully accepts. Patti, "The Maiden," enjoys a spiritual connection with D.C., a cat who shares their home. The sisters' attitudes toward D.C. make clear a distinction between "old" and "new" thinking. Ingrid refers to D.C. as "their" cat, implying ownership. Patti is quick to tell everyone he's a friend, who stays with them sometimes, free to wander whenever he wants. As the flower-children of the late sixties put it:

> *Let a thing go and, if it chooses*
> *To return, you'll have it forever.*

"Forever" is what Patti and D.C. share. She alone senses this Siamese's connection to ancient gods.

When D.C. wanders home one night with a wristwatch around his neck, Patti notices the letters "HEL" scratched on the back. Connecting with the cat, Patti—who, other than possessing heightened powers of insight, seems normal in every respect—is able to discern the truth. A kidnapped woman (Grayson Hall) scratched those letters, desperately slipping her watch around the stray cat's neck, hoping someone would discover the message and rescue her. Though everyone, including well-intentioned FBI agent Zeke Kelso (Dean Jones), tells Patti she's a kook, the girl—like all Disney heroines—believes in her own vision and perseveres.

She is, eventually, proven right, the hostage saved moments before the lowlives (Neville Brand and Frank Gorshin) attempt to kill her. As a result of all that occurs, Ingrid arcs, growing less conventional. Eventually, she

EVERYTHING I NEEDED TO KNOW ABOUT LIFE, I LEARNED FROM MY CAT. Most Disney films positively portray cats, the most popular companion to female Wiccans. In *That Darn Cat*, Dorothy Provine plays a pseudosophisticated woman who grows more natural (and bewitching) as she grows ever closer to her own cat. (Copyright 1964 Walt Disney Productions; courtesy Buena Vista Releasing.)

dumps Gregory to date the danger-loving but sensitive Kelso. The theme is signified by the "HEL" message on Margaret Miller's watch. If she had managed to scratch the entire word "HELP," the plot wouldn't be significantly altered, though the film's Wiccan subtext would be. "HEL" is the ultimate Wiccan term for the Great Goddess on earth.[8]

The most significant post-Walt cat film, *The Cat from Outer Space* opens (four years before *E.T.—The Extra-Terrestrial,* which it inspired) with an image of an unidentified flying object, dropping down into a rural area. We note a single house, inhabited by a simple family: the husband, an aging throwback to frontier types; his wife, strong and silent; their dog, loyal and fretful. As in the upcoming Spielberg film, a small visitor from outer space, left behind, must somehow find a means of returning to the mother ship, possible only through the help of an eccentric human. Wilson (Ken Berry), a throwback to Disney's genial insider/outsider figures—played during the 1960s by Fred MacMurray—is a brilliant but iconoclastic scientist whom the extraterrestrial cat instinctively realizes he can trust. When cat and companion flee well-intentioned but misguided military pursuers, they fly a motorcycle up into the sky, across the moon. That image, slightly reimagined, would shortly constitute the insignia of Amblin Entertainment.

In addition to the offbeat male (Wilson wears casual clothes, not the suits and ties of conformist scientists), there's a liberated woman present. Dr. Elizabeth Bartlett (Sandy Duncan) is the highly educated but engagingly flaky female lead, an equal with Wilson in defying both military and political powers to do what's right, if treasonous by conventional standards—returning the cat to his distant home. While on earth, the cat becomes their familiar. The feline possesses powers associated with cat gods, including levitation, and is able to alter the future by aligning his will with primal forces in the universe.

To return him home entails an elaborate plan that will surprise those who cling to the myth that Disney films are simplistically moralistic. The heroes fix horse races, betting on the outcome, winning enough to purchase the necessary rare, missing element to complete the craft and send the cat home, without thought of personal profit. That's made clear by their foil, a neighbor (MacLean Stevenson) who dreams of using the cat's power for raw capitalistic gain.

A Weird Way with Beasts
The Three Lives of Thomasina (1964)

The most ambitious of Disney's familiar films, its title refers to a cat who narrates (voice provided by Elspeth March) about her relationships with Mary McDhui (Karen Dotrice), a child growing up in the Scottish highlands, circa 1912, and Lori MacGregor (Susan Hampshire), a strange young woman who makes her home deep in the wood. Lori's abode appears a throwback to an earlier age, bereft of modern conveniences. She labors on an ancient loom, symbol of the Wiccan woman, the cottage itself surrounded by high-reaching trees, various animals all the while circling this loving incarnation of Hicks's *Peaceable Kingdom.*

Fortuitously, Lori finds the near-dead Thomasina and nurtures the cat back to health. Owing to her unique lifestyle, the locals fear Lori as a witch. Nonetheless, Geordie (Matthew Garber), a child who has learned (by "imitation" of his elders) prejudice, overcomes the narrowness of society and instinctively brings a hurt toad to her cottage. He senses this Wiccan woman is benign and positive; working in the Romantic tradition, Disney depicts the youngest child as first to open up to Lori. Geordie's pals, each older than the next, prove (in ascending order of age) more difficult to convince. But as each in turn is won over, Disney systematically demystifies "the witch" for his youthful audience.

The adults eventually learn of Lori's gentleness from their children ("the child is father to the man"). Early on, Lori—dealing with locals who wonder where her magical broom might be—seizes the one she's been using to clean her cottage, gleefully shaking it at the terrorized citizenry. The audience laughs with her, at them. We, like Geordie, quickly come to view Lori as the positive figure. There exists that rare adult, in touch with primal sympathy, who "understands." Here, it is Andrew's housekeeper, Mrs. MacKenzie (Jean Anderson), who defends Lori. Confronted with slurs regarding Lori's witchcraft, Mrs. MacKenzie replies:

> Lori's a bit strange. She has a weird way with beasts.

Lori is indeed a witch, though only in a sense stripped of that word's negative connotations—precisely the film's ambition and outlook. A practicing Wiccan, Lori—like others of her ilk—exists in continuing communion with nature, which endows her with curative powers. Initially, Andrew—the most logical, modern, scientific townsperson—scoffs when villagers cease bringing sick animals to him, turning instead to the supposedly mad girl in the woods:

> So you're going back to witchcraft? And the old superstitions!

Ordinarily, a Hollywood film would view their regression as Andrew does: Moving backward to something old and evil. Disney takes the opposite view. Andrew transforms from disbeliever ("No more talk about witches and magic," he tells little Mary. "Eat your supper, say your prayers, go to bed.") to Lori's most die-hard convert. "They call you a witch," Andrew initially tells Lori. "If you can get all the creatures to live here in peace, there may be some truth to it." She answers: "I love them!" Like early Wiccans, and those Earth Mothers so admired by the late-sixties counter-culture, Lori brings about peace through love in nature.

Another element of witchcraft—the benign spell of romantic love—has its place here. When Andrew comments on Lori's healing powers, she laughingly reminds him of the long-standing prejudice against her.

> LORI: I'm a witch. Remember?
> ANDREW: You must be. You've cast a spell over me.

Andrew realizes and accepts that he too has been "bewitched," though without negative implications. Lori achieves her greatest good when her spiritual and emotional gifts are aligned with Andrew's scientific and logical skills. This combining of old and new wisdoms, symbolized by the eventual marriage of the characters signifying them, is perfectly in line with Disney's ongoing approach. The yin/yang combines the best of both worlds, traditional values and progressive thinking held in perfect harmony.

This first occurs when Lori and Andrew work together to save a wounded animal. Later, Mary lies near death with pneumonia, having (like Pollyanna) temporarily lost her faith and, with it, the will to live. After modern medicine and traditional prayer fail to restore her, Andrew seeks out Lori, who calls back Mary's fading spirit. Andrew saves Mary by praying again, this time calling out not to Christ, as he earlier did with Reverend Peddie (Laurence Naismith), without notable result. Andrew now invokes the Great Goddess. At that moment, Thomasina appears at the window, restoring Mary's will to live.

The final image—Andrew and Lori married, Mary and Thomasina re-united—offers something more than merely a conventional happy ending. We encounter a satisfying variation on Disney's ongoing guardedly optimistic vision. Despite darkness in the world, positive results may (and will) be achieved if only logic and emotion are combined, by adults who listen together to the primal wisdom found in animals and children. As all four characters (Thomasina included) sit down to dinner, we realize this positive outcome has been achieved through Disney's paradigm for wisdom, happiness, and peace on earth.

The Maiden
Snow White and the Seven Dwarfs (1938)
Moon Pilot (1962)

The first stage in a Wiccan woman's life is the Maiden, a virgin who lives close to nature. Snow White is that film's representative Wiccan maiden. She necessarily deserts civilization for a more natural life in a wood. In the Green World, the Maiden fully acknowledges her heretofore dimly realized connection with the animal kingdom, sensing its potential for generating positive change. This allows Snow White to enact great good by transforming cold (male) technocrats of mining (the dwarfs) into responsive, fully realized humans, inducing them to dance at night with the animals they previously ignored.

Disney brought the Maiden out of the Dark Ages and into a contemporary setting with *Moon Pilot*. Bewitching Lyrae (Dany Saval) harks from another galaxy. As with the Maiden in all pro-Wiccan literature, she is associated with the moon, and serves as one of its minions. Her planet Beta Lyrae, as we learn from a song by Richard M. and Robert B. Sherman, is distinguished by its seven moons—that number closely associated with Wiccan culture, indicating why numerous New Age bookstores bear the name Seven Rays. Though as a Maiden Lyrae is implicitly virginal, she is also (true to the Wiccan tradition) highly sensuous in a positive way. Another song informs us that "True Love's an Apricot," fruit associated with romance, though not in the negative sense of the Judeo-Christian Bible's forbidden apple. Like all the best Wiccans, Lyrae arrives to harness positive powers of the universe and effect good. Lyrae knows, through her greater (female) wisdom, that America's first manned spacecraft will explode. She has come to provide a formula that, if applied to the surface, will ensure safety.

The space program's chosen astronaut is Captain Richmond Talbot (Tom Tryon), not surprisingly another of Disney's charmingly eccentric male heroes. Talbot is regarded as something of a Beatnik (and prehippie) by his straight-laced colleagues, allowing him to accept Lyrae in a manner impossible for a conventional astronaut. Following a safe takeoff, Talbot agrees with Lyrae that they ought to confiscate the rocket and head for her planet, so he can meet her parents and begin a period of proper courtship. This is in defiance of the patriarchal system at Space Command. Talbot is one more of Disney's unlikely rebel heroes who rightly abandons all patriotic ties for the sake of a woman he loves.

The Maiden and the Mother
Babes in Toyland (1961)
A Tiger Walk (1964)

Snow White "dies" only to rise again, owing to a sensual experience, her first *real* kiss. At movie's end, the Maiden appears completely comfortable with her upcoming move to the next natural stage in her development, the Mother. Likewise, Lori has, at the end of *Thomasina*, entered into that second aspect of the Great Goddess. Whereas the Maiden represented and reflected the earth in its untouched form, the Mother symbolized the land that had been cultivated, yielding up bounty for the future.[9] Few filmmakers have offered more positive portraits of mothers than Disney. "Your mother, and mine," Wendy sings to the lost boys; shortly, we sense, she will make the move from girl to woman.

The Mother and the Maiden, operating in tandem, dominate the action in Walt's reinterpretation of Victor Herbert's family-oriented operetta. First, though, we meet the familiar, Sylvester J. Goose, a talking animal companion of good witch Mother Goose (Mary McCarty). Her identity as a Wiccan is established by the hats she wears: Alternately, the traditional black cone and a bright wicker bonnet adorned with flowers, signifying her oneness with nature. The wall surrounding her house is a bright green, preferred color of Wiccans owing to its associations with nature. With her innocent ward Mary Contrary (Annette Funicello), this eternal Mother figure gently rules the magical realm of Mother Goose Land.

The female principle remains healthily earthbound; high up on a hill, in a dark castle, the villainous male patriarch Barnabas (Ray Bolger) peers down, intent on making mischief. Barnabas schemes to ruin the impending wedding of Mary to Tom Piper (Tommy Sands). He orders his helpers Gonzorgo (Henry Calvin) and Roderigo (Gene Sheldon) to kill Tom, so he can then marry Mary himself—such a loveless relationship of men with power and women of beauty always the target of Disney's wrath. A vivid incarnation of Disney's representative villain, Barnabas suffers not so much from lust (which might be forgiven) but capitalism at its rawest: greed for the considerable fortune Mary will inherit. His cohorts are, likewise, financially motivated. "We Won't Be Happy till We Get It" is the title of an extended song-and-dance routine in which the three celebrate riches they hope to acquire. In contrast, there's Mary's garden—nature perfected by the hardworking hands of a Maiden who appreciates silver bells, cockleshells, and pretty maids all in a row. Likewise, Mary's relationship with Tom portrays a combination of natural instincts and self-conscious restraint. "Just a whisper away," they sing in a restaging of the balcony scene from *Romeo and Juliet,* expressing their desire to consummate a burning love while remaining aware of the necessity of, for the time being at least, restraint.

When Bo Peep (Ann Jillian), Little Boy Blue (Kevin Corcoran), and several other children become lost in the Forest of No Return, it momentarily appears as if Disney will reverse his long-standing belief in nature as the source of goodness. Monstrous trees come to life, surrounding the little ones, seemingly spelling their doom. In fact, the children have more to fear from the human villains, watching from hiding. For reality belies appearance. The trees escort the children, as well as Tom and Mary, to Toyland, where the fussy Toymaker (Ed Wynn) and his eccentric assistant Grumio (Tommy Kirk) try their best to meet Santa's Christmas deadline. We realize that, as in the rightfully famous sequence depicting Snow White's first night in the forest, we have nothing to fear from nature. The darkness humankind sees there is nothing more than a false projection of "civilized" concerns onto the natural world. Mary is reunited with Mother Goose, though she'll doubtless be a mother herself soon. Bo Peep is ready to assume the role of Maiden, Mother Goose moving on to the Crone stage.

Complementary images of Mother and Maiden are also combined in ostensibly more "realistic" projects. *A Tiger Walks* concerns the efforts of Pete Williams (Brian Keith), a macho but fair-minded sheriff, to track down an escaped jungle cat, loose in his isolated Northwest community. Quickly, though, Disney shifts the focus to the females: Pete's daughter Julie (Pamela Franklin), this film's Maiden, and Pete's wife, Dorothy (Vera Miles), an incarnation of the Mother. Though they are straightforward women (Julie and Dorothy might have been painted by Norman Rockwell), each is, unbeknownst to herself, something of a Wiccan. Julie is at once associated with a pet cat, a virtual miniature of the title figure. Visually, we have been informed she's one of "the cat people," though without the negative stigma in Val Lewton's legendary 1942 horror film of that name. Here, both the small pet and its larger counterpart are positive. Julie's near-mystic relationship with her cat transfers to the tiger, who will not harm her, sensing something special and positive about a female who is "different."

Though Dorothy attempts to live a conventional life, she possesses more of a primal sympathy than even she initially realizes. During the narrative, Dorothy arcs from an identity in which she is primarily Wife (supporting her husband as he admonishes his strange daughter) to Mother (standing in unison with her daughter against a patriarchal system). The film's moment of crisis occurs when Pete, determined to kill the escaped cat, finds himself face-to-face with Dorothy and Julie. They say nothing, but make clear through their female/spiritual body language that they wish him to do otherwise. Pete proves himself one of Disney's enlightened males by respecting their silent request, finding a nonviolent means of bringing the cat back to life.

The Earth Mother Incarnate
Mary Poppins (1964)

The title character, an aging Maiden, serves a positive purpose by acting as surrogate Mother. Though a far cry from the strange curmudgeon created by P. L. Travers, Julie Andrews well served Walt's purpose. Andrews's persona stretched beyond the book's aura of twentieth-century fairy tale, reaching into the more complex territory of full-blown myth. The opening image returns us to sedate London, jumping off place for so many previous adventures *(Alice in Wonderland, Peter Pan, 101 Dalmatians)*. Director Robert Stevenson's camera pans across the city, moving from right to left. Such a movement entails a reversal of what audiences traditionally experience in a film's opening,[10] suggesting the chaos and disorientation just beneath 1910 London's calm surface. Eventually, the camera veers upward, where we spot Mary Poppins, sitting on a cloud. Her positioning is identical to Zeus's in *Fantasia's Pastoral* Symphony; it wouldn't surprise us to see her hurl down a thunderbolt. Instead, this incarnation of the Great Goddess will pay a personal visit, though not before applying makeup. Disney's progressive feminists always maintain their traditional surface aura of femininity.

The camera drifts down to Hyde Park, the Green World in otherwise drab London. There, we meet Bert (Dick Van Dyke), a lovable lowlife, a street musician, and self-styled painter when not working as a chimney sweep. In tune with his own primal sympathy (implied by his love of music, art, and nature), Bert senses something spiritual before it happens:

Wind's from the East,
Mist coming in!
I feel that what's about to happen
Has all happened before!

As in *Peter Pan* ("All this has happened before, and all this will happen again"), the visit initiates a secular version of religious ritual. The arrival of this Mary (there are as many Marys in Disney films as there are Katherines in Shakespeare's plays) to the Banks home may be viewed as the descent of a pagan goddess or a long-overdue female incarnation of the Christian God.

Either way, she will prove to be the family's savior. When a series of prospective nannies line up at the Banks home, they are blown away by a sudden wind. All cling to umbrellas, looking witchlike, recalling Margaret Hamilton as the twister whisks her away from Kansas in *The Wizard of Oz*. Once they're gone, the true witch (quite lovely, with rosy cheeks) makes her decidedly unwitchlike appearance. Disney reverses an audience's expectations: Normals look like conventional witches; the witch seems supremely normal. Adults, who have lost the ability to closely consider anything, don't even notice. Children are another matter. "Perhaps she's a witch," Michael (Matthew Garber) whispers to sister Jane (Karen Dotrice) as Mary Poppins slides *up* the banister. Michael, of course, is right, if not in the precise manner he implies. Frightened that Mary Poppins may be dangerous, he and his sister are shortly delighted to discover she is, in fact, benign.

Her "witchcraft" has as much to do with perception as reality. Though Mary can make objects dance about in the air, her greatest gift resides in an ability to teach children to turn work (cleaning the nursery) into a game. By altering their line of vision (their perception of chores), Poppins transforms work into a pleasurable experience, precisely paralleling what Snow White earlier achieved for her beloved dwarfs. Once the work is done, Poppins hurries them off to the park. Previous nannies tried to keep the little ones away from this single natural spot. There, they meet Bert, genial scrivener, using chalk to draw temporary works of art on the sidewalk. The film grows reflexive, as Bert represents Walt himself, framing pictures of rural life for children to slip into, something Michael and Jane quite literally achieve here. Yet Walt's alternative world is hardly sacrosanct. Cartoon characters hunt a fox, and would kill the little creature if Bert didn't save him. Animal rights activism, so dear to Disney's heart, intrudes even into seemingly escapist projects.

Though childless, Mary Poppins embodies that aspect of the Great Goddess called the Mother—Disney's suggestion is that a biological relationship is not necessary. A predecessor to Vida Downey Siddons (Vera Miles) in *Follow Me, Boys!,* Mary Poppins adopts lost children (Wendy, the Maiden on the verge of becoming a Mother, did precisely that in *Peter Pan*) to compensate for having none of her own. Disney's Earth Mother incarnate, she is neither the perfect matron of sentimental Hollywood films—*I Remember Mama* (1948)—or her opposite, the fiercely dominating mom in *Portnoy's Complaint* (1972) or virtually any Hitchcock thriller. Tough but fair, she proves a stern taskmaster, yet amply rewards the little ones when tasks are completed.

Like Lori in *Thomasina* (though the context has changed from grim realism to fanciful musical), this Wiccan woman can talk with the animals. Her warlock relative, Uncle Albert (Ed Wynn), admits, "I love to laugh," transforming the screen warlock from a frightful thing into a lovable figure for the children in the film, and those watching. He also reflects Disney, who similarly said: "I am interested in bringing pleasure, particularly laughter, to others."[11] When Mr. Banks, outraged by the spontaneity Poppins has brought into his household, insists on the need for order, Mary surprises him (and, perhaps, us) by admitting: "I quite agree." Disney would hardly offer a champion of anarchy as a positive character (thus, a role model) in his movie. What Mary Poppins hopes to achieve is not chaos (though that stage must be passed through, briefly if painfully), but rather a more enlightened order than what exists in the male-dominated microcosm we initially witness. When this has been achieved, she moves on to other people and places where her "white magic" may be needed.

The Crone
Trick or Treat (1952)
Bedknobs and Broomsticks (1971)

Among the ancients, the Crone served as the third aspect of the Great Goddess: woman worshiped in her final state on earth, a noble figure employing her carefully acquired natural wisdom (herbs, grasses, etc.) to a "practice of the healing arts."[12] *Snow White*'s black-garbed villainess might seem a contradiction to the notion that Disney offers a more enlightened view. She became locked in the public imagination, along with the Wicked Witch of the West from *The Wizard of Oz* (1939), as one of Hollywood's frightening icons. This shape-shifter is one of the rare Disney women who willingly surrenders to her worst impulses. However terrifying she may seem, slipping through the forest with her poisoned apple, such an icon would soon be replaced.

Having humanized young, attractive Wiccans, Disney felt a need to accomplish the same for their older counterparts. *Trick or Treat* (1952) opens on a Halloween night in Eisenhower-era suburbia. Witch Hazel, a typically grotesque-looking crone from the folk tradition, rides her broomstick down into contemporary society. She glances about happily as children of middle-class residents (Donald's nephews, Huey, Dewey, and Louie) don costumes, temporarily becoming minions of the moon. To her horror, Donald (ever a negative caricature of the era's adult male at his absolute worst) plays vicious tricks on the innocent kids. Offended, Witch Hazel invokes the ancient Wiccan curse, popularized in *Macbeth* owing to Shakespeare's familiarity with King James's volume *Daemonologie* (1599): "Bubble-bubble, toil and trouble." The notable difference in impact has to do with artistic context. In Shakespeare, the invocation served to signal an abrupt entrance of evil into a seemingly safe and sound *demi-monde*. In Disney, the phrase eliminates evil from the everyday world, where it's practiced by white-bread "normals." Witch Hazel's spells provide poetic justice. Donald is terrified, the children rewarded. The Wiccan woman has brought moral decency into a corrupt (male-dominated) world. Only the uncorrupted young are open enough to appreciate her.

That concept was extended for the highly ambitious *Bedknobs and Broomsticks,* released five years following Disney's death, and one of the final films he personally put into production. If, in the pre-Woodstock years, *Poppins* had dared to advance the issue of Wiccan women, *Bedknobs*—released at the beginning of the new posthippie era—pushed the envelope further. Opening credits were superimposed over paintings of witches, gleefully riding broomsticks through the air, accompanied by cats and their other favorite "familiar," rabbits. Yet the music that underscores these traditional images was celebratory rather than spooky. Disney's revision of audience attitudes began with his contrast between what we see and hear.

The heroine, Miss Eglantine Price (Angela Lansbury), allows three London kids to enter her rural home in hopes of escaping the Blitzkrieg.

THE "FAMILIAR." A follow-up to *Mary Poppins, Bedknobs and Broomsticks* (the last semi-animated project Walt set into production before his death) furthers the earlier theme of a benign Wiccan woman (Angela Lansbury), seen here with an animal companion. (Copyright 1970 Walt Disney Productions; courtesy Buena Vista Releasing.)

No sooner have they arrived than Carrie (Cindy O'Callaghan), Paige (Roy Smart), and Charley (Ian Weignill) witness her midnight rituals, including flying on a broom in the moonlight. She proves to be a positive character, explaining her spells thusly: "The work I'm doing is so important to the war effort!" More correctly, *anti*war effort: One more of Disney's pacifistically inclined females (and lauded in the film's context as such), she would, if possible, prefer to employ white magic to stop the fighting before it claims more lives.

Miss Price has bypassed the Mother stage ("children and I don't get on!") to self-consciously become a Crone, if a highly attractive one. During the course of the narrative, she will (as another of Disney's nonbiological Mother figures) learn the importance of enjoying every stage of life's journey. Reversing her attitude about children, Miss Price will become their surrogate mom—and, in that position, nurturer. Always, she obeys the Wiccan code. The children are dismayed to learn she forsakes meat, feasting on cabbage buds, rose hips, and lentils—vegetarianism as much a hallmark of ancient Wiccan thinking as of the New Age lifestyle. Disney's demystification of the witch/Crone is completed with images of her awkward attempts to fly. All three children (and those in the audience) overcome their fear of Miss Price, instead finding her charming.

At the end, this woman—previously scorned as a witch—emerges as something of a saint. For she has—with the help of her warlock friend Browne (David Tomlinson)—employed magic to defeat the invading Nazis. In Disney, though, life is always a two-way street. Miss Price has not only taught the world an important lesson, but learned one as well. She is finally able to embrace the sensual side she heretofore denied, kissing Browne good-bye as he marches off to fight the last good war. Also, she is now in touch with the only side of her Wiccan nature that had proven elusive. For she has mothered and nurtured children and is finally complete.

When Things Were Rotten
Fantasia ("The Sorcerer's Apprentice") (1940)
The Sword in the Stone (1963)

As Browne proves in *Bedknobs and Broomsticks,* male Wiccans can also make a positive contribution to society. Disney's first significant portrait of the male Wiccan occurs in "The Sorcerer's Apprentice." Adapting Paul Dukas's music for Mickey had been Walt's initial incentive to mount *Fantasia,* the remaining segments added one by one during this concert feature's gestation period.[13] The initial image is of the Sorcerer, plying forbidden skills. Though he appears every inch the stereotype—tall, elderly, wearing a cone-shaped hat covered with pentagrams, "the devil's star"—Disney undermines the cliché by having a lovely butterfly rise out of the mist that this Sorcerer summons up, rather than some hideous ancient demon.

Mickey, the apprentice, is dutifully involved with drudgery tasks, keeping the tower clean and hauling water from the well. He doesn't enjoy this, reflecting the filmmaker for whom the Mouse had long since become an onscreen alter ego. Walt shunned hard physical labor as much as he loved creative work. No sooner has the Sorcerer left than Mickey dons the magical hat, employing its powers to bring a broom to life, commanding it to work. The results prove disastrous. As Mickey naps, the broom inadvertently floods the room. After Mickey smashes it, splinters from the broom handle take life and continue the task until the returning Sorcerer restores order.

This cautionary fable expresses Disney's values. The apprentice's flaw was not so much laziness (as in the source) but unearned ambition—a desire to get out of the only work he is, at this point, fit to perform. There's nothing wrong with the Mouse (like the man who created him) despising grunt work or preferring artistic endeavor. But the latter cannot be undertaken until one has reached a certain level of maturity. In terms of offering another of his thinly disguised autobiographies, Disney here split himself in two: Mickey signifies the young Walt, eager to leave busywork behind, not yet accomplished enough in craft to successfully manage that; the Sorcerer represents the mature Disney, a Prospero-like magician/artist who insists his underlings—matte artists, cell animators, and the like—quietly continue with their daily chores until ready to leave and create their own studios, if they dare try.[14] Yet here, as in Shakespeare, the quality of mercy is not strained. The Sorcerer first glares at the apprentice with stern eyes, then reveals a touch of amusement. He too was young once. Instead of consigning the apprentice to some terrible fate, Disney's Sorcerer whacks him once with the broom, sending Mickey scurrying off to do those tasks that, at least for now, constitute his lot in life.

Nearly a quarter century later, Disney provided an unofficial sequel with *The Sword in the Stone*. At one point, brooms again come to life and bounce about, doing the assigned work of yet another youth in an image that stirs memories of the earlier film. More significant, though, is the difference between the two. Mickey's experiment failed because he attempted to employ powers he didn't completely understand, while doing so for all the wrong reasons. Here, it is the sorcerer who exerts the magical influence—and not to free the youth from responsibility, but "busywork." No sooner are the brooms performing their chores than Merlin whisks young Arthur away for a higher form of work—intellectual study, signifying Disney's ongoing belief in education as positive. We grasp, then, that things would have turned out very different for Mickey if, once freed from drudgery, he had opened a book and read rather than simply dozing off.

To effectively transform the Arthur legend into a work of personal expression, Disney took considerable liberties not only with T. S. White's highly regarded children's book, but the legend as it dates back through Tennyson to Malory. In most versions, Merlin is advisor to the unfortunate Uther, instructing the dying warlord to pierce a stone with his sword. The weapon then becomes a test by which knights attempt to prove their worthiness by drawing it forth and claiming the crown. Merlin hides young Arthur with Sir Ector and his son Kay. As Arthur (nicknamed Wart in White) grows to manhood, Merlin hovers about, waiting for the right moment to reveal he is England's rightful king.

In Disney's version, the "miracle" of the sword in the stone is never explained. Moreover, it's positioned in London town, in the middle of a churchyard, rather than in some remote forest. Merlin, when we first meet him (and he is, significantly, the character we meet first), knows nothing about either the sword or Arthur, only that someone important will soon pay a visit. The initial image is of Merlin, retrieving water from the well near his forest cottage, slipping on the way and dunking himself. "One medieval mess," he complains about the current state of affairs. He has, in this version, traveled through time and knows full well of the technical wizardry to come. Not that things will be any better: "One modern mess," Merlin complains after revisiting the twentieth century. The twin gags reflect Disney's view: Though society may improve on a technical level, the quality of life itself remains constant over the years.

The youthful audience is induced to laugh at and/or with Merlin early on, resulting in a demystification of a figure who, if judged on looks, is the scary sorcerer incarnate. He lives deep under the ground, his subterranean hovel filled with an alchemist's equipment. Also present is a familiar, Archimedes, an irritable owl—this animal as closely associated with the wizard as cats have been with the witch. Yet Disney's Merlin is (in contrast to the conception of another American, Mark Twain, in *A Connecticut*

Yankee in King Arthur's Court) entirely benevolent. To the as yet unknown person unwittingly hurrying to meet him, Merlin says:

> Fate will deliver him to me, so I may guide him to his rightful place in the world.

The dark forest surrounding Merlin's lair is swarming with wolves, though they too are treated with surprising sympathy. As Wart—frightened but courageous—pushes deep into the wood, he's stalked by a hungry wolf that reappears throughout the film. Initially, the animal looks dangerous. As the narrative progresses, he is reduced from fairy-tale symbol of male predator to a comic figure, not unlike Wylie Coyote of MGM's animated shorts.

Whatever the wolf does proves to be a mistake. Arthur is barely aware the creature even exists, though it's forever attempting to catch and eat the boy, suffering humiliation at each turn. Diverse expressions of despair and disgust cross the wolf's face, until Disney's desired effect is achieved. Audiences leave the film with a less negative impression of the much-maligned species.

Disney's Romantic vision is fully expressed. The child, too long subject to civilization (and the violent "lessons" a squire learns there), has to be reeducated by the natural world's purity. Always antisentimental, Walt insists that Wart's alternative education will introduce the boy not only to nature's abundance of life, but also its potential for instant death. The beauty, one experiences emotionally. The danger, a person avoids intellectually. In the opening narration, we were told "these were dark ages, without law and order," and that "the strong preyed on the weak." These words do not merely set the stage, but serve as the essence of this film's theme and its auteur's vision. Wart is transformed by Merlin's shape-shifting abilities into a fish, a squirrel, and a bird. In each guise, he comes in contact with some essential truth that he must master if he is to survive. These experiences concern everything from sex (in the form of a determined female squirrel) to death (a hawk that swoops down on the smaller bird). Though the strong threaten to destroy the weak, brainpower defeats simple brawn. As Merlin sings:

> *The strong will try to conquer you;*
> *And that is what you must expect,*
> *Unless you use your intellect.*

Nineteenth-century Romantics rejected just such "wisdom" from the Age of Reason. Disney insists on a harmonious balance between the two. Merlin moves into the tower of Ector's castle, so as to better mentor Wart. He points to a pile of books, insisting the boy must read all of them: "Books come first." They always have for Disney, who opens almost every film with the image of a book, inviting the viewer to enter. The great unstated hope was to employ the film medium not as an alternative to, but a means of hooking children on, reading.

"Don't get the idea that magic will solve all your problems," Merlin insists. "It won't." Inside the castle, Ector confronts his guest:

ECTOR: I hope you don't go in for any black magic.
MERLIN: Oh, no, no, no. My magic is used strictly for educational purposes.

Merlin's desire is to "educate" Wart away from the violent ways of Kay and other "normal" boys, winning the youth over to a more pacifist approach. This in time will lead to the creation of the Round Table, with its peaceful solutions to problems and democratic value system.

Wart also serves as a surrogate for Walt. When Ector and Kay speak of Merlin in derogatory terms, the boy seizes the moment and (to their surprise) stands up to them:

He's not an old devil. He's good! Just because you can't understand something, doesn't mean it's wrong.

There is such a thing as black magic. Wart confronts it in the form of Madame Mim, a sorceress who happily admits:

> I find delight in the
> Gruesome and grim.
> I'm the magnificent
> Mad Madame Mim.

Merlin defeats her not because his skills are any greater, rather because "Righteousness and wisdom is the real power!" This is the wisdom Wart takes with him when he heads for London, as Kay's squire, there pulling the sword from the stone. In, significantly, a churchyard: "It's a *miracle*, ordained by *heaven*," an onlooker proclaims. True, though one that could not have been achieved without the constant guidance of a wizard. Christianity and Wicca are not, in Disney's vision, antithetical after all.

Delightfully Evil Days
The Shaggy Dog (1959)

Wilby Daniels (Tommy Kirk) appears a precursor and virtual model for the post-Woodstock youth hero Harry Potter. This live-action comedy, released at the tail end of the fifties, closed off the Eisenhower era with a broad but effective rejection of the culture of conformity. Once again, Walt turned to Felix Salten, author of *Bambi* and *Perri,* for inspiration—in this case *The Hound of Florence* (1923). Professor Plumcutt (Cecil Kellaway) relates, early in Disney's film, the tale of a young Italian commoner who assumes the form of a dog to defend his beloved noblewoman from an evil aristocrat. In Walt's version, the story is reimagined as a comment on the Generation Gap conflict and a paradigm for much of what would occur in the 1960s.

An establishing shot reveals the suburban home of Wilson Daniels (Fred MacMurray). A mailman (who never seems to work), he desires nothing more than to live a quiet life with his wife, Frieda (Jean Hagen). The middle-class sterility into which the couple has fallen is visually signified by their morning ritual of a near-kiss, one more white-bread couple who no longer make physical contact. Results of an earlier, more sensuous period abound in the presence of two sons, little Moochie (Kevin Corcoran) and teenager Wilby. The latter brings elements of nature (mice, a tortoise) into their cellar. Wilby also expresses Disney's ongoing contempt for organized religion; his initial stunt is getting the new dean of the divinity school thrown into jail.

In due time, Wilby will bite a cop, then steal his police car. Such activities are presented, in context, as harmless fun rather than (as most teen flicks of the late 1950s would have portrayed it) the actions of a dangerous juvenile delinquent. Wilby is another of Disney's future-minded heroes who also appear, however incongruous the combination, to be throwbacks to America's pioneers. He experiments with rocketry, launching a homemade missile through the house's roof, becoming a signifier of the recently emerged American teenager as outsider:

> MOOCHIE: Pop sure was sore.
> WILBY: Yeah. I always seem to rub him the wrong way.

Their "gap" reaches its zenith when Wilby turns into a protohippie. His crew cut gives way to long, white hair that, a generation later, would do

"WONDERFULLY WICKED DAYS." In *The Shaggy Dog,* a warlock (Cecil Kellaway) introduces Tommy Kirk (playing a predecessor to Harry Potter) to the joys of the dark side, gloating over re-created moments from history's more gruesome side. The film applauds rather than condemns such activity. (Copyright 1959 Walt Disney Productions; courtesy Buena Vista Releasing.)

rocker Edgar Winter proud. This occurs after Wilby visits a museum, meeting Plumcutt (shortly to become Wilby's Leary-like guru) in a side room reserved for the dark arts. Seemingly a harmless old eccentric, Plumcutt allows his secret identity as a Wiccan to become known to Wilby. A frightful mock-up of a witch moves toward the teenager, though he (and we) quickly realize it's manipulated by Plumcutt. When Wilby reveals he's not afraid (as other, more "normal," teens would be), Plumcutt senses that he's found a disciple.

Like the Sorcerer and Merlin, Plumcutt is presented as a positive figure. He serves as a foil for Mr. Daniels, the seemingly perfect American father, if in Disney's daring context a negative role model. Wilby spots a painting of Lucrezia Borgia, wearing an ancient ring, accompanied by a large dog. Noting Wilby's interest, Plumcutt sweetly sighs before saying: "In the delightfully evil days of the Borgias here, something interesting happened to people every day." This, in contrast to the dullness of then-contemporary America. Audiences were expected to agree with him, then cheer as a genially rebellious teenager turns merry prankster and explodes the fast-fading fifties ennui.

Wilby embraces Borgia's forbidden arts. After first growing scraggly long hair, this embryonic hippie disturbs the quiet neighborhood with one "happening" after another, to his mentor's delight:

PLUMCUTT: There are moments on dark and lonely nights when something stirs within us, reviving ancient beliefs!

Those beliefs include shape-shifting, the borrowing of someone (or something) else's body. Wilby assumes the form of a huge dog, rather than the expected wolf of lycanthropy films. These include a then-recent youth-oriented version, *I Was a Teenage Werewolf* (1957), in which another teen antihero (Michael Landon) was destroyed by his surrender to "the beast within." Wilby, conversely, achieves great good for himself, his family, even society at large, winning the girl (Roberta Shore) while foiling enemy spies. For the first time, lycanthropy has been presented in a totally positive light.

At one point, Mr. Daniels reads a newspaper while Wilby (in the guise of a dog) sits nearby, trying his best to communicate. The typical suburbanite is so used to peering past and through (rather than looking at) his son that he initially fails to notice the transformation. More satiric still, Disney includes a pointed put-down of the white-bread gun nut. In mid-film, Wilson darts about the neighborhood, firing his shotgun wildly at the neighbors' "pet," failing to realize it's his own son in a dog's guise—a comedic turn on George Waggner's *The Wolf Man* (1941). That film did indeed end tragically, the father (Claude Raines) mistakenly killing his son (Lon Chaney Jr.). No less profound, Walt's outcome transcends any concluding happiness in the superficial sense by implying a possibility of reconciliation. Parents can (and, Disney hopes and trusts, will) learn to accept their offspring, despite the younger generation's nonconformist ways. Before this can happen, though, the middle-aged, middle-class, middlebrow public must be reeducated about many things—including Wicca. And made to see that what conventional society has come to perceive as an immoral throwback to paganism can also have highly positive consequences.

NOW WE DON OUR GAY APPAREL. In the Disney Westerns, hardy pioneers and rugged mountain men are often depicted as setting aside their traditional macho demeanors in order to come to grips with their potent feminine sides, dressing in drag to dance together, as occurs in *The Saga of Andy Burnett.* (Copyright 1957 Walt Disney Productions; courtesy Buena Vista Releasing.)

8

Beyond the Celluloid Closet
Disney and the Gay Experience

The love that dare not speak its name.
—OSCAR WILDE, 1868

Different strokes for different folks.
—SLY STONE, 1968

$\mathcal{L}$ong after various other groups had achieved major inroads into the American mainstream, gay liberation remained a final taboo for those of a conventional mind-set. Openly gay persons in such areas as San Francisco's Haight-Ashbury or New York's East Village continued to be routinely hassled by local police. On June 28, 1969, at the Stonewall Inn, a gay bar in Manhattan's Greenwich Village, the victimized fought back in what would soon be mythologized as the movement's Bunker Hill.[1] One year later, the newly formed National Gay Task Force emerged as the original political activist group for homosexuals. In response, the American Psychiatric Association in 1974 reversed a long-held position, announcing that homosexuality did not in and of itself constitute a mental "disturbance."[2]

Changing public attitudes could only occur via a major alteration in media presentations. During the spring of 1973, the Gay Activists Alliance demanded a meeting with members of the Association of Motion Picture and Television Producers, at which guidelines for more enlightened screen portrayals were presented. With the loosening of Hollywood's Production Code during the previous decade, the open depiction of homosexuals in Hollywood films—nonexistent during the waning studio era—had become a screen staple, ironically creating even greater image problems. David Lean's *Lawrence of Arabia* (1962) portrayed an Arab sheikh (Jose Ferrer) who forces himself on the title character (Peter

O'Toole). Though T. E. Lawrence had been bisexual,[3] Lean transformed him into a conventional "straight" who recoils in horror at the (villainous) homosexual's touch.

This set the tone for a new iconography. In the late-sixties films, movies ranging from the serious drama *The Sergeant* (1968) to a lowbrow exploitation item such as *The Gay Deceivers* (1968) presented gays as deeply neurotic or half-human jokes. No wonder film critic/gay activist Arthur Bell complained: "Our revolution came late in 1969, but our stereotypes continue. Our screen image is alive and sick and in need of a euthanistic ending and a liberated beginning."[4] The occasional positive portrait was largely confined to imports like John Schlesinger's *Sunday, Bloody Sunday* (1971). Conversely, Hollywood's vision reached its low point in *Cruising* (1979), a gross caricature of a small and marginal subculture (black leather sadists) presented as representative of the vast and varied gay community. The surprise success of the import *La Cage aux Folles* (1978) suggested a belated sea change. The watershed year was 1980. *Tootsie* and *Victor/Victoria* portrayed both cross-dressing and homosexuality in a nonpatronizing manner, within the context of major releases. This ran against the grain of what Bell described as a longtime misconstruing of the gay experience by "heterosexual [filmmakers] who are either unconscious of what they're doing or homophobic enough to want to perpetrate age old stereotypes that gay is bad."[5]

One heterosexual filmmaker always provided happy alternatives to the polar visions of harmless sissy-victims or dangerously violent criminals. Disney's positive portraits of gays were so advanced that, following his death, rumors abounded that Walt had been a closeted homosexual.[6] He may, in his youth, have been sexually molested by urban rednecks who objected to his father's socialist politics.[7] In truth, though, Disney was a righteous heterosexual, a point missed even by gay film historians. "Walt Disney may not have liked hearing it," Vito Russo argued, "but there are gay overtones to the relationships of more than one pair of beloved animated figures of the classic years."[8] However apt his observation, Russo's conclusion (based on the ongoing prejudice against Disney, supposedly a reactionary) proves wrongheaded when one considers internal evidence in the films.

Now We Don Our Gay Apparel
The Dog-Napper (1934)
The Three Little Wolves (1936)
Hawaiian Holiday (1937)
The Hockey Champ (1939)

Yet another key incident from Disney's early life diminishes the sense of surprise so many viewers experience upon recognition of cross-dressing in his films. Growing up on a farm in rural Missouri, the young prankster once slipped into his mother's clothes and hurried around the house to the front door. Pretending to be a lost lady, he engaged Flora in lengthy conversation before she realized who he was.[9] At age thirty-nine, Disney reflected on the warmth of heavy dresses favored by farming women, admitting: "Sometimes I wished I might have worn skirts myself!"[10] A surprising number of his characters live out that fantasy on the screen.

An early example occurs in *The Dog-Napper*. When Minnie's pet Fifi is seized by villainous (and ultramacho) Pete, Mickey and Donald follow in hot pursuit. Pete's hideout is in a secluded sawmill, where a series of melo-dramatic confrontations take place. Donald hides in a shabby vanity, finding himself entangled in some hidden garment. To Don's great surprise, it turns out to be a girdle, though there's no evidence of a woman sharing the place with Pete. After revealing this to Mickey, the heroes appear considerably less threatened by Pete's surface show of toughness. Essentially, they have "outed" him. The two employ the girdle as a means of capturing (emasculating) Pete, tying him up in the contraption, displaying him to the public, and fully revealing Pete's secret self to all. The scene's significance is less that a villain has such a hidden life than that a character who, in previous cartoons, was accepted as simplistically masculine is revealed to be far more complex.

Another macho villain voluntarily makes a similar revelation in *The Three Little Wolves*. The Big Bad Wolf hatches a plan to disguise himself as Little Bo Peep, searching for her sheep. The pigs will be conned into helping, while little wolves hide under sheepskins, popping out to eat the porkers. Only the scheme goes all wrong, largely because Father Wolf becomes so enamored of Bo Peep's clothing, particularly her undergarments, that he loses control. Even after grabbing the two more gullible pigs and dragging them back to his lair, he refuses to divest himself of the lingerie—dancing about while his pups, stunned, stare in rapt amazement, which allows the pigs to escape.

Had Disney reserved cross-dressing for his villains, he would be guilty of furthering the same negative stereotype as his more adult-oriented contemporaries. Heroes reveal their kinks as well. The experience with Pete apparently impacted heavily on Donald. In *Hawaiian Holiday*, the Duck joins the other cartoon regulars on a stretch of isolated surf. When no one is looking, he slips into a woman's hula outfit. Directly addressing the audience and taking us into his confidence in a way he would not do were Mickey around, Donald gleefully shouts: "Boy, am I *hot!*" This is hardly an isolated incident. In *The Hockey Champ*, Donald ventures onto an icy pond to practice his skating. Noticing that no one is around, the Duck gleefully ruffles his hair, transforming himself into a precise replica of Sonja Henie, a popular skating star. "Who is this Sonja Henie?" Donald shrieks in falsetto, all the while cutting a demure figure, moving in perfect mimicry of a woman. His nephews appear, discovering Donald's secret. In awkward response, he reverts to his masculine self (i.e., his cover), challenging Huey, Dewey, and Louie to a hockey game. Donald believes that by besting them, he will reassert his now questionable manhood. As the boys put Donald to shame, he grows ferocious, then hysterical. The seven-minute short remains one of the most striking portrayals of homosexual panic in Hollywood history.

Boys Will Be Girls/Girls Will Be Boys
The Three Caballeros (1945)
The Story of Robin Hood and His Merrie Men (1952)
The Sword and the Rose (1953)
Ten Who Dared (1960)

This theme was first extended to the feature-length format with *The Three Caballeros*, ostensibly a tribute to Latin culture. As the titles roll, a second agenda is suggested in song: "We're three caballeros, three *gay* caballeros."[11] Donald opens a package from friend Joe Carioca and discovers his present to be a home-movie projector with films of various Central and South American settings. No gay subtext appears in the first three episodes, though each does deal with Disney's positive preoccupation with being different (i.e., "queer," in a more all-encompassing sense): the first, a South Pole penguin, Pablo, who hates snow; the second, a young Uruguayan gaucho, discovering a winged burro, gaily flying off to an alternative existence; and third, species of *aves rares* ("strange birds"), selected for study here owing to uniqueness.

Then, Donald dives headlong into a book on Brazil, joining Joe. The film's style turns surreal as the tone becomes sensual. Swaying samba music accompanies images of flowers, opening wide with provocative wetness, while exotic birds cuddle close in romantic embrace. As Donald responds, Joe transforms before his eyes (or is it only in the Duck's mind?) into a woman—much to Donald's delight! In a small Bahian village, the two gay caballeros encounter a real-life woman (Aurora Miranda) singing and dancing. The boys compete for her attentions, though she's surrounded by actual men, leaving the animated Donald ignored and upset. As humans couple off, woman to man, Donald and Joe find themselves alone. Fantasizing about beautiful girls, Donald turns into one, this time to Joe's delight. Rejected by humans—particularly the woman—male cartoon characters dance together, one momentarily assuming the role of female, then vice versa, realizing they can function on their own, discovering true happiness together.

Mexican *charro*-rooster Panchito joins them. His matched six-guns constantly leap out of their holsters, firing wildly. But Panchito's overstated macho image may be a show. "Now," Joe sighs, "we truly are *three* 'gay' caballeros!" The two kiss Donald on either cheek, though he—his self-image threatened—responds according to the dictates of masculine role-playing. In places like Vera Cruz and Acapulco Beach, they spot beautiful women whom Donald covets but cannot have. In the former, he embraces his companions after a señorita rejects him for what she senses is a "true" man; in the latter, he makes such ridiculous plays for bathing beauties that, following initial anxiety, they cease taking him seriously, sensing his overexaggerated interest suggests a kind of overcompensation.

Blindfolded by his buddies, Donald kisses Joe. Shock upon realizing this transforms from denial to acceptance. Later, when he attempts to embrace his fantasy woman (Dora Luz), she disappears. Donald finds himself kissing Panchito instead. Again, Don quickly recovers from brief discomfort. "Three *gay* caballeros!" Joe and Panchito constantly remind Donald as he now obsessively searches for a girl. Suddenly alone on the desert, he meets his Latino inamorata—a dark lady of cinematic sonnets—in the form of Carmen Molina, dancing toward him. The woman appears in drag: dressed like a macho caballero, wielding a black leather S&M whip. Don crumbles under the pressure, responding by accepting and projecting the female role via effeminate motions. This relationship "works": The macho woman and feminized male dance off together into a sunset composed of hot pink, powder blue, and lavender—colors associated with gayness since the late nineteenth century.[12] Returning to his "gay" companions, Donald appears altered via experience.

Disney's live-action films extend the concept. Women in the British films often don drag outfits, closely resembling Shakespeare's gamin heroines of romantic comedy. Like the Bard's beauties, Disney's male-attired women create great confusion as to the issue of sexual identity for those men who love them. For the young women attract their men most intensely while passing themselves off as boys. Maid Marian (Joan Rice) in *The Story of Robin Hood and His Merrie Men* slips into a page boy's outfit before running away from the castle, entering the woods in search of Robin (Richard Todd). As they again meet, following a long separation, it's impossible to tell whether Robin's flirtations occur because he recognizes this is his beloved, or if he simply enjoys the young lad's company. Mary Tudor (Glynis Johns) in *The Sword and the Rose* likewise disguises herself as a page boy when she sneaks off to sail for America with Charles Brandon (Richard Todd). Having remained in control of his feelings for her up to this point, the hero takes one glance at the now-boyish Mary in drag, then seizes her in his arms for a tense embrace. In each case, the woman's appeal is of a highly androgynous nature. Like Viola transformed into Cesario, each wins the heart of her prince only after becoming his longtime companion. Conversely, seemingly simple heroes experience an identity crisis that can be traced to *Twelfth Night*'s erotically confused and sexually challenged Duke Orsino.

Though it occurs less often, men in live-action films also slip into drag. This occurs even in the context of that most masculine of genres, the Western. Shortly after arriving at the Alamo, Crockett (Fess Parker) and Russel (Buddy Ebsen) attempt to raise the men's spirits by playing a spirited song. The fort's defenders match off and dance together, something that occurs in none of the numerous other Alamo movies produced during the twentieth century. Such an idea is extended in *Ten Who Dared*, as John Wesley Powell and members of his 1869 expedition camp for the night. Several sing a song, "Jolly Rovers" (by Lawrence E. Watkin and Stan Jones). Suddenly, Billy "Missouri" Hawkins (L. Q. Jones), most blatantly macho of the explorers, dons a towel as a makeshift skirt, affects feminine mannerisms, and flirts with still-seated explorers. Any initial shock gives way to enthusiasm at his ever more outrageous actions. The following day, as the trek continues, there is no sense of embarrassment on his part or that of his companions.

In the Company of Men
Cinderella (1950)
Pinocchio (1940)
Snow White and the Seven Dwarfs (1937)
Treasure Island (1950)
Davy Crockett, King of the Wild Frontier (1955)

In *The Celluloid Closet,* Russo points out that in *Pinocchio* (1940), "Honest John and Gideon, a fox and a cat, are best friends who procure lost boys for sale to an evil coachman. . . . They seduce Pinocchio with the hit song 'Heigh Diddley Dee' (the second line of which is 'Heigh diddley day, an actor's life is *gay*'), and away he goes—twice."[13] The author might have added that Honest John constantly extends a small finger, a key method employed by early moviemakers to imply a character's gayness.[14] Such a pairing holds true not only for animated villains, as Russo also reveals:

> In *Cinderella* (1950), everyone's favorite mice, Jock and Gus-Gus, volunteer to help finish Cinderella's dress in time for the ball. But they are quickly admonished by a female mouse to "leave the sewing to the women" and told to go find "some trimmin'" for the dress. Their relationship grows . . . later, when Cinderella describes how she was swept off her feet by the handsome prince, Gus-Gus, sighing evenly, puts an arm around Jock's shoulder and holds him close. After a minute, Jock realizes they are sitting on a log at the side of the road in each other's arms, and homosexual panic set[s] in. Pulling away quickly, he gives Gus-Gus a quizzical look of wary scrutiny, as if to say, "Hmmmm, there's something funny about this mouse."[15]

Implying a homoerotic bond between beloved characters, if one that probably goes unconsummated, hints that in Disney, gays are as likely to be good characters as villains.

This tolerant view can be found in the least likely contexts, including *Snow White and the Seven Dwarfs.* "A fine bunch of water lilies you turned out to be," Grumpy snarls when his companions wash before dinner. There's little question as to his meaning. The redneck male incarnate, Grumpy insults his friends owing to their willingness, under Snow

White's guidance, to get in touch with their feminine sides. Disney hardly condones Grumpy's attitude: He is the only dwarf who must dramatically arc, if he's to, in time, find salvation. Grumpy is Disney's presentation of a narrow-minded cracker who believes that deep-seated (and heretofore unquestioned) bigotry represents some sort of simple folk wisdom.

The first step in Grumpy's moral growth is conveyed visually. The others—sensing Snow White's positive influence—tackle Grumpy, adorning him with the very objects he's ridiculed. As they pull away, Grumpy is revealed in blue bows and yellow flowers. He looks like precisely what he implied the others are: a gay man, and a flamboyant one at that. If his later arousal at Snow White's kiss makes clear that Grumpy's heterosexuality remains intact, he has been rendered more tolerant, accepting that gay behavior is nothing to be ashamed of.

Treasure Island plays as *Snow White and the Seven Dwarfs* without Snow White. In this adaptation of Robert Louis Stevenson's 1883 novel of buccaneers steering a course between Britain's West Coast and the wild Bahamas, circa 1765, Jim Hawkins (Bobby Driscoll) signifies Disney's innocent child hero, swept into adventures with pirate Long John Silver (Robert Newton). Jim's innkeeper mother is mentioned but never seen, nor does any other woman have a speaking role. Seven men are left to survive on their own, doing so with notable dysfunction and characteristic affection, much as in the films of Howard Hawks. "All my films," that producer/director once reflected, "are really love stories between men."[16] Most notable among them is *Rio Bravo* (1959), in which John Wayne kisses Walter Brennan, not Angie Dickinson. Hawks's supposed he-man films contain a homoerotic subtext that's always made them as popular within the gay community as with the mainstream.[17] Likewise, *Treasure Island* concerns the growing love of two men, innocent Jim and evil Long John. Each ultimately rejects the dynamics of his specific male group (honest seamen and murderous mutineers, respectively) to discover a deep, abiding sentiment for the other. It is Long John who gives Jim a gun, ongoing universal screen symbol for male sexuality, which the boy keeps hidden, appropriately enough, just beneath his belt buckle. Later, Jim—ignoring conscience, surrendering to instinct—pushes Long John's skiff off a sandbar, allowing the murderous pirate to escape. The confusion in Jim's eyes makes clear his lack of rational understanding as to his instinctive act of pure love. A physical relationship between Jim and Long John is never in any way suggested, yet the growing emotional bond—the love story between men—is at the film's very core.

Significantly, *Treasure Island* was the first Disney film put into production following World War II, a period when the "all-male environment of the armed services forced to the surface a confusion about the inherent sexuality between two men who preferred each other's company but always chose women to prove their masculinity."[18] This aptly describes *Davy Crockett,* in which Davy (Fess Parker) and George Russel (Buddy Ebsen) are never portrayed as anything other than die-hard heterosexuals. Still, their relationship—not Davy's with his wife Polly—is the one that sustains them. Though their pairing initially evokes the conventional hero/sidekick of run-of-the-mill Westerns, Disney does so only to reverse and transcend every cliché. This begins (in the longer TV version) with the image of Russel riding up to the Crockett cabin; Davy bids Polly goodbye and the men ride off together. The depth of their emotional bond could not be construed as anything other than a love (however nonphysical) between two men. Still, we witness a predecessor of what film historians would eventually perceive as the great hope for 1970s cinema: "emotion once condemned in men as feminine is now possible in a heterosexual hero."[19]

Reimagining the Sissy
Melody Time (1948)
Ichabod and Mr. Toad (1949)
The Sign of Zorro (1960)

Overtly homosexual characters were absent from Disney films for the same reason they did not appear in more adult pre-1966 movies. The Production Code forbade any graphic depiction of heterosexual, much less homosexual, love. In *Stagecoach,* John Ford's 1939 vision of American society in miniature, that filmmaker was unable to identify a prostitute (Claire Trevor) by the correct term, or even invoke the word "pregnant" for a married woman (Louise Platt). One can readily grasp, then, the restrictions on depicting gayness. Yet onboard Ford's moving microcosm were an all-American he-man (John Wayne) and a fussy salesman (Donald Meek). Though the latter constantly refers to wife and children in Kansas City, Meek nonetheless embodies the homosexual ethos in that era's Hollywood films:

Webster defines *sissy* as the opposite of male, and the jump from harmless sissy characters to explicit reference to homosexuality was made well before sound arrived. The line between the effeminate and the real man was drawn routinely in every genre of American film[, allowing for] the explicit leap to the homosexual possibilities inherent in such definitions.[20]

Sissies, mama's boys, and any "sensitive" male interested in arts or intellectual pursuits proved suspect. Ford's appropriately-last-named character actor is the first to be wounded when Apaches attack. In contrast, Wayne climbs up on top, where he seemingly could have decimated Geronimo's tribe had ammunition not run out. The sissy functions as the foil by which we appreciate a hero's machismo.

Not, however, in Disney. "Sissies" were presented as worthy of standing center stage. *Melody Time,* an anthology of featurettes, featured a Meek-style sissy in "Johnny Appleseed" and a Wayne-like macho man in "Pecos Bill"—both presented with a revisionist attitude and surprising results. "Pecos Bill," derived from numerous Texas folk tales about the "toughest critter west of the Alamo," features the most grotesquely masculine of all Disney heroes. Able to (according to balladeer-storytellers Roy Rogers and the Sons of the Pioneers) "out-lope the antelope, out-jump the jackrabbit, and out-hiss the rattlesnake," Bill is the compleat cowboy. Yet as the ironic tone makes clear, this is less a celebration of the wild 'n' woolly personality than an extremely cruel caricature of such conventionally boyish behavior. Bill—the young John Wayne as an animated caricature—does accomplish worthwhile mythic tasks, creating the Gulf of Mexico and the Rio Grande. Yet what seems to be shaping up as a mini-epic about an American Hercules is blocked by Bill's lack of social sensibility, a key characteristic of Disney's preferred hero, Davy Crockett. By the final fade-out, Bill appears an abject failure. He has lost Sluefoot Sue, the love of his life, owing to a flaw worthy of Greek tragedy: hubris as a roping star, compounded by the cowboy's Achilles heel, love for his horse. All Bill has achieved is forgotten. What we remember is a shrill shadow of his former self, as—having learned humility—he howls at the moon alongside the wild dogs among which he was raised.

Nothing could be further from the ending of "Johnny Appleseed." Here, the hero expires, but does so aware of having accomplished everything he set out to achieve. If Bill's fate establishes a man who reached the heights in his *demi-monde* only to end up worse than dead, Johnny does achieve epic stature. The meek little man's impact casts a shadow—great in size and scope, positive in effect—that ultimately covers the entire country.

AN ALTERNATIVE AMERICAN HERO. In addition to shows about more masculine heroes like Daniel Boone and Davy Crockett, the "Johnny Appleseed" segment of *Melody Time* allowed Walt to positively present as equally valuable a softer, sensitive, effeminate, and (as the theme song tells us) "gay" frontiersman. (Copyright 1948 the Walt Disney Company; courtesy RKO Radio Films.)

Loosely derived from stories about the real-life John Chapman, Johnny's initial image seems that of the prototypical sissy, a man who on first glance pales beside Bill. The narration makes Disney's take completely clear. "In the pages of American folklore," we learn, "are legends of mighty men" as well as violent symbols of their strength: Paul Bunyan's axe, John Henry's hammer, Davy Crockett's rifle. We are then told, regarding a satchel of seeds in plain view: "Strangely enough, these are the symbols of one of the most powerful men of all."

Johnny, whistling while he works at a Pennsylvania apple orchard, appears pink and white, an overgrown baby. "Just to look at him," the narrator admits, "you knew Johnny never would make a pioneer." Not, that is, a *conventional* pioneer. But in Disney, initial appearances can conceal the true reality. The film's early macho men serve as foils for the sissy, rather than (as in all other films of the era) the other way around. Johnny sadly stands behind a fence, closing him off from the community. Rugged types—women and children as well as men—pass by in covered wagons. Johnny imagines being one of them, perceiving himself in buckskins and coonskin cap, carrying a long rifle. Quickly, any such dream of normality passes. Feeling inferior, Johnny trudges back to his "working, singing, carefree, and *gay*" life.

Disney provides no hint of John's sexual orientation. Compared to Pecos Bill, he seems, if anything, asexual. Yet in Hollywood movies made before 1967, while "At first there was no equation between sissyhood and homosexuality, the danger of gayness as the consequence of such behavior lurked always in the background."[21] Johnny's guardian angel, something of a cracker-barrel philosopher, convinces him to go west despite Johnny's admission: "I'm about the puniest man alive." The angel insists Johnny can accomplish more without a gun (traditional symbol of male sexuality as well as male violence) than others can with one. What occurs, we are told, is "a miracle," if one of a special order: Johnny's self-realization that he's as valuable as others, if decidedly different. Also, belated acceptance of his uniqueness, accompanied by growing self-esteem.

By implication, the angel has outed Johnny, who afterward accepts his appealingly unique identity. A key sequence reveals him watching a community of pioneers celebrating happily with apples from trees that Johnny has planted, while our meek hero—the catalyst for their good fortune, yet always sensing his own basic difference—gazes on from the nearby woods. At least he now accepts his lot in life, with a bittersweet smile, afterward moving on to plant more fields of apple trees. Before Johnny's death, he (and we) note the orchards he has seeded. The sissy is not a sissy at all, but a true pioneer—if only we understand that term at its most inclusive. "Johnny Appleseed" stands as the rare positive example of an ordinarily negative syndrome in which "the sissy remained asexual while serving as a substitute for homosexuality."[22]

Clearly, though, intelligence and homosexuality have always been synonymous in the redneck mentality. This explains why "a certain amount of anti-intellectualism is basic to the ingredients of the sissy stereotype."[23] Disney's version of "The Legend of Sleepy Hollow" (half of the two-part film *Ichabod and Mr. Toad*) provides a rethinking of the 1820 yarn. In Disney's version, the sissy—a notably heterosexual Ichabod Crane, tormented by that gross-caricature of macho behavior, Bram Bones—survives and flourishes beyond anything imagined in Washington Irving's original. Disney's reimagined Ichabod arrives in what would eventually become Tarrytown, New York, nose buried in a book, oblivious to all around him. Yet books have, in films featuring tomes opening for us to share, consistently served as a positive symbol. There's no reason to believe such an attitude will not continue here.

Shortly, we meet the Sleepy Hollow Boys, predecessors of the deadly Paxton Boys in the live-action feature *The Light in the Forest* (1958). Lazy louts, they waste time while waiting for their macho, posturing leader to arrive. A cartoon prototype of *Light*'s evil Uncle Wilse, Bram Bones approaches on horseback, wearing a coonskin cap of the type associated, in our popular imagination, with such heroic figures as Daniel Boone and Davy Crockett.[24] But Bram is a bully and blowhard, and an odious one at that. Disney here matched, in a single story, Pecos Bill's macho man and Johnny Appleseed's softer hero from *Melody Time*. As the bully downs a mug of beer, he notices Ichabod through the glass bottom. Ichabod's bookish image provides humor for Bram, who considers the intruder a harmless sissy he can victimize. Since the audience momentarily shares Bram's vision (this is the film's only point-of-view shot), it appears Disney assumes moviegoers will perceive Ichabod, and the situation, as Bram does. Any man who reads is a sissy; any sissy is something other than a "real man." Walt, however, invokes this subjective view only to dispel it during the course of the story. Bram will learn how wrong this assumption was. And so, with him, will the audience.

Disney insists it's wrong to make assumptions about an intellectual's sexual proclivities. "Maybe he's odd," singing narrator Bing Crosby intones, "and maybe he ain't!" Ichabod seduces Sleepy Hollow's widows, particularly good cooks, through his mastery of "culture." In contrast, we witness "masculine" bullyboys in continual bonding—mocking Ichabod as less than a true man while never, like him, involving themselves with women. It's the bullyboys who—judged on actions rather than appearance—ought to be "suspect." Ichabod's appearance is "questionable": He wears his hair in a ponytail, tied with red bow; alone among the town's men, he sports a flower in his lapel.

Macho men, particularly Bram, do not like to dance. Ichabod is a master dancer, music passing through his body (as it does for every positive character in the Disney canon) and motoring his movements. The key contrast is between a "sissy" who acts like a ladies' man and a "bullyboy" who prefers the company of men. Still, Bram hopes—like every local fellow—to marry Katrina von Tassel, beautiful daughter of a wealthy farmer. While Bram remains content to hang with his homeboys, assuming sooner or later Katrina will fall into his hands, Ichabod ardently pursues the pretty flirt. This threatens Bram, who then plays on Ichabod's superstition, a fear of the Headless Horseman. Whereas Irving's Ichabod dies or disappears into oblivion, Disney's enjoys the last laugh, feasting at a table, surrounded by his pleasingly plump wife and assorted children. Bram, who wins fair Katrina's hand, seems less happy, for his bride clearly hasn't mended her flirtatious ways. In Disney, the sissy not only survives but succeeds, forcing a reevaluation of audience assumptions.

The ultimate reimagination of the sissy occurs in Disney's *Zorro,* both the weekly TV series (1957–1959) and the feature film version released in 1960.[25] Don Diego de la Vega is a casually masculine swordsman who returns to Southern California in 1820 after an extended stay in ancestral Spain. Discovering Los Angeles under the control of a tyrant, Monastario (Britt Lomond), Diego passes himself off as a fop, living a double life as Zorro, masked protector of the downtrodden. Happily, Disney's Diego never opts for the limp-wristed antics and mincing manner of previous screen incarnations (Douglas Fairbanks Sr., Tyrone Power, etc.), avoiding any condescending caricature of that type eventually parodied by George Hamilton in *Zorro, the Gay Blade* (1981).

Diego allows for Disney's most extreme depiction of the openly visible sissy as closeted hero. Initial disgust characterizes the reaction of Diego's father, Don Alejandro, toward a son who appreciates the finer things in life: music, poetry, flowers, and the like. Alejandro would, at least at first, prefer a more conventionally masculine son. Over the course of the series, Alejandro arced in a way that did not occur in earlier or later versions. Viewers witnessed a gradual acceptance of his son's prissiness, followed by Alejandro's final realization of the young man's true bold nature. Alejandro emerged as an audience surrogate, the older man's slow movement toward enlightenment suggesting that middle-aged mainstream viewers would be smart to do the same regarding their own "different" children.

The Reclamation of Manhood

Bath Day (1946)
Tonka (1958)
Lambert, the Sheepish Lion (1952)
Peter Pan (1953)

A key variation on the sissy theme is the reclamation of a male's sense of self: "The effeminate mama's boy is forced to prove his manhood by fighting a local band of thugs. This theme was a staple of American film, occurring naturally in various contexts."[26] When handled properly, this paradigm results in a nonpatronizing view of any character perceived as gay by the public at large. In Disney's *Bath Day*, Figaro (the cat from *Pinocchio*) is forced by Minnie Mouse to endure a bubble bath (powder-blue bubbles, Minnie's dress a corresponding hot pink) in which he is rinsed with lavender-mist perfume. Afterward, a red bow is placed around his neck. Out in the yard, a macho tom cat mocks Figaro's movements with exaggerated effeminate gestures. Angered by the idea that assumptions attributing weakness to him can arbitrarily be drawn from how he happens to appear, Figaro attacks his larger opponent in a striking premonition of Stonewall. His enemy defeated, Figaro hisses at the male gang; they panic and run. In the denouement, Figaro—red bow intact, if disheveled—proudly heads home, his "reclamation of manhood" complete. In Disney, not only every dog has his day, but every cat as well.

That theme is turned inside out in *Lambert, the Sheepish Lion,* after a well-intentioned stork misdelivers a cub to an expectant mother sheep. Initially ostracized for his inability to bleat, the ferocious-looking Lambert adopts the cowardly attitudes of his herd, denying the lion within. But when a wolf menaces them, homing in on Lambert's beloved nonbiological mother, Lambert draws upon the king-of-beasts element he has long repressed. The male youth heroes of numerous Disney films could be tagged as mama's boys—Bobby Driscoll in *Song of the South, So Dear to My Heart* (here, the maternal figure is a grandmother), and *Treasure Island* (even offscreen, the mother remains a significant presence). Additionally, each is, like Figaro, forced to undergo a thorough scrubbing and slip into fancy clothes at some point in the story. Yet each belies the Little Lord Fauntleroy stereotype.

A striking example occurs in *Tonka*. Early on, White Bull's maturity— and, with it, his masculinity—are called into question, forcing him to give up hunting and "walk with the women." Disney does not invoke the Sioux term "berdache,"[27] tribal epithet for men who live in such a manner (essentially, gay Indians), though this is implied. However, White Bull makes a vow to his young mother Prairie Flower (Joy Page): "No more will they call you the mother of a son who does not know how to be a man!" White Bull soon proves himself a warrior, though he (in comparison with the other Lakota youths) is apparently uninterested in the band's young women. White Bull's only male-female relationship is with attractive, dominating Prairie Flower—the father/husband absent without any explanation—consistent with what has traditionally been perceived as a recurring gay family dynamic.[28] White Bull's other loyalty is to a constant companion, Strong Bear, played by Rafael Campos with notable (though never demeaning) feyness.

The very casting of Sal Mineo as White Bull ensured a homosexual sub-text. After engaging in complex relationships with James Dean and Rock Hudson during the filming of *Giant* (1956), Mineo was one of the first Hollywood stars to live an openly gay life, at a time when others (notably Hudson) remained carefully closeted.[29] Disney had to be aware, as was every producer, of Mineo's orientation, which soon cost him key roles at other studios. Nonetheless, Walt hired the actor, allowing Mineo to play an implied gay character—without, happily, even a touch of sissiness.

Perhaps no film encapsulates Disney's attitude better than *Peter Pan,* which, after all, was "a fairy tale; grown men had real responsibilities that necessarily included growing up and settling down to marriage with a woman."[30] Hollywood's notion of "homosexuality and promiscuity [was] as the stuff of adolescence, habits to be discarded when one is ready to face adulthood and maturity . . . homosexuality [depicted as] a bid to stay forever young."[31] As in James Barrie's 1902 fable for post-Victorian children, Peter literally lives "underground"—physically incarnating an early term for homosexuals.[32] Venturing aboveground, Peter flirts with pretty women—Wendy, Tiger Lily, the mermaids—without ever attempting to consummate such relationships. In the opening sequence, Peter admits to Wendy he doesn't even know what a kiss is. At night, Peter sleeps with a group that is all male except for Tink, too small to be anything other than ornamental.

Besides, she's been identified as a "fairy," even if Disney was concerned enough about that phrase's double meaning in the 1950s to instead la-bel her a "pixie." Peter, in the stage tradition, had always been played by a young woman in drag, most famously Mary Martin. Peter is, after all, not really boy or man, rather inhabiting a state halfway between the two. While he occasionally needs a casual relationship with some female, he will not commit. When Wendy wants to become a mother, she—now considered a threat to Peter's extended adolescence—is promptly re-turned to London. Yet Peter is anything but a traditional "sissy," despite the sometimes pink, sometimes lavender feather he sports in his cap in the Disney Version.

Pan is, in the popular idiom, "butch," be he/she Martin's live-action conception or Disney's animated one. Crowing like a rooster, Peter serves notice to all that the girl/man/boy should not be mistaken for a weak-

ANAL FIXATION. Disney emphasized a situation implied in James Barrie's *Peter and Wendy*—that Captain Hook and Mr. Smee are gay—through cinematic iconography. The "elegant" Hook's face is superseded by a seagull's rear end, though pink and pudgy Smee fails to notice. (Copyright 1953 the Walt Disney Company; courtesy RKO Radio Films.)

ling. Captain Hook is more flamboyant, strutting about in grotesquely tight pants and black leather boots. A lavender shirt leads to a frilly ascot; his maroon hat, in certain lights, likewise appears lavender. Even the bow on the present that Hook sends to Pan (with a bomb inside) is the gay-associated lavender, as is most of his ship's surface.

In privacy, Hook plays classical music on the piano. Dominant Hook is cared for by recessive Mr. Smee, a pudgy, pink-faced lackey attending to Hook's every need, accepting verbal assaults without question. The ultimate anal gag passes between them, for Disney added a bizarre sequence in which nearsighted Smee, while shaving his captain, mistakes a seagull's rear end for Hook's face. Diligently, Smee cuts away feathers before lovingly massaging the bird's derriere. When the crocodile pursues Hook, he becomes the terrified cinematic cliché of the gay as hapless victim. When he plots against Peter, Hook is a polar stereotype, the gay as villain. Significantly, Disney combines the two clichés for the first time, satirizing both mercilessly. His Hook is a burlesque of both Old Hollywood clichés, simultaneously decimating these yin/yang stereotypes. In their place we find Pan: neither victim nor villain, rather an implied gay as nonsissified hero. The ongoing hatred between Pan and Hook can best be understood by recalling the intense dislike that developed between young, radical bisexual James Dean and older, traditional homosexual Rock Hudson on the set of *Giant.* Young Dean, always assuming a sensitive-macho pose, took a cruel kind of pleasure in tormenting a man who represented a retro-flamboyant style of gay behavior.[33] Their conflict was waged even as Disney's *Peter Pan,* with its similar contest, reached theater screens.

Attainable Assimilation
Alice and the Wild West Show (1924)
Shanghaied (1934)
Cookie Carnival (1935)

Disney's plea for tolerance appeared early on in *Alice and the Wild West Show.* As the butch heroine performs a cowboy act for neighborhood kids, an immediately identifiable sissy (glasses, straw hat, fancy suit) sits in the front row with a girl rather than back with the "regular boys." One roughneck taunts the sissy, pushing his hat down over his eyes. Other filmmakers of that era might have let the situation go at face value. Disney suggests something can be done, things can be altered. As the show progresses, the sissy moves back and, in time, is fully accepted by the other boys.

Such an image of attainable assimilation was furthered once Disney reached Los Angeles. In *Shanghaied,* Mickey rushes to the rescue of Minnie, abducted by Pegleg Pete and an unsavory crew in identical striped shirts. One sailor, however, is clearly "different." As Pete's crew dances in unison to a chorus of "The captain's got a girl," a crosscut carries us to the upper deck, where, alone, a gay pirate offers his fey version. The captain is a prototypical gay basher, and his immediate reaction is to punch this sailor in the face. The villain is not the gay, then, but the basher—hinting to the mass American audience that it ought to seriously consider the source of such an approach. Mickey makes no prejudicial distinctions. Entering into combat, he treats all pirates the same. Portraying the gay's abilities during this fight, Disney reveals him as equal; once the battle begins, the gay sailor submerges into his group, no more or less efficient at derring-do than the others. Though he's one of the "bad guys," his ho-mosexuality does not matter. He's bad only because he fights against the hero. Disney judges the gay as an individual rather than gender type. The movie's subtext is that we all ought to follow suit.

One year later, Disney solidified his notion of an ideal society by casu-ally including gays in *The Cookie Carnival,* a *Silly Symphony* set within a sugar-frosted alternative universe. The demure winner of this utopia's beauty pageant must pick a king from males who, in twosomes, dance before her. She, and we, watch antics of hipster Candy-cane Kids, Old-Fashioned Cookies, and nice but naughty Devil's Food Cakes. Also, the sweet Angel Food Cakes, who dance and fussily sing:

> *We're the angel food cake,*
> *we want it understood;*
> *You should marry one of us,*
> *because we are so good.*

Though exaggerated to the edge of cliché, the moment doesn't play as patronizing, owing to context. Since other twosomes were similarly cari-catured, we accept this as the overall approach, rather than something that is reserved for gays alone. The implication is that gays have as much of a right to live openly in Cookietown as anyone else. This place, like the eventually created Disneyland and Walt Disney World, is all-inclusive.

Blue Movies
Ferdinand the Bull (1938)
The Reluctant Dragon (1941)
Two Chips and a Miss (1952)
Mickey's Nightmare (1932)

Disney's definitive statement about gays is to be found in his "blue mov-ies." Leonard Maltin noted that *Ferdinand the Bull* and *The Reluctant Dragon* are reminiscent of each other "in depicting a supposedly ferocious animal who in reality is rather peaceful,"[34] though this merely scratches the surface of similarity in conception, tone, and status as plea for toler-ance. Both begin with a traditional "Once upon a time" narration, elicit-ing an audience expectation of conventional entertainment—an expecta-tion that will be undermined at every turn.

Dragon takes place in an exaggerated fairy-tale portrait of Western Europe during the Middle Ages, *Ferdinand* in a relatively realistic rendering of contemporary Spain. Both films ridicule macho posturing and, as a preferable alternative, present poetic and lovably fey flower-power figures. Disney employs symbolic color to identity his title characters. Though Ferdinand's physique is no different from that of other bulls romping in the pasture, his tuft of hair is powder blue, while his soft, vulnerable inner ears are hot pink. These hues are likewise employed for the dragon, whose effeminate mannerisms are complemented by blue-on-pink color composition with lavender flourishes. "Why don't you go and play with the other bulls, and hit heads?" Ferdinand's mother asks, her son luxuriating in the shade of a tree. In a sympathetically rendered falsetto, Ferdinand replies: "I like to sit here, and smell the flowers." She accepts this, as do, perhaps surprisingly, other bulls. The film insists Ferdinand's alternative choice is worthy of respect.

Similarly, in *Dragon*, a child—brainwashed by books filled with stereotypical portraits of fire-breathing beasts—seeks out the title character in his cave, where the little boy is initially disappointed to discover a peace-loving poet. A "punk" poet at that, the film insists; the term was widely accepted during the 1940s and '50s as the equivalent of "gay." [35] *Dragon* chronicles the boy's alternative-education toward acceptance of the dragon's reality as compared to society-at-large's limiting myth. Unlike Ferdinand, who could "pass" were it not for voice and values, the dragon is flamboyantly gay. We first see him (as does the child hero) singing while bathing, then gaily prancing off to write poetry and sip rare teas (small finger extended) from delicate cups. A caricature, to be sure, though hardly vicious. It's those who do not understand and accept the dragon (in the film, and in the audience watching) who are chastised.

Disney employs parallels between effeminate dragon and his would-be killer, knight of the realm Sir Giles, making clear even macho males have a feminine side, however much they deny this to maintain a "proper" public image. When the child hero first comes across Sir Giles, the knight sings in the shower, an echo of the dragon's demeanor; Sir Giles is "a bit of a bard" himself, as he admits to (and *only* to) the dragon, for fear his public might suspect him of . . . . Elderly Giles is caricatured as upper-crust Brit on the surface, eager to reveal his hidden self after finding a kindred soul in the flaming (in more ways than one) dragon.

With both films, the moviegoing audience becomes at one with the public-at-large attending Giles's duel with the dragon and the matador's confrontation with Ferdinand. The two audiences experience something different from what they expect, then afterward are asked to accept the alternative and grow in the process. Disney—while effectively providing entertainment—hopes to convert moviegoers, even as playgoers within his movie, at one with the American mainstream watching his film, are "converted." Giles and the dragon are glimpsed, when the smoke clears, dancing in one another's arms, flirting rather than fighting. Ferdinand kisses the matador, who crumbles with surprise and, incredibly, pleasure. Ferdinand, returning to his hillside, is last glimpsed smelling wildflowers, gazing into a blue-and-pink sunset. "He is very happy," the narrator insists, his tolerant tone eliciting audience acceptance for this choice. Likewise, the dragon crawls back to the cave, where epicene poetry ("Ode to an Upside-down Cake" among his verses) is the order of the day. Whether Giles will retire there with him, we are not told.

Disney did, however, provide a coming-out short, *Two Chips and a Miss*. Here, Chip 'n' Dale ultimately accept the very sort of relationship *Cinderella's* Jock and Gus-Gus earlier recoiled from. The film begins with a montage of shots illustrating Manhattan's neon nightlife. Signs for the Stork Club and other hot spots attract jaded big-city customers. Walt's camera pulls back to the countryside, where chipmunks make ready for sleep. Wearing identical nightshirts, they exchange pleasantries and slip into parallel beds, much in the manner of Laurel and Hardy, the screen's most homoerotic male comedy team.[36] No sooner are the lights turned off, however, than each embraces a love note from Clarise, beautiful young entertainer at a pint-size saloon. The film concerns their attempts to outdo one another in ever more desperate (and, seemingly, uncomplicated heterosexual) competition. At one point, libido literally overtakes the proceedings. The chipmunks, decked out in tie and tails, are driven so mad by Clarise's sexually charged performance that they beat the table with little paws, like Tex Avery's wolves going mad at the sight of "Red." Chip 'n' Dale actually frighten one another with the extremity of each other's hysteria.

In time, they settle for something less threatening—performing with Clarise as musicians, Chip on piano, Dale on guitar. She rewards each with a peck on the cheek. When they attempt to kiss Clarise on the mouth, she strategically slips back, causing them to inadvertently kiss one another. Their initial shock is followed not by the expected show of disgust or humiliation. Instead, there are surprising smiles of acceptance on each chipmunk's face. Apparently, this is what they always wanted, extreme heterosexual activity only a form of denial. Knowing them better than they do one another, Clarise winks into the camera. Her decision to have both chipmunks court her at the same place, same time, was not what it seemed—female game-playing for the satisfaction of her ego—but an attempt to help them come out of the closet, in a way Gus-Gus and Jock were unable to. Good-naturedly relieved by their admission, Chip 'n' Dale embrace one another instead of Clarise. She sweetly looks on, as happy to have been a catalyst as was Joanne Dru, forcing Wayne and Clift to admit their love for one another, in the last scene of Hawks's *Red River* (1948).

Every bit as important as this couple's implicitly admitting their feelings and finally daring to openly embrace is every individual's need to understand and accept, if not necessarily subscribe to, the lure of an alternative lifestyle. Lars Eighner articulates this in relationship to the Religious Right's unwarranted homophobic paranoia. "Those who now advocate so-called 'family values,'" he explains, devoutly believe in a "common heterosexual fantasy": Since the dawn of man, the recipe for perfect happiness has been embodied in the "heterosexual couple, [in] their little hut or cave, [with] perhaps a few mewling infants crawling about." Essentially, this is a mythic notion of modern romantic man-woman coupling, comfortably compatible with pre-Victorian notions of familial responsibility. It leads to an insistence on the viability of "a kind of family that never existed."[37] The current divorce rate provides ample proof that the ideal is not so easily achieved. Any attempt to point that out, however, is quickly written off as homosexual heresy—i.e., a frontal attack on family values—by the Religious Right.

In *Mickey's Nightmare*, Disney early on offered a vision that could be perceived by the Right as an attack on everything they stand for. The short opens with Mickey returning home from a date with Minnie, hopping into bed and dreaming about a potential marriage. The fantasy, however, turns into a nightmare. Their first child briefly appears a blessing from heaven, drawing the two closer together. But Mickey and Minnie shortly find themselves desperately attempting to care for dozens of children, all screaming and/or misbehaving like banshees from hell. "Surreal" is the only word to describe the pit of horror into which Mickey descends. He's woken by his male dog, Pluto, licking his face—a gesture Mickey initially believes to be (and as such rejects) open-mouth kissing on the part of Minnie. Discovering the actual source, Mickey breathes a sigh of relief.

Whether or not he will put that dream aside and continue his court-ship of Minnie, we are not told. Clearly, though, Minnie remained a sometimes-companion rather than joined with Mickey as half of a com-mitted couple. Disney is not strident enough to suggest that rejection of traditional family values is the only answer. On the other hand, he is en-lightened enough to positively illustrate another possibility.

"A Gentleman Does Not Go Back on His Word"
The Adventures of Bullwhip Griffin (1967)

Disney here returned for the last time to the Westerns that had sustained him throughout the late 1950s. This broad yarn about a runaway boy (Bryan Russell) surviving adventures in 1849 San Francisco plays like Twain's *The Adventures of Huckleberry Finn* as rewritten by Bret Harte. *Bullwhip* boasted Disney's signature attention to period detail, now ren-dered with a post–*Cat Ballou* (1964) satiric sensibility toward American frontier history, once taken completely seriously. The title character (Roddy McDowell) is yet another of Disney's seemingly sissy heroes—a slim, stuffy butler. "Although extremely frail and physically doomed to fail," George Bruns's song informs us, "he had plenty of heart in back of him." This allows Griffin, like Johnny Appleseed, to reclaim manhood by surpassing seemingly more appropriate candidates for pioneer heroism. Griffin even bests the gigantic Mountain Ox (Mike Mazurki) in a fight by using brains to defeat brawn. Their duel transforms into a dance resem-bling the one between Sir Giles and the title character in *The Reluctant Dragon*.

Death is a real presence, despite the light tone. *Bullwhip* opens with the reading of a worthless will. The passing of Boston's Mr. Flagg sends fam-ily and servants off to earn their livings elsewhere. Flagg's niece Arabella (Suzanne Pleshette) is another of Disney's liberated ladies, sexually, emo-tionally, and intellectually. Though former maids fear for Arabella's fate following the loss of her family fortune, Arabella scoffingly insists that she can make her way in the world. She accomplishes this by becoming a provocative San Francisco cancan performer. Even in this déclassé situation, Arabella maintains independence and self-respect by refusing to become mistress to saloonkeeper Sam Trimble (Harry Guardino). By film's end, she owns his establishment, and he works for her. Arabella did not resort to deviousness to achieve this. She also teaches Griffin the necessary techniques her chosen man needs to know if he's to win his fight.

Arabella furthers another recurring Disney theme, the overturning of old and restrictive class distinctions. She romantically pursues her former butler, despite Griffin's own belief that Arabella is above him. Disney's attitude toward capitalism is consistent with depictions in his earlier films. Greedy miners who, in the first half, arrive on the Gold Coast with Midas-like dreams of getting rich quick are seen starving on the streets in the second part. On the other hand, growing rich slowly, through diligent work, is as admired as ever. Griffin employs his considerable skills (he's master of everything from gourmet cooking to hairstyling) to sustain himself and friends. The Establishment is satirized in the person of Judge Higgins (Karl Malden), law-and-order proponent eventually revealed to be a phony. Classic literature is supported when Quentin Bartlett (Richard Haydn), a seeming con man spouting Shakespeare, turns out to be a decent sort. The desire of real people to live up to mythic conceptions is present. Little Jack is inspired to seek adventure after reading dime novels about fictional "Bullwhip Brannigan," then helps his initially wary butler/companion to realize that even as unlikely a choice as Griffin can achieve such mythic stature—and, not insignificantly, wield a mean bullwhip.

Minorities are treated with sensitivity. Though Hispanic outlaws who rob a stagecoach initially appear broad stereotypes, their leader (Joby Baker) reminds our heroes: "Please, do not complain. The land belonged to us. You came and take our gold? We take yours!" A Chinese coolie laboring in the gold camp, at first appearing a less than politically correct screen incarnation of an Asian, sets up a key gag. Higgins (master of disguise) escapes by passing himself off as an honest Oriental worker. As with the child hero in *Treasure Island,* innocent Jack is inexplicably drawn to the dark side Higgins represents. So is the film's viewer, who can never fully condemn this charming villain. In presenting a supposed sissy who reclaims his manhood as the centerpiece of a comedy-epic Western, Disney also manages to again reveal his enlightenment in other areas.

Dare to Be Different
Dumbo (1941)

Ultimately, Disney's sympathetic portrait of the gay or presumably gay individual is one manifestation of his larger, greater sensitivity to the very concept of being different, whether or not that status involves sexuality. Essential to the Disney films from their very outset, this element was first explored in depth in *Dumbo,* the fifth full-length animated film. Walt's enlightened sensibility, as expressed in this brief (sixty-four minutes) movie, would provide the basis for variations on this theme throughout Disney's career.

Dumbo is set at a circus. As the opening credits roll, the words and names initially pass over images of conventional big top acts—pretty female bareback riders and the like. But as the title segment draws to a close, such upbeat images give way to something more on the order of the traveling carnival as depicted in Edmund Goulding's 1947 film of William Lindsay Gresham's novel *Nightmare Alley:* the sideshow acts, filled with freaks including the Strong Man. The sequence introduces Disney's story structure for the film that follows, as well as for all his subsequent motion pictures: Swiftly present the expected mainstream images, then move on to the real substance at hand, that being the disenfranchised minorities who are marginalized in life, as in the itself-marginalized microcosm of the circus.

That idea—the circus as a symbol for life—pervades the film. The behind-the-scenes elements—particularly hard work and the need for communal activity, with humans and animals cooperating as equals— are absolutely necessary for survival, much less success. And, shortly, we meet Disney's consistently despised elite, the pillars of society who set the pace for the pachyderm subworld of this notably sleazy *demi-monde.* Viciously satirized, these snobs will shortly ostracize the title character owing to the size of his ears. First, though, Dumbo must be delivered to his mother. Even in this conventional depiction of the fabled storks, Disney has an opportunity to reveal his love of genial eccentrics. First, we see the conventional storks, all flying in perfect order and harmony, each identical to the next. Dumbo, however, will be dropped off by a notably unique individual, his voice provided by Sterling Holloway, employed by Walt for just such parts (Winnie the Pooh, Kaa the Snake) over several decades.

The character immediately involves the child viewer in a way that the more ordinary storks did not. Though this serves merely as a prologue to the narrative proper, it effectively conveys the Disney outlook on life. The unique individual, rather than the conformist mass, should be the object of our emotional involvement. Though the prejudice against Dumbo is immediately directed toward his large ears, the baby elephant is clearly intended as the progenitor of Walt's gay (if by implication only) characters. Though he's initially named after his father ("Jumbo, Jr."), Jumbo is absent. Perhaps this is meant to suggest (again, by implication rather than statement) that Jumbo has died before the story even began (a recurring plot device in Disney). Then again, there are no other male elephants on view, nor do we see the males of any other species. This is clearly a matriarchy, and Dumbo (as he will be nicknamed by the unpleasant society matron among the elephants) is clearly a mama's boy and a sissy.

Even his best friend, Timothy Mouse, complains about Dumbo's being a crybaby. When the clowns make the little elephant a part of their act, they draw inspiration for the painting of his face from Dumbo's essential personality, doing him up in pink, baby blue, lavender, and white. Most significantly, they transform "him" into a girl-child for the act in which Dumbo will drop down from a faux burning building into a net that the clown/firemen hold out for him. Dumbo is, in the words of the insensitive elephants, a "f-r-e-a-k" in more ways than one—at least in comparison to supposedly "normal" characters, a theme that is at the heart of the Disney canon.

The ending of *Dumbo* encapsulates all of Disney's most often overlooked themes. Most significant among them is Walt's far-seeing positive portrayals of those who are different, and the need for others—purportedly more "normal" types, if that term has any valid meaning—to accept and include those who are different in the American mainstream. Such a quiet revolution can only strengthen the society at large by drawing on the unique gifts of the diverse types that have all too often been marginalized in the past. Dumbo maintains his friendship with his brown companion, the diminutive Timothy. He has not forgotten his black friends, either, without whom he could not have achieved self-realization. And, in time, acceptance—both by the crowd and by himself, for himself. He has been reunited with the female principle, his mother—not disparaged, as in the anti-Momism literature of the times (and simultaneously caricatured onscreen via Alfred Hitchcock's horrific mother figures), but presented as intelligent and independent. He has been drawn into the community at large without surrendering his individuality.

Dumbo lives out the enlightened dream of achieving inclusion without having to so fully assimilate that his uniqueness is diminished. This is the vision of the most forward-looking among us today, yet of no other film-maker from Hollywood's studio era than Walt Disney.

MAIN STREET, U.S.A. In Disneyland, Walt re-created the small town of his memory. Though his nostalgia has been employed to damn Disney as a conservative sentimentalist, such iconographic ideology appears in the work of leftists Orson Welles *(The Magnificent Ambersons)* and Rod Serling *(The Twilight Zone)*. (Copyright 1955 Walt Disney Productions.)

Popular Culture and Political Correctness
In Defense of Disney, Part 99

> Instead of political convictions, he occupied himself with myth-making and the creation of a world—the creating of the world anew.
> —RUSSIAN POET MARINA TSVETAYEVA, ON THE DEATH OF THE
> (PURPORTEDLY) REVOLUTIONARY ARTIST MAX VOLOSHIN, 1932

> If he had any politics at all, they were the politics of nostalgia.
> —RICHARD SCHICKEL, ON THE DEATH OF THE
> (SUPPOSEDLY) REACTIONARY ARTIST WALT DISNEY, 1969

*T*he place where [Disney] operated most comfortably in the late Fifties and early Sixties," according to Richard Schickel, "was the American small town."[1] With unmasked contempt, he added: "Only in Disney films has it remained unchanged."[2] The first half of his assessment is true; the second, I hope to prove, could not be more misleading or patently false. The syndrome of which Schickel speaks—exploiting the public by marketing "nostalgia for a carefully falsified past"[3]—is most manifest in Main Street, U.S.A., the entry route to Disney theme parks. A visitor must pass through this romanticized vision of turn-of-the-century America—implicitly presented as superior in all ways to our current lifestyle—before heading on to other attractions. An attack on Disney owing to this key decision in the parks' design derives from the long-held belief that any aggrandizement of a bygone Golden Age qualifies the creator as reactionary.[4] How else explain Walt's preference for a lifestyle, more mythic than actual, in sharp contrast to the way we live today?

Yet during that very time period in which Walt proffered this vision, not only in the park but on episodes of his weekly TV show, Rod Serling—interpreted as a popular artist of liberal leaning—projected precisely the same value system. Two of the most memorable (and characteristic of that writer-producer) *Twilight Zone* episodes, "Next Stop, Willoughby" and "Walking Distance," deal with middle-aged men (respectively played by Gig Young and James Daly) who long to leave their ultramodern Madison Avenue careers and pseudosophisticated suburban existence behind. Serling's heroes want nothing less than to slip back to a bygone America where everyone knew everyone else's name and band concerts were a daily occurrence. Similarly, the first Mickey Mouse cartoon ever released in color—*The Band Concert* (1935), which Serling (an avid moviegoer) likely saw while growing up in Ithaca, New York—offers an idealization of such quasi-rural pastimes. That cartoon could easily have set the pace for *Zone*'s image of the mythic past as preferable to our then-present reality.

Various charming sequences in "Willoughby" and "Walking Distance"—depicting a vision of small-town life, truer to our national collective unconscious than our actual history, bespotted with its social turmoil—might well have been filmed at Disneyland's Main Street, U.S.A. From the park's opening day, band concerts greeted those disembarking from the Disneyland antique railroad. Not coincidentally, perhaps, Daly steps down from just such a train in "Willoughby." Considered from this perspective, Main Street, U.S.A., enables visitors to experience firsthand what Serling's lost souls long to do in their secret fantasies: get back in touch with, if not a past reality, then some idea of who we once were—members of a generous, easygoing, positive community. However faux, such a grand illusion sustained us during the troubled postwar period when Americans were victims of anomie, each a fragment of the lonely crowd.

Clearly, Disney was not (as Schickel insists) "alone" in offering such a vision. Such a nostalgic conception had earlier been implied by Orson Welles in *Citizen Kane* (1940) and further developed in *The Magnificent Ambersons* (1942). In the former, Charles Foster Kane's chances for happiness are destroyed at that moment when, as a child, he's yanked from the simple nineteenth-century Western setting where he happily played in the snow. Afterward, Kane matures in a sophisticated twentieth-century Eastern environment where moral complexity and raw capitalism corrupt the onetime idealist. Not only a sled or corresponding paperweight, Rosebud constitutes what both objects signify in Kane's mind, what he hoped to reachieve by finding the former in life or hanging tight to the latter at his moment of death—the innocence of our American Dream as it once was, or, more accurately, as we need to believe it to have been. Such a lost Eden is even more vividly portrayed in Welles's adaptation of Booth

Tarkington's best-loved novel. *Ambersons* begins with a montage of small-town America shortly before the turn of the century that might well have served, however unconsciously, as Disney's model for Main Street, U.S.A. As this beloved place gives way to a modern city, the protagonist (Tim Holt) gradually dissipates, at least in part as a result of the fading of a time and place that, in their delicate beauty, sustained him. Yet people continue to perceive Welles as a liberal and think of Disney as conservative.

Either—each—and others (Serling, Tarkington) expressed a vision not easily tagged by the dichotomized labels critics pin on artists in the process of deciding if they are acceptable today: revolutionary or radical, traditional or progressive, Classicist or Romantic. The vain attempt to impose ideological structure aside, what this vision, when fully understood, actually addresses is an inherently populist notion of what it means to be an American. Just as specific sequences in Disney films must, for fair assessment, be viewed in the context of the entire movie, so should Main Street, U.S.A., be analyzed from the perspective of the whole park. After experiencing that fin de siècle pavilion, visitors could drift to one side and recover an earlier, even more traditional aspect of our past in Frontierland; turn the other way and peek into a remarkably accurate preview of what H. G. Wells once tagged the shape of things to come in Tomorrowland; or continue straight ahead and, after passing through Cinderella's castle, enter an alternative realm of fable and folktales, drawn from European literature, in Fantasyland.

Past and present. Fantasy or reality. Here, there? What Disney accomplished in building his world is a distillation of the human condition, experienced through the wondrous eyes of a child, then offered back to the public (children and the child that still exists somewhere in every adult) in crystallized form. However disparaged by highbrow critics, the remarkable and ongoing commercial success (lest we forget, in 1954, the "word on the street" was that Disneyland would quickly fail, bankrupting Walt) suggests his conception did connect with the only critics Disney cared about: the people. Likewise, the durability of his films resides in just such an approach, best described as universality—not only in terms of the extent of the public reached and touched at the time of each release, but the ongoing appeal of these movies for the radically different audience of today.

But financial success can work against an artist's acceptance by the cultural elite. In American intellectual circles, commercial viability is more often than not equated with a loss of moral values on the part of the creator and, correspondingly, within the creation. So we encounter the disparagement of those who, working in a dramatic tradition that reaches back through Shakespeare to Sophocles, aim squarely for the mass—highborn, lowbrow, and everyone in between; people with nothing in common but their essential humanity. As to this success-based line of attack, *Time* put a particularly nasty spin on Disney's popularity. The week after Walt's death, that magazine decried that the once humble company had transformed into "a giant corporation whose vast assembly lines produced ever slicker products to dream by."[5] This argument rang hollow when an anonymous scribe added: "Many of them, mercifully, will be forgotten." Virtually none of Disney's creations, including those from that later scorned period, has dropped out of the public consciousness. These works live on, thanks to videocassettes, DVD, cable channels, and theme parks. "The Disney Studio," a critic could complain, solved "the ancient Hollywood problem of achieving financial stability when the success of the basic product depends on such unpredictable factors as fads and fashions in stories and stars"[6] by retelling public domain narratives and creating its own animated "celebrities" who could not demand raises.

There is no reason, though, why this ought to be given a negative spin. From the outset, Disney reached for—and more often than not achieved—the eternal rather than the momentary. The public might fall in and out of love with the current reigning stars at MGM or Columbia, as the ever rising or waning box-office appeal of such people proves. Mickey—Chaplin's Little Tramp, anthropomorphically rendered as the ultimate (and immortal) icon in American popular culture—proved, conversely, to be the compleat star, with an appeal that promises to last forever. Like Chaplin, Disney was (whatever one thinks of his output) a populist. Though the creation of the theme parks has been perceived by many intellectuals as the ultimate commercialized exploitation of whatever shard of integrity yet resided in his work, there is another way to read the situation. Every artist, whether he or she is consciously aware of it or not, plays God by realizing a unique world. This holds as true for the creation of supposedly realistic fiction and painting as in creating more fantastical works—the only distinction being the degree to which any one practitioner hews to Aristotle's age-old dictum that art is an imitation of life. As Aubrey Menen put it, "the strongest desire an artist knows is to create a world of his own where everything is just as he imagines it."[7]

In the entire history of creative discourse, Disney—and Disney alone—achieved that, via the creation of parks which allowed those already familiar with his vision (thanks to those uniquely twentieth-century art forms, film and television) to enter and experience it firsthand. If one accepts Menen's thesis, what Disney achieved establishes Walt not only as *a* legitimate artist, but *the* über-artist. Not, however, that this led to a self-contained universe, some solipsistic alternative to reality. James Rouse, one of the country's most significant and innovative city planners, pointed to Disneyland—with its moving sidewalks and other forward-looking devices for efficient displacement of people—as "the greatest piece of urban design in the U.S. today."[8] Walt's initial conception had in fact been less the theme park that emerged in 1954 than an actual town where people could live and work in the most progressive of settings while simultaneously returning to a community ripe with traditional values. Though this ultimately proved too far-reaching for even him to then manage, Disney began blueprinting just such a place even before Disneyland opened.

The result would be Walt Disney World, finished after his death. WDW featured everything Walt ever dreamed of in meeting the demands of an enlightened public—from ecology-oriented wildlife sanctuaries to an actual town, Celebration—combining our ongoing nostalgia for America's mythic past with a modern technological environment. Now, people could not only walk down Main Street, U.S.A., for a single day's visit but actually live there. For Disney's harshest critics, though, his personal empire building (and that of the company since his death) threatens to encompass the entire globe. *It's a Small World,* for those who see a dark aspect to any commercial success, plays more like "Tomorrow, the World." Chyng Feng Sun argues:

> Media conglomeration raises fundamental concerns about its impact on democracy. Because enormous conglomerates like Disney own so much of the media, they exercise unprecedented control over the images and messages we are exposed to.[9]

Essentially true, her statement doesn't take into account that the various media conglomerates ("like Disney" in size and scope, though not necessarily ideology) run the gamut from archconservative to openly liberal. Rupert Murdoch's right-wing viewpoint, projected by Fox TV and various newspapers, could not be further from, say, Ted Turner's long-term leftish leanings. Feng Sun can argue that the result is, we're constrained "by a very limited world-view, skewed and dominated by corporate institutions." Still, the output of each operation varies in terms of who is in charge, and what that person's politics happen to be. To truly understand today's Disney, we ought not to assume any media conglomerate's output is necessarily reactionary in intent or impact. With this in mind, we should recall that Michael Eisner, Disney's long-term CEO, is a political liberal. As a Jew, he's also a member of an ethnic minority—as such, sensitive to issues of diversity.

With this in mind, it's important to note that whether Disney's contribution to popular culture is or is not deemed acceptable according to politically correct values ought to be considered within the context of a larger issue. Much of what has, in our time, come to be considered proper evaluation of the arts and/or entertainment hails from ideas first espoused by Theodor Adorno, founder of the Frankfurt School. Aesthetic and intellectual concepts originally formulated by Adorno led to an attitude Chyng Feng Sun may have had in mind when she offered her assessment of Disney: Most of what we refer to as popular culture, however seemingly devoid of ideas, is political—indeed, most political when seeming not to be political at all. Moreover, such work is almost invariably designed to uphold the status quo.[10]

Such an assessment is hardly invalid. Much handsomely crafted work, produced in recent times and within a medium as modernist in its mechanical basis as the commercial cinema, may first appear revolutionary but reveals itself on close examination as reactionary. Most famously, John Steinbeck's *The Grapes of Wrath* concluded with the uprooted Okies unable to find work and facing total despair. At the end of John Ford's Oscar-winning 1940 film, however, they head off to a good new job and, like America itself, are reborn. A pessimistic novel was transformed into an optimistic film. Almost invariably, a book offers one person's individual vision, while a major motion picture involves a multimillion dollar investment for a large corporation that must earn back its money. To do that, it provides the legendary audience-appeasing "happy ending."

If Hollywood's most acclaimed (and apparently mature) works fall into this trap, Walt Disney's supposedly genial entertainments would likely rate as the worst offenders. The purpose of this book has been to illustrate through example that the opposite is true. Disney films, cheered and/or jeered as genial middlebrow family entertainment, provided—like the proverbial wolf in sheep's clothing—that rarest of rarities: ideologically iconoclastic narratives discovered where we would least expect to find them. In so doing, they expressed the man who made them. Always, there was something of the puckish, nonviolent, antisocial outlaw about Walt, obvious even in his early years. Whereas other struggling commercial art-

BEYOND POLITICS. A Democrat in his youth and a Republican in later years, Disney set aside such considerations at his park and greeted (clockwise, from upper left) liberal Democrat John Fitzgerald Kennedy in the company of President Sekou Toure of Guinea; conservative Republican Dwight Eisenhower with his wife, Mamie; former President Harry S Truman and his wife, Bess; Republican Richard M. Nixon and his entire family. (Copyright 1959, 1961, 1957, and 1959, and reprinted courtesy Walt Disney Productions.)

ists set mousetraps in their humble Kansas City offices, Walt left water and bits of cheese for them to consume after working hours. When he left for California, the young artist rounded up his pack of rodents and set them loose "in the best neighborhood I could find," so they would then annoy the filthy rich.[11] Significantly, this attitude did not alter after he became rich himself. Living in one of those "best" neighborhoods after achieving success in California, Walt refused to allow his wife, Lillian, to set traps that would kill off the rodents that daily destroyed whatever she grew in their backyard garden. His own immediate situation may have changed, but something essential-—and essentially anti-Establishment—in Disney's makeup did not.

Always, he saw himself (as his alter ego Mickey makes clear) as one of those rodents who never quite won full acceptance into the status quo. His love of such creatures hardly endeared Disney to the harshest of political rightists. One of the first official acts of the Third Reich, upon seizing power, was to banish Disney entertainment. "The Mouse was the most miserable ideal ever created," a Hitler spokesperson announced, since "mice are dirty."[12]

So, was Disney a liberal or a conservative? Happily, he defies easy labeling. But if the historical record is any indicator, it's worth recalling that during the 1930s, Mickey was damned in Hitler's Germany as too dangerously democratic and from Yugoslavia for appearing too revolutionary. On the other hand, the Mouse was beloved in Russia as a symbol of the common man, a cartoon hero who always somehow overcame the adversity created by a totalitarian state. Nonetheless, critics very much want to tag Disney as the prime reactionary. One key line of attack insists that Disney films, seemingly escapist fare, are actually teaching tools. Elizabeth Hadley (African American Studies, Simmons College) flatly states: "Disney is dangerous because it's a sublime kind of education; it's absorbed by our young people as entertainment."[13] Perhaps Hadley meant to say "subliminal," implying that those who choose to see Disney films only as entertainment are also being educated, even though they remain unaware of the process. Ironically, another Disney critic, Margaret Moody, complains that there is no patina of education in Disney entertainment, insisting: "I really believe that as an entertainer, you have a responsibility to be a teacher as well."[14]

That precisely describes Walt Disney's aim. He intentionally set out to destroy the old dichotomy between education and entertainment by making the learning process fun rather than tedious. One early effort, *Tommy Tucker's Tooth* (1921), explained dental hygiene to boys and girls by captivating them with the appealing title character. The desire to merge education and entertainment would reach its ambitious apex in the thrill rides at Florida's Epcot Center, including the journey through audio-animatronic dinosaurs. A relationship between such extinct beasts and modern oil supplies is effectively conveyed even as the audience has a good time. "We like to have a point to our stories," Walt admitted, though it ought to be "not an obvious moral but a worthwhile theme."[15] That is, essentially moral yet never obviously—or conventionally—moralistic. The most basic idea for this current book has been that what Disney taught us are the very precepts for political correctness, and that who we are today derives in large part from what we learned from him.

But Disney is perceived, at least in some academic and intellectual circles, as a potently racist force in popular culture. Complaining about *The

Jungle Book (1967, the final animated film supervised by Walt), Jacqueline Maloney (Du Bois Institute, Harvard) implies that Mowgli, lost child of the outback, is a representative Anglo, surrounded by "orangutans that sound like black people."[16] Mowgli is not Anglo, of course, but a native of India—a person of color, as the film's vivid tableaus reveal. In refusing to overly Anglicize the character, even during that violent era of ghetto burnings and street confrontations, Disney provided American children, including those in the deep South, with their first animated youth hero of color.

More significant, the animated orangutans were voiced not by black performers but by whites. Their leader, King Louis in Disney's version of the Kipling tale, represents the studio's long-held technique of "character animation." The celebrity who will eventually voice any character is chosen before the animation process begins. Animators then employ this well-known performer as their physical model—in this case, Louis Prima, an Italian American jazz singer. Prima's unique voice was recognizable (at least to the audience that saw the film during its initial run), while his striking personality was represented by the cartoon character he posed for. Like his followers, Louis is anything but a caricature of blacks. Indeed, the Disney team appears to have gone out of its way to avoid the racial situation it is accused of creating.

Still, accusations abound. Speaking of her daughter, Marisa Penalta recalls in *Mickey Mouse Monopoly* something troubling that the child (experiencing an epiphany) said after observing the way things work in media portrayals of the world around us: "Mommy, why is it that dark people are always doing bad things?"[17] The question is excellent, in the old "from the mouths of babes" tradition. Children, with their fresh take on everything, see directly to the heart of the matter on issues involving cultural baggage that, to adults, are old hat—and, as such, often going unquestioned. Notable here, though, is the documentarian's decision to at this moment cut to an onscreen image of *Fantasia's* evil monster Chernobog from Mussorgsky's *Night on Bald Mountain*. The little girl was not necessarily speaking about Disney entertainment in general, much less this particular moment, when she noticed—and rightly questioned—the old and unfortunately ongoing stereotype.

Feng Sun's editing decision confuses a significant issue by fusing the child's sharp observation to a pop-culture icon that the little girl did not likely have in mind. This clever if unfair fusion of sight and sound apparently indicts Disney as the most striking perpetuator of the black-as-evil myth.

In fact, Disney hardly rates as the most notable or extreme practitioner, as anyone who has seen Lucas's original *Star Wars* trilogy (1977–1983) can attest. Villainous Darth Vader wears a black costume. His voice, alone among those in the first installment, was provided by an African American actor, James Earl Jones. Moreover, *Star Wars* was filmed in the midseventies, even as politically correct thinking emerged. It should, then, be more (not less) sensitive to such an incendiary issue than a 1941 film.

Dr. Hadley complains of the 1999 version of a venerable Edgar Rice Burroughs tale that Disney's is "a *Tarzan* film without black people at all." [18] While this is true, her comment makes clear the difficult (impossible?) situation modern filmmakers, desperate to do the right thing, find themselves in—confounded by political correctness taken to its extreme. Spielberg, the modern Disney, did not include any Indians in *Hook* (1991), his riff on Disney's 1953 *Peter Pan*. Amblin Entertainment, like the modern Disney company that eight years later remade *Tarzan*, found itself in a no-win situation. Include Indians or Africans and caricature them (along with the Anglos) to maintain the tone of burlesque so necessary for a broad entertainment, and a producer will be accused of perpetuating an odious cliché. If, on the other hand, the studio did not portray Indians or Africans, it would be attacked for less-than-benign neglect. Dr. Deidre Almeida complains that in *Pocahontas* (1995), Disney co-opted Native American culture, more or less insisting that "we can change your history, portray you to look as we want, put your picture on lunch boxes, [allow] kids to dress up like you at Halloween—and you can't do anything about it!" (her words, not Disney's, of course). [19]

Exasperated, Spielberg chose the route of "neglect" for *Hook*. The modern Disney company did the same with *Tarzan*, though it dared navigate the other, perhaps more perilous path with *Pocahontas*. Native Americans have long complained that they are seldom if ever allowed to take center stage in a major Hollywood movie. Even Kevin Costner's overpraised *Dances with Wolves* (1990) is nothing more than a conventional Anglo romance, set against a Native American background that, in truth, was not accurately portrayed. The Disney company alone allowed a Native American to assume the lead role. It's worth noting that the only previous sound-era film version of this story clearly placed its emphasis on the Anglo male hero, as the title of Lew Landers's *Captain John Smith and Pocahontas* (1953) announced. It mattered little, though, that Disney played Pocahontas as the true protagonist and depicted most Anglos as endangering the natural world that Native Americans appreciate, or that numerous Native Americans (including outspoken activist Russell Means) were hired as historical advisors so that their culture would be realistically as well as positively portrayed.

The film—however beloved by the public—was attacked by the same people who would have taken Disney to task if the company failed to at least try and address Native American issues. The Disney studio was damned if it did, damned if it didn't. It did, and a precious few found fault because Pocahontas was portrayed as conventionally beautiful. The negative claim insisted this qualified the movie as sexist as well as racist. But like the heroines of films released while Walt ran the show, Pocahontas is not limited by her beauty. She is bright, caring, and righteous. Though she does happen to be physically attractive, she is not defined by her good looks. Pocahontas is a beautiful person, not yet another image of the female reduced to beauty object. With this icon of a full and rich loveliness—intellectual, emotional, and spiritual, as well as physical—Disney added a woman of color to its gallery of leading ladies.

In *Mouse Monopoly,* the camera focuses on several little (Anglo) girls playing Pocahontas, cutting back and forth between them and Vanessa Williams singing "Colors of the Wind." The documentarian's point, apparently, is that these girls have been conditioned by endlessly watching the video into modeling themselves on Disney's character. Certainly, that is the case, though the implication that this constitutes negative conditioning hardly holds up. They are imitating a woman of color who is an environmentalist and pacifist. How could anyone ask for a more politically correct role model than that?

Yet Gail Dines notices and criticizes the similarity in Disney's female leads, asserting that the Disney vision of beauty has not notably changed over the decades. "Not that Disney invented [the stereotype of flirtatious females], but what they do with the roles is caricature them."[20] Her statement is precisely correct, if not necessarily in the negative manner intended. Rather than presenting female sensuality at face value, as other filmmakers (past and present) do, the Disney company of today (in *Aladdin, Hercules, Who Framed Roger Rabbit,* etc.), like Walt himself, makes us laugh at what other filmmakers take seriously. Disney does not *represent* but does *caricature* (Dines's own word) all images of overripe female sexuality—performed specifically for, to borrow from Laura Mulvey, the male gaze. Jessica's exotic song/dance number draws (pun intended) such activity to the point of ridiculousness, as the laughter heard at any screening anywhere in the world made clear. George Bernard Shaw once claimed that a joke is an epitaph of an emotion. Disney's humorous portrayal makes clear that such an outrageous image of women ought to be as dead and gone as the period during which that film takes place: the 1930s.

Far worse than the charge of stereotyping women is the more damning assertion that *Beauty and the Beast* (1991) legitimizes abusive behavior by men toward women. "A great deal of my work in my professional life," Dr. Carolyn Newberger (Psychology, Harvard Medical School) explains, "is [working with cases of] family violence. And when you look at the film through that eye, the abuse is horrific." Her unique "eye," however, is not necessarily enlightening. Such a perspective can result in an intellectualized tunnel vision. Such a highly specified background can distort the work by predetermining how a unique person receives the film's universalized text. "She [Belle] reinterprets his [the Beast's] abuse and rage as [mere] temper."[21] Actually, Belle intuits that abuse, rage, and/or temper—whatever the term one chooses to refer to such abominable behavior—is, semantics aside, utterly intolerable.

Belle does not make the (sadly common in our society) mistake of denying that rage and temper are interchangeable as a pretext for continuing in an abusive relationship. Disney's Belle never entered into any relationship with the Beast so long as he remained abusive. Rather, she forces him to reinvent himself. Then, and only then, Belle becomes involved. "He screams at her," Newberger notes. "His behavior is without question frankly and horribly abusive."[22] That is what he initially does. What Newberger utterly fails to take into account, though, is what then transpires in that sequence, as the Beast insists Belle join him for dinner:

> BEAST: Come out or I'll break the door down.
> MRS. POTTS (mentoring): Gently . . . gently . . .
> BEAST (repentant): Join me . . . please?

Lowering his voice, the Beast expects her to immediately appear. She does not, so he reverts to his previous unacceptable behavior. From this, Belle learns he has not changed—not yet—only temporarily modified his behavior in hopes of achieving immediate gratification. She informs the Beast that even when he does speak politely, he cannot assume she will do anything he wants, thereby initiating the Beast's moral education.

"The whole thrust of the story," Newberger continues, "is that she . . . excuses him . . . and then falls in love with him." Belle never once excuses him; she *changes* him. Under Belle's guidance, he arcs. Only then does Belle fall in love. "This is a movie," Newberger concludes, "that is say-

CONTINUING THE FEMINIZATION OF FAIRY TALES. Few old stories are as sexist as the original "Beauty and the Beast," in which the female lead accepts abuse by the brutal male. The contemporary Disney organization continues the approach that Walt insisted on by having Belle reject the Beast until he not only modifies his behavior but actually alters his attitude. (Copyright 1991 Walt Disney Productions; courtesy Buena Vista Releasing.)

ing to our children, 'overlook the abuse.'" It "says" nothing of the sort. Disney's *Beauty and the Beast* tells the modern young woman, who may very well identify with Belle, that under no circumstances should abuse be tolerated. "It's your job to kiss the beast," Newberger explains in terms of what she believes the film means to little girls, "and bring [the prince] out. That's a dangerous message."[23] If that were the message, "dangerous" would be far too mild an admonition. Though just such a message may be implicit in earlier *Beauty and the Beast* retellings, it's precisely what the Disney Version warns us against. In comparison to previous Belles, Disney's heroine never kisses the beast before he becomes a prince, in the truest (that is, nonphysical) sense. Only after an internal reformation is complete does she kiss him. His supposedly "ugly" appearance means nothing to her. He is no longer a beast but a prince, at least in her eyes (the modern woman's eyes) because of his ability and willingness to grow after accepting the wisdom of a protofeminist woman.

Her kiss, then, does not change a beast into a prince, rather acknowledges that the beast is gone and a prince has taken his place—even though he does not yet look any different. At that point, his looks alter; the physical change mirrors the far more significant inner change that has already occurred. The documentarian then turns the camera on "Melissa," a nine-year-old girl. Asked how she would feel if the film's heroine happened to be a friend of hers, she replies without hesitation: "I'd probably say, keep being nice and sweet and that will change him. And, in the movie, it does." [24] Melissa's reading—drawn from a close (and objective) viewing, arrived at without the blinders of Newberger's professional baggage—is a precise description of what transpires.

Dr. Justin Lewis (Journalism, Media, and Cultural Studies, Cardiff University) notes:

> Because Disney [is] such a large media conglomerate, and [its] products are so ubiquitous and so widespread globally, the stories that Disney tell[s] will be the stories that form, or help form, a child's imagination over the world, and that's an incredible amount of power. When you have that kind of power, you're becoming a dominant storyteller for children globally. We have to begin asking very serious questions about what kind of stories are being told. Are they the kinds of stories we would want to be told? [25]

We absolutely should ask that question, but only if we do so as freethinkers: Approaching Disney without the prejudices that those on the far right and far left bring to any discourse on Disney (or, for that matter, any other subject), such attitudes predetermining what their answer will be. I asked my friend the Fulbright scholar, whose anti-Disney ideology was mentioned in this book's introduction, how he felt about *Pocahontas*. The reply was that, in his opinion, today's Disney corporation is *too* politically correct. This, he insisted, represented another case of a media conglomerate co-opting the PC values of our emerging diversity-oriented society. Such a complaint suggests that, from a radical intellectual point of view, *anything* offered by a media conglomerate is bad and unhealthy for us and our children—an attitude totally different from (even the polar opposite of) that expressed by Dr. Lewis.

The Fulbright scholar's retort suggests, however inadvertently, that Disney films do pass the test that Lewis rightly poses. The more radical approach—wishing that all media conglomerates would cease to exist—strikes me as dangerous in its mixture of idealism and naïveté. They aren't

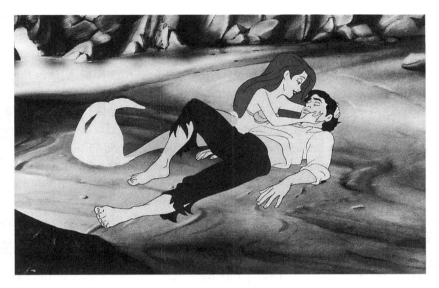

CONTINUING THE TRADITION. Critics complained that *The Little Mermaid*'s happy ending violates Hans Christian Andersen's story. An alternative reading notes that Ariel is here *not* destroyed for defying Triton's patriarchal order, reversing the antifeminist cautionary fable aspect of the original. Also, the heroine saves the helpless male in most Disney films, another happy reversal of a long-standing stereotype. (Copyright 1989 the Walt Disney Company; courtesy Buena Vista Releasing.)

going to go away. But the best among them can and sometimes do react in positive ways to an enlightened public's demand for mass entertainment that furthers the values of multiculturalism. Walt Disney instigated that; today's Disney furthers such an approach. Also, my friend's words make me more aware than before of something I have long since come to believe: that reactionaries on the far right and radicals on the far left, despite seeming polarization, always end up saying the same thing, occasionally even doing so for the same reason. In this case, they both hate today's Disney films because those films are politically correct and further those very ideas of diversity that Walt Disney himself first presented to the public—ideas that have finally been absorbed into mainstream thinking.

In a free society—one in which neither the polarized minorities of the Religious Right nor the radical left presume to prescribe for the middle-American mass audience—such an honest and open asking of questions will be undertaken by parents, each with his or her own set of values. As Henry Giroux noted with shock and disappointment after attempting to "enlighten" such people via radio interviews, the public approves of

Disney more or less wholeheartedly, as does its children. As yet another little girl puts it: "I think Disney makes movies because people like their movies." The statement is simple enough to rate as profound. That has always been the case. Any attempt to boycott Disney from either end of the social-political spectrum finally stems from nothing more than a desire to exert the tyranny of a minority over the vast and wide audience with which a populist artist like Disney so completely connects.

This book has not been intended as the final word on Disney, only as an alternative to the current alternative view. While there is nothing inherently wrong in challenging Disney (or any other national institution), an academic corrective to giddy acceptance of anything Disney has for so long been in place that a corrective is now needed for the corrective. *Multiculturalism and the Mouse* is then offered as an attempt to face up to Dr. Lewis's hard but fair question and come away with what I believe to be the correct response: Yes, Disney provides precisely the kinds of stories we (that is, most of us) want our children to be told. I hope my interpretation will at least provoke a new discussion that may allow for a climate in which Disney films are considered with an open mind—interpreted after close scrutiny rather than recklessly written off following a cursory examination, followed by damnation as so many reactionary texts.

The Frankfurt School's notion that all commercial commodities, however liberal they may appear, contain conservative paradigms is an attitude I by and large agree with. My only objection is the failure to acknowledge that there are rare but significant (indeed, significant in large part because they are so rare) exceptions to that rule. Even those who would heartily agree with me here are likely to be surprised, perhaps outraged, by my essential argument: Disney, seemingly the most conventional of all middlebrow offenders, is actually the most subversive among Hollywood entertainers. As such, Disney (now, as in the past) ought to be lauded for providing in the form of easily accessible popular culture the most iconoclastically envisioned alternatives to supposed social norms—positively presented to impressionable mainstream children—rather than attacked as an easily targeted enemy of politically correct thinking.

Notes

Introduction. I Had a Dream Is a Wish Your Heart Makes: In Defense of Disney, Part I

1. Dave Smith, *Disney A to Z* (New York: Hyperion, 1998), p. 291.

2. Ibid.

3. Steven Watts, *The Magic Kingdom: Walt Disney and the American Way of Life* (Boston: Houghton Mifflin, 1997), pp. 416–417.

4. Richard Schickel, *The Disney Version* (New York: Avon Books/Discus Edition, 1969), p. 145.

5. Chyng Feng Sun, *Mickey Mouse Monopoly* (videotape) (Let's Talk Media, 2001); all interview quotes in the introduction are taken directly from this documentary.

6. Smith, *Disney A to Z*, p. 291.

7. Schickel, *The Disney Version*, p. 254.

8. Richard L. Plant, "Of Disney," *Decision*, July 1941, p. 84.

9. Schickel, *The Disney Version*, p. 34.

10. Mary Ellen Snodgrass, *Encyclopedia of Frontier Literature* (New York: Oxford University Press, 1977), p. 382.

11. Schickel, *The Disney Version*, p. 86.

12. "Taking on Disney: Southern Baptist Convention and Other Organizations Boycott Disney," *60 Minutes* (Anchor, Lesley Stahl), Sunday, November 23, 1997.

13. Peter Conrad, *Modern Times, Modern Places* (New York: Knopf, 1998), pp. 391–393.

14. Henry Giroux, *The Mouse That Roared: Disney and the End of Innocence* (Lanham, Md.: Rowman and Littlefield, 1999).

15. Schickel, *The Disney Version*, p. 74.

16. José Ortega y Gasset, *The Dehumanization of Art and Other Essays* (Princeton, N.J.: Princeton University Press, 1948), p. 47.

17. Rudolf Arnheim, *Film as Art* (Berkeley and Los Angeles: University of California Press, 1957), p. 82.

18. Schickel, *The Disney Version*, p. 175.

19. Ibid.

20. Ibid., p. 27.

21. Ibid., p. 187.

22. Ibid., p. 81.

23. Review of *The Living Desert*, *Time* magazine, November 16, 1953.

24. Mark Van Doren, "Fairy Tale in Five Acts," *Nation*, January 22, 1938.

25. Joseph Campbell, *The Hero with a Thousand Faces* (New York: MJF Books, 1949), pp. 3–9, 18.

26. Joseph Campbell, *The Masks of Eternity* (videotape) (PBS Video).

1. Return of the Vanishing American: Disney and the Native Experience

1. Leslie Fiedler, *The Return of the Vanishing American* (New York: Stein and Day, 1968), pp. 150–153.

2. Philip French, *Westerns* (New York: Viking Press, 1973), p. 8.

3. Dee Brown, *Bury My Heart at Wounded Knee* (New York: Washington Square Press, 1970), pp. 189–221.

4. Fiedler, *Return of the Vanishing American*, pp. 88–89.

5. D. H. Lawrence, *Studies in Classic American Literature* (New York/Boston: Thomas Seltzer, 1923), p. 49.

6. *Life* magazine, in its February 1969 issue, demonstrated an awareness of this social fissure via a cover story, "Dusty and the Duke," acknowledging the Generation Gap split that had older moviegoers attending *True Grit* even as younger viewers flocked to *Midnight Cowboy.*

7. French, *Westerns,* p. 89.

8. George N. Fenin and William K. Everson, *The Western: From Silents to the Seventies* (New York: Grossman Publishers, 1973), pp. 370–375.

9. Sergei Eisenstein, *Film Form* (San Francisco: Harcourt, Brace, 1969), pp. 126–129.

10. Fiedler, *Return of the Vanishing American,* p. 21.

11. French, *Westerns,* pp. 79–80.

12. Though "Georgie Russel" is fictional, there was a George Russell. He was the son of Major Russell, the historical Crockett's commander during the War of 1812. Though Crockett and young Russell did scout together at the time, there's no indication the two ever saw each other again.

13. There was no chief named Red Stick; however, one Choctaw band of the Tennessee Creeks was referred to as Red Sticks by Jackson, owing to small red sticks worn in their headbands.

14. The Seminoles are the southernmost extension of the Creek Nation, essentially Choctaws who had adjusted their lifestyle from forest living to the swamps.

15. French, *Westerns,* p. 95.

16. This legislation called for forced removal of peaceful Cherokees from their homeland, resulting in the Trail of Tears; numerous men, women, and children died en route, during a fierce winter, to the far West, where tribes hostile to the Cherokee awaited their arrival.

17. The historical Crockett left Congress after failing to win reelection for a fourth term in 1835; to his credit, though, Crockett lost the election largely because Jackson campaigned against him—a member of Jackson's own Democratic Party—owing to their break on the Indian Bill issue.

18. Disney's is the only film or TV program about the Alamo that includes a Native American among "Crockett's Company."

19. In reality, Crockett's company numbered somewhere between twenty-one and thirty-two men; Disney reduced the group's numbers for easier comprehension by children.

20. Leonard Maltin, *The Disney Films* (New York: Crown Publishers, 1973), p. 139.

21. Robin Wood, *Hitchcock's Films* (London: Tantira Press, 1965), p. 128.

22. Maltin, *The Disney Films,* p. 140.

23. George Armstrong Custer, *My Life on the Plains* (Lincoln: University of Nebraska Press, 1966), pp. 216–230; some consider the book dubious history at best, though, and one of Custer's own disgruntled officers liked to refer to the tome, at least when under the influence of alcohol, as "My Lie on the Plains."

24. Richard Slotkin, *People,* January 12, 1983, pp. 87–89.

25. The last line of *Hondo,* based on a Louis L'Amour Western and produced by Wayne himself, has the title character watching the defeated Apache Nation crawl back into the Chiracahua Mountains of Southern Arizona. "End of a way of life," he sighs wistfully, adding, "Good way, too." Then, he turns his back on the scene, shrugs, and mutters: "Too bad." This is the Social Darwinist approach, favored by true conservatives, in a nutshell.

26. Intriguingly, Corey—who never before or again worked for Disney—appears to have been chosen less owing to acting ability than his personality. The part seemingly reflected his own well-known

off-screen personality. Kirk Douglas, who performed in one Broadway play and one film with Corey, mentions him in his autobiography, *The Ragman's Son* (New York: Simon and Schuster, 1988): "People passed on to me some of the things this minister's son said about me, like 'That Dirty Jew.' . . . Wendell became increasingly reactionary and a drunk" (p. 128). Perhaps Douglas's friend Disney cast Wendell less out of admiration for Corey the actor but to have the last laugh on Corey the man.

27. Steven Spielberg, often referred to as the modern Disney, employs Goethe (Ralph Fiennes) similarly (bigot and exploiter of young women under his power) in *Schindler's List* (1993).

28. The film here anachronistically refers to an all-too-true massacre of Christianized Delawares that occurred seventeen years later; in March 1782, Colonel David Williamson and about one hundred self-appointed militiamen embarked from Fort Pitt, entering Ohio. There, they executed the inhabitants of a peaceful village of forty men, twenty women, and thirty-four children, who begged only that they be allowed to pray to Jesus in hopes that he might save their souls (this wish was granted before the Delawares were systematically bludgeoned to death with hammers). Chronicled in *Daniel Boone: The Opening of the Wilderness* by John Mason Brown (New York: Random House, 1952), pp. 124–126.

29. Fiedler, *The Return of the Vanishing American*, p. 111.

30. Ibid., p. 95.

31. Maltin, *The Disney Films*, p. 138.

32. Comanche had been wounded twenty-six times; all other cavalry horses had either been run off or killed during the battle.

33. Integral, for example, to the pomp and circumstance at the burial of President John Kennedy in 1963.

34. Disney dropped the original title for fear his film might be confused with a B Western called *Comanche* that was currently making the rounds; the title of that movie, incidentally, referred to the tribe of Native Americans, not the horse referred to in the novel's title.

35. French, *Westerns*, p. 82.

36. There was a historical White Bull among the Lakota, and some insist it was he who shot and killed Custer; confusion arises, however, since there was a White Bull among their cousins, the Cheyenne, as well. In Disney's film, White Bull does not kill Custer, so the point is, in this context, moot.

37. Alvin Josephy, *The Indian Heritage of America* (New York: Knopf, 1968), pp. 49–121.

38. French, *Westerns*, p. 80.

39. Ibid.

40. Britt Lomond, who portrays Custer as a megalomaniac in the film, had recently been playing the villain, Captain Monastario, on Disney's ABC-TV series *Zorro.*

41. Paul Mitchell Marks, *And Die in the West* (New York: Touchstone Books, 1989), pp. 4–6.

42. Here I speak firsthand, from the experience of seeing the film in the company of my father in March 1959 at the Rialto Theatre in Patchogue, New York.

43. Maltin, *The Disney Films*, pp. 150–151.

44. Evan S. Connell, *Son of the Morning Star* (New York: Harper and Row, 1984), pp. 324–327.

2. Together in Perfect Harmony: Disney and the Civil Rights Movement

1. Schickel, *The Disney Version*, p. 225.

2. Maltin, *The Disney Films*, p. 52.

3. Watts, *The Magic Kingdom*, p. 91.

4. A DVD version is available as an import from Japan.

5. "Needed: A Negro Legion of Decency," *Ebony* 2 (February 1947): 36–37.

6. Thomas Cripps, *Black Film as Genre* (Bloomington: Indiana University Press, 1978), p. 44.

7. *Time* review, 1946, quoted in Maltin, *The Disney Films*, p. 77.

8. Herman Hill, *Song of the South* review, *Pittsburgh Courier*, November 5, 1946.

9. Thomas Cripps, *Slow Fade to Black: The Negro in American Film, 1900–1942* (London: Oxford University Press, 1977), p. 384.

10. Ibid., p. 385.

11. Thomas Cripps, "The Dark Spot in the Kaleidoscope: Black Images in American Films," in *The Kaleidoscopic Lens: How Hollywood Views Ethnic Groups*, ed. Randall M. Miller (Englewood Cliffs, N.J.: Jerome S. Oser, Publisher, 1980), p. 24.

12. "Walt Disney Presents 'Song of the South,'" *Sepia Hollywood*, December 1946.

13. Jack Kinney, *Walt Disney and Assorted Other Characters: An Unauthorized Account of the Early Years at Disney* (New York: Harmony Books, 1988), pp. 1–32.

14. Snow White was banned in Britain, at the time of its initial release, for being too horrific for those very young children the film targeted as an audience. In the years following this decision, the British censors came to look extremely silly for having ever doubted the Disney studio, once Walt's company came to be perceived as the world's great purveyor of wholesome family entertainment. Though hardly fair in censoring dark, complex entertainment for children, the British had been quite correct in arguing that the film was a considerably less potent version of the old fairy tale than Disney's detractors would have had it.

15. Marc Eliot, *Walt Disney: Hollywood's Dark Prince* (New York: Lyle Stuart, 1993).

16. NAACP position paper, quoted in Maltin, *The Disney Films*, p. 78.

17. Maltin, *The Disney Films*, p. 78.

18. Donald Bogle, *Toms, Coons, Mulattoes, Mammies, and Bucks*, rev. ed. (New York: Continuum Press, 2001).

19. James Baldwin, "Life Straight in de Eye," *Commentary*, January 1955.

20. *Song of the South* review, *Variety*, November 1946.

21. Cripps, *Slow Fade to Black*, p. 27.

22. Thomas Cripps, "The Dark Spot in the Kaleidoscope," p. 28.

23. George Schuyler, "Views and Reviews," *Pittsburgh Courier*, November 9, 1946.

24. Schickel, *The Disney Version*, p. 34.

25. Bogle, *Toms, Coons, Mulattoes, Mammies, and Bucks*, p. 136.

26. Cripps, *Slow Fade to Black*, p. 385.

27. *Song of the South* review, *Tribune*, November 22, 1946.

28. Cripps, *Slow Fade to Black*, p. 121.

29. William Loren Katz, *The Black West* (New York: Touchstone Books, 1996), p. 34.

30. Tim Brooks and Earle F. Marsh, *The Complete Directory to Prime Time Network and Cable Shows, 1946–Present*, 8th ed. (New York: Ballantine, 2003).

31. Bogle, *Toms, Coons, Mulattoes, Mammies, and Bucks*, p. 57.

32. Ibid.

33. William Grant Still, "How Do We Stand in Hollywood?" *Opportunity*, 1945 (publication of the National Urban League).

34. Robert Benchley, "Hearts in Dixie: The First Real Talking Picture," reviewed in *Opportunity* magazine, April 1929.

35. Ossie Davis, "The Wonderful World of Law and Order," in *Anger and Beyond*, ed. Herbert Hill (New York: Harper and Row, 1966), p. 27.

36. Huey Newton, quoted in James Haskins and Kathleen Benson, eds., *Sixties Reader* (New York: Viking, 1988), p. 45.

37. James Baldwin, *Commentary*, January 1955.

38. Bogle, *Toms, Coons, Mulattoes, Mammies, and Bucks,* p. 114.

39. Ibid., p. 39.

40. National Urban League public statement.

41. Stokely Carmichael, quoted in Haskins and Benson, *Sixties Reader,* p. 121.

42. Peter Noble, *The Negro in Films* (New York: Arno Press and New York Times, 1970).

43. Bogle, *Toms, Coons, Mulattoes, Mammies, and Bucks,* p. 10.

3. Beat of a Different Drum: Ethnicity and Individualization in Disney

1. Watts, *The Magic Kingdom,* p. 302.

2. Ibid., p. 90.

3. Ibid., p. 89.

4. Ibid., p. 91.

5. Smith, *Disney A to Z,* p. 433.

6. Schickel, *The Disney Version,* p. 182.

7. Ibid., p. 183.

8. Smith, *Disney A to Z,* p. 434.

9. Gordon W. Allport, *The Nature of Prejudice* (Reading, Mass.: Addison-Wesley, 1954), p. 200.

10. Mark Reisler, *By the Sweat of Their Brow: Mexican Immigrant Labor in the United States, 1900–1940,* (Westport, Conn.: Greenwood Press, 1977), Chapter 6.

11. *Variety,* April 2, 1941, p. 14.

12. Press release (not dated), contained in the South American Stories file at the Disney Archives, Burbank, California.

13. Allen L. Woll, "Bandits and Lovers: Hispanic Images in American Film," in *The Kaleidoscopic Lens: How Hollywood Views Ethnic Groups,* ed. Randall M. Miller (Englewood Cliffs, N.J.: Jerome S. Ozer, 1980), p. 66.

14. Ibid., p. 58.

15. Ibid., p. 68.

16. Juan N. Seguin, *The Revolution Remembered* (reprint; Austin: State House Press, 1991).

17. Woll, "Bandits and Lovers," p. 59.

18. Schickel, *The Disney Version,* p. 37.

19. Ibid., p. 76.

20. Ibid., p. 37.

21. Ibid., p. 129.

22. Patricia Erens, "Between Two Worlds: Jewish Images in American Films," in Miller, ed., *The Kaleidoscopic Lens,* p. 116.

23. Neal Gabler, *A Kingdom of Their Own: How the Jews Invented Hollywood* (New York: Crown Publishers, 1988).

24. Erens, "Between Two Worlds," pp. 116–117.

25. *Time,* December 27, 1954.

26. Plant, "Of Disney," *Decision,* July 1941, p. 84.

27. Edward G. Smith, "St. Francis of the Silver Screen," *Progress Today,* January–March 1935, p. 43.

28. Walt Disney, "The Cartoon's Contribution to Children," *Overland Monthly,* October 1933, p. 138.

29. Joe Grant and Dick Huemer, "Laughter Knows How to Fight," in *Dispatch from Disney,* 1943 (World War II Miscellany file in Disney Archives, Burbank, California).

30. Randall Miller, ed., *Ethnic Images in American Film and Television,* specifically Miller, "Ethnic Pictures and Ethnic Fate: The Media Image of Italian Americans," (Philadelphia: Balch, 1978), p. 94.

31. Golden, p. 75.

32. Ibid.

33. Ibid., pp. 77–78.

34. Richard Gambino, *Blood of My Blood* (Toronto: Guernica Editions), p. 27.

35. Smith, *Disney A to Z,* p. 53.

36. Annette Funicello, *A Dream Is a Wish Your Heart Makes* (New York: Hyperion, 1994), p. 93.

4. Racial and Sexual Identity in America: Disney's Subversion of the Victorian Ideal

1. Erika Doss, *Elvis Culture: Fans, Faith, and Image* (Lawrence: University Press of Kansas, 1999), p. 170.

2. Trent Hill, "The Enemy Within: Censorship in Rock Music in the 1950s," *South Atlantic Quarterly* 90 (1991): 691.

3. Doss, *Elvis Culture,* p. 135.

4. Molly Haskell, *From Reverence to Rape,* p. viii.

5. Herbert S. Stone, public statement, June 15, 1896.

6. Quoted in Jeremy Pascall and Clyde Jeavons, *A Pictorial History of Sex in the Movies* (London: Hamlyn, 1975), p. 53.

7. Watts, *The Magic Kingdom,* p. 328.

8. Maltin, *The Disney Films,* p. 37.

9. Pascall and Jeavons, *A Pictorial History of Sex in the Movies,* p. 53.

10. Benita Eisler, *Private Lives: Men and Women of the Fifties* (New York: Franklin Watts, 1986), p. 129.

11. Schickel, *The Disney Version,* p. 204.

12. Watts, *The Magic Kingdom,* p. 330.

13. Eisler, *Private Lives,* p. 127.

14. Maltin, *The Disney Films,* p. 144.

15. Eisler, *Private Lives,* p. 130.

16. Ibid., p. 129.

17. Elise Finn, "The Three Caballeros Is Bright, Gaudy, Gay," *Philadelphia Record,* June 3, 1945.

18. Review of *Three Caballeros, New Yorker,* June 1945, quoted in Maltin, *The Disney Films,* p. 67.

19. Eisler, *Private Lives,* p. 128.

20. Ibid., p. 114.

21. Apparently this sequence caused problems for the people currently running the Walt Disney Home Video company. When the film was belatedly released on videocassette and DVD in the summer of 2000 (the last Disney classic, other than *Song of the South,* to reach the public in such formats), the "Rustic Ballad" sequence had been entirely removed. Most likely it was less the intense sexuality than the depiction of the female lead as a harridan following her marriage that caused such self-censorship for "politically correct" purposes. Nonetheless, the public has apparently forever been denied the possibility of seeing this work by Walt Disney in its original form.

22. Schickel, *The Disney Version,* p. 24.

23. Eisler, *Private Lives,* p. 142.

24. Doss, *Elvis Culture,* pp. 43–47.

25. Eisler, *Private Lives,* p. 128.

26. Watts, *The Magic Kingdom,* p. 330.

27. Eisler, *Private Lives,* p. 128.

28. Ibid., p. 110.

29. Doss, *Elvis Culture,* 128.

30. Eisler, *Private Lives,* p. 67.

31. Grace Metalious, *Peyton Place* (orig. 1956; reprint, Boston: Northeastern University Press, 1999), p. 134.

32. Maltin, *The Disney Films,* p. 109.

33. "Peter Pan: Real Disney Magic," *Newsweek,* February 16, 1953, pp. 78–79.

34. Watts, *The Magic Kingdom,* p. 326.

35. Eisler, *Private Lives,* p. 141.

5. "If It Feels Good, Do It!": Disney and the Sexual Revolution

1. Eisler, *Private Lives,* p. 128.

2. L. Berg and R. Street, *Sex Methods and Manners* (New York: Archer House, 1953), p. 14.

3. Eisler, *Private Lives,* p. 133.

4. Maltin, *The Disney Films,* p. 118.

5. Ibid.

6. Review of *Vanishing Prairie, New Yorker,* 1954, p. 57.

7. Eustace Chesser, *Love without Fear: How to Achieve Sexual Happiness* (London: Rich and Cowan, 1941), p. 82.

8. David Crockett, *A Narrative of the Life of David Crockett of the State of Tennessee* (orig. 1834; reprint, with an introduction

by Paul Hutton, Lincoln: University of Nebraska Press, 1987).

9. Funicello, *A Dream Is a Wish Your Heart Makes*, p. 59.

10. Gordon Badge, "The Dolly Princess," *TV Radio Mirror*, July 1958.

11. Watts, *The Magic Kingdom*, p. 342.

12. *The American Dream: The 50s* (Alexandria, Va.: Time/Life, n.d.), p. 70.

13. Eisler, *Private Lives*.

14. Robert Pattison, *The Triumph of Vulgarity* (New York: Oxford University Press, 1987), pp. 69–70.

15. Robert Salmaggi, review in the *New York Herald-Tribune*, July 1964, quoted in Maltin, *The Disney Films*, p. 223.

16. Maltin, *The Disney Films*, p. 225.

17. Cover story, "The California Girl," *Life*, October 13, 1968.

6. Our Bodies, Ourselves: Disney and Feminism

1. Simone de Beauvoir, *The Second Sex* (New York: Bantam, 1961), p. 346.

2. Betty Friedan, *The Feminine Mystique* (New York: Dell, 1963), p. 94.

3. Germaine Greer, *The Female Eunuch* (New York: Random House, 1970), p. 108.

4. Haskell, *From Reverence to Rape*, p. 44.

5. Pascall and Jeavons, *A Pictorial History of Sex in the Movies*, p. 41.

6. Midge Decter, *The New Chastity* (New York: Berkley, 1972), p. 132.

7. Una Stannard, "The Mask of Beauty," in *Women in Sexist Society*, ed. Vivian Gornick and Barbara K. Moran (New York: Basic Books, 1971), p. 121.

8. J. L. C. and W. C. Grimm, *Grimm's Fairytales* (Hertfordshire, England: Wordsworth Editions, 1993); all quotations from the fairy tales—"Snow-white," "Cinderella," and "The Sleeping Beauty"—are taken from this version.

9. "No More Miss America!" (independently printed and distributed leaflet for September 7, 1968, protest and demonstration, Atlantic City, New Jersey).

10. Stannard, "The Mask of Beauty," p. 124.

11. Grace Slick, as quoted by James R. Petersen in "The Joy of Sex," *Playboy*, October 1998, p. 70.

12. Decter, *The New Chastity*, p. 72.

13. Walt Disney, *Famous Quotes*, ed. Dave Smith (New York: Walt Disney Company, 1994), p. 96.

14. Decter, *The New Chastity*, p. 61.

15. Maltin, *The Disney Films*, pp. 28–29.

16. Decter, *The New Chastity*, p. 19.

17. Marge Piercy, "The Grand Coolie Dam," in *Sisterhood Is Powerful*, ed. Robin Morgan (New York: Random House, 1970), p. 423.

18. Petersen, "The Joy of Sex," p. 82.

19. Decter, *The New Chastity*, p. 143.

20. Ibid., pp. 198–199.

21. Ibid., p. 74.

22. Michelle Wallace, *Ms.*, February 1978, p. 34.

23. Decter, *The New Chastity*, p. 82.

24. Shulamith Firestone, *The Dialectic of Sex* (New York: Bantam, 1971), p. 141.

25. Caroline Bird, *Born Female: The High Cost of Keeping Women Down* (New York: Pocket Books, 1969), p. 143.

26. Decter, *The New Chastity*, p. 126.

27. Ironically, in 1991, the current Disney corporation released a remake of *Father of the Bride*.

28. Vivian Gornick and Barbara K. Moran, *Women in Sexist Society* (New York: Basic Books, 1971), p. xiii.

29. Firestone, *The Dialectic of Sex*, p. 74.

30. Decter, *The New Chastity*, p. 111.

31. Anne Koedt, "The Myth of the Vaginal Orgasm," in *Voices from Women's Liberation*, ed. Leslie B. Tanner (New York: Signet/New American Library, 1970), p. 166.

32. Firestone, *The Dialectic of Sex*, p. 140.

**7. Something Wiccan This Way Comes:
Walt's Wonderful World of Witchcraft**

1. Scott Cunningham, *The Truth about Witchcraft,* 2d ed. (St. Paul: Llewellyn Publishers, 1998), p. 21.

2. Stephen L. Harris and Gloria Platzner, *Classical Mythology: Images and Insights,* 2d ed. (Mountain View, Calif.: Mayfield Publishing, 1999), pp. 84–91.

3. Campbell, *The Hero with a Thousand Faces,* p. 221.

4. Cunningham, *The Truth about Witchcraft,* p. 34.

5. Disney, *Famous Quotes,* p. 81.

6. Lady Jane Wilde, *Ancient Legends of Ireland* (Dublin and London: Ward and Downey, 1887), p. 124.

7. Janet and Stewart Farrar, *A Witch's Bible: The Complete Witch's Handbook* (Blaine, Wash.: Phoenix Publishing, 1996).

8. Harris and Platzner, *Classical Mythology,* p. 152.

9. Ibid., pp. 94–96.

10. Louis Giannetti, *Understanding Movies,* 9th ed. (Upper Saddle River, N.J.: Prentice-Hall, 2002).

11. Disney, *Famous Quotes,* p. 34.

12. Cunningham, *The Truth about Witchcraft,* p. 42.

13. Frank Thomas and Ollie Johnson, *The Illusion of Life: Disney Animation* (New York: Hyperion, 1995).

14. Watts, *The Magic Kingdom,* p. 92.

**8. Beyond the Celluloid Closet:
Disney and the Gay Experience**

1. Bruce Bawer, "Notes on Stonewall," *New Republic,* June 13, 1994, pp. 23–24.

2. Jonathan Katz, *Gay American History* (New York: Dutton, 1992), p. 23.

3. Jeremy Wilson, *Lawrence of Arabia: The Authorized Biography* (New York: Atheneum, 1990), pp. 23–34.

4. Arthur Bell, "Let the Boys in the Band Die," *New York Times* (Leisure section), April 8, 1973.

5. Ibid.

6. Susan Schindehette, "Growing Up Disney," *People,* December 21, 1998, p. 52.

7. Schickel, *The Disney Version,* p. 45.

8. Vito Russo, *The Celluloid Closet* (New York: Harper and Row, 1981), pp. 74–75.

9. Watts, *The Magic Kingdom,* p. 11.

10. Letter from the personal collection of Miss Daisy Beck, from Walt Disney in Hollywood, dated September 27, 1940.

11. Some observers insist that "gay," as a synonym for "homosexual," dates back to the 1920s; others claim "gay" acquired its contemporary meaning in 1938, following the release of Howard Hawks's screwball comedy *Bringing Up Baby.* Cary Grant, caught wearing Katharine Hepburn's clothes, leaps into the air, spins about, and announces in a fey voice: "I've just suddenly gone *gay!*" Either way, "gay" was unquestionably a well-known code term for "homosexual" by the time of *Pinocchio's* release in 1940.

12. Dennis Altman, *Homosexual Oppression and Liberation* (New York: Outerbridge Dienstsrey, Dutton, 1971), pp. 101–114.

13. Russo, *The Celluloid Closet,* p. 75.

14. Richard Dyer, *Now You See It: Studies on Lesbian and Gay Films* (New York: Routledge, 1990), pp. 27–35.

15. Russo, *The Celluloid Closet,* p. 74.

16. Todd McCarthy, *Howard Hawks: The Great Fox of Hollywood* (New York: Grove Press, 1997), p. 63.

17. Donald C. Willis, *The Films of Howard Hawks* (Metuchen, N.J.: Scarecrow Press, 1975), pp. 49–52.

18. Clifford M. Sage, "Curtain Going Up," *Dallas Times Herald,* August 4, 1950.

19. Russo, *The Celluloid Closet,* p. 68.

20. Ibid., p. 230.

21. Ibid., pp. 16–17.

22. Ibid., p. 6.

23. Ibid.

24. Historians long ago concluded that Boone never actually wore one, and they doubt whether Crockett did either. As to the continuation of this image on TV and in the movies despite that common knowledge, we can refer to John Ford's famed line about the West in *The Man Who Shot Liberty Valance* (1962): "When the legend becomes fact, print the legend." Apparently, that goes for celluloid as well as paper-and-ink printing.

25. There were seventy-eight half-hour TV episodes between 1957 and 1959, plus four additional hour-long installments during the 1960–1961 season of *Walt Disney Presents;* a 1960 film, *The Sign of Zorro,* was composed entirely of clips from the first thirteen episodes of the show's first season on ABC.

26. Russo, *The Celluloid Closet,* p. 16.

27. Joseph Agonito, "Half-Man, Half-Woman: The Native American Berdache," in *True West* 36, no. 3 (March 1989): 22–29.

28. Joseph Nicolosi, "The Importance of the Father-Son Relationship," in *Homosexuality,* ed. Robert M. Baird and M. Katherine Baird (Amherst, Mass.: Prometheus Books, 1995), pp. 51–61.

29. Susan Braudy, *Who Killed Sal Mineo?* (New York: Wyndham, 1982), pp. 36–43.

30. Russo, *The Celluloid Closet,* p. 70.

31. Ibid., p. 110.

32. Richard Dyer, *Brief Encounter* (London: British Film Institute, 1994), pp. 111–121.

33. Paul Alexander, *Boulevard of Broken Dreams* (New York: Viking, 1994), pp. 123–127.

34. Maltin, *The Disney Films,* p. 48.

35. Alexander, *Boulevard of Broken Dreams,* pp. 187–189.

36. Vicki K. Janik, *Fools and Jesters in Literature, Art, and History* (Westport, Conn.: Greenwood, 1998), pp. 281–288.

37. Lars Eighner, *Gay Cosmos* (New York: Masquerade Books, 1995), pp. 89–95.

Conclusion. Popular Culture and Political Correctness: In Defense of Disney, Part II

1. Schickel, *The Disney Version,* p. 256.

2. Ibid.

3. Ibid., p. 66.

4. Giannetti, *Understanding Movies,* p. 121.

5. "Disney Obituary," *Time,* December 19, 1966, p. 44.

6. Schickel, *The Disney Version,* p. 15.

7. Aubrey Menen, "Dazzled in Disneyland," *Holiday,* July 1963, p. 38.

8. James Rouse, "Rouse on Problems and Wifely Help," *Life,* February 24, 1967, pp. 46–47.

9. Chyng Feng Sun, *Mickey Mouse Monopoly.*

10. Theodor Adorno and Max Horkheimer, "The Culture Industry: Enlightenment as Mass Deception," in *Dialectic of Enlightenment* (orig. 1944; reprint, London: Verso, 1995), pp. 120–167.

11. Schickel, *The Disney Version,* p. 94.

12. Ibid., p. 132.

13. Feng Sun, *Mickey Mouse Monopoly.*

14. Ibid.

15. Walt Disney, "The Cartoon's Contribution to Children," p. 32.

16. Feng Sun, *Mickey Mouse Monopoly.*

17. Ibid.

18. Ibid.

19. Interview included by Feng Sun in *Mickey Mouse Monopoly.*

20. Feng Sun, *Mickey Mouse Monopoly.*

21. Ibid.

22. Ibid.

23. Ibid.

24. Ibid.

25. Ibid.

Index

Page numbers in boldface type indicate photographs. Films are listed with dates.